GETTING RID OF ANGER

I asked her to try to describe her feeling of anger. She expressed annoyance and irritation at the request.

"What good would that do? I don't want to feel the anger! I want to get rid of it!"

But I persisted, and gradually she began to describe feelings of tension in her chest and a tight knot in her stomach.

Then she exclaimed, "I feel indignant, I feel enraged, I feel: how can he do this to me?"

Then to her astonishment, the anger began to dissolve. Another emotion emerged in its place: anxiety. I asked her to describe her anxiety.

"My God!" she cried, "I'm afraid of being left alone."

I asked her now to sink more deeply into her fear of being left alone.

"I'm afraid of what I might do when he's gone," she said suddenly. "You know—other men; I might get involved with another man. I don't trust myself."

By now, the anger was gone, the anxiety had dissolved, the fear of loneliness had faded away. A problem remained that had to be dealt with—but now, since it was admitted into conscious awareness, it was *capable* of being dealt with.

THE
DISOWNED
SELF

Nathaniel Branden

BANTAM BOOKS
TORONTO · NEW YORK · LONDON · SYDNEY · AUCKLAND

THE DISOWNED SELF

*A Bantam Book / published by arrangement with
Nash Publishing Corporation*

PRINTING HISTORY

Nash edition published January 1972
2nd printing .. February 1972   3rd printing .. September 1972
Bantam edition / June 1973

2nd printing ..... April 1974	6th printing .... July 1979
3rd printing ..... April 1975	7th printing .. December 1980
4th printing .. December 1976	8th printing ...... May 1982
5th printing ...... May 1978	9th printing ...... May 1984

ISBN 0-553-24557-0

Published simultaneously in the United States and Canada

Bantam Books are published by Bantam Books, Inc. Its trademark, consisting of the words "Bantam Books" and the por-
trayal of a rooster, is Registered in U.S. Patent and Trademark
Office and in other countries. Marca Registrada. Bantam
Books, Inc., 666 Fifth Avenue, New York, New York 10103.

PRINTED IN THE UNITED STATES OF AMERICA

H   18 17 16 15 14 13 12 11 10 9

Contents

A PREFATORY NOTE
TO THE BANTAM EDITION

Some months after the original publication of **THE DISOWNED SELF**, I gave an interview to REASON Magazine which appeared in May, 1973. In it, I discussed certain issues in psychology and psychotherapy that further elaborated the thinking behind my previous work. I am grateful to the editors of REASON Magazine for permission to include this interview as a special Epilogue to the Bantam edition of this book.

Preface

Sixteen years ago, when I began the practice of psychotherapy, I was struck by the fact that, regardless of the particular problem for which a client or patient sought help, there was one common denominator: a deficiency of self-esteem. Always, at the base of the individual's symptoms, there was intellectual self-doubt, moral self-doubt, feelings of inadequacy, helplessness, guilt. The effort to defend himself against this self-esteem deficiency—and to avoid the fact of the deficiency—was clearly central to his motivation and behavior.

It became evident that there was the most intimate tie between self-esteem and mental health. Yet, to my astonishment, I could not find any illuminating discussion of this issue in the professional literature; not, at any rate, in terms applicable to the phenomena I was encountering in my practice. Thus I was led to an urgent concern with such questions as: What *is* self-esteem? What are the facts of man's nature that give rise to his *need* of self-esteem? On what conditions does its fulfillment depend? What is the nature of the relationship between self-esteem and mental health? What is the effect of a person's self-esteem (or lack of it) on different aspects of his life, such as work, ambition, creativity, love relationships, sexual psychology, friendship, esthetic responses, and so forth? My answers to these questions are presented in *The Psychology of Self-Esteem* (Nash Publishing, 1969).

Central to that book is the thesis that the individual plays a profoundly important role in determining the course of his own psychological development and in the strengthening or destroying of his self-esteem. In it I maintain that:

■ Since man's faculty of reason is his basic means of survival, the development of his mind, the development of his ability to think, is the foremost requirement of his well-being.

■ Since the choice to think or not to think, to exercise his reason or to suspend it, is volitional, man is uniquely a self-determined and self-created being.

■ Since man's emotions and desires are the product of conscious or subconscious value judgments, the premises, conclusions and values he arrives at or accepts, and with which he "programs" his subconscious, are essential to an explanation of his behavior.

■ Since man's life depends on his cognitive contact with reality, the ability to achieve such contact, unobstructed by reality-avoiding blocks and distortions, is the necessary standard of mental health.

■ Since man must achieve self-esteem by his own volitional effort—since man must make himself into an entity able to live (able to deal with reality efficaciously) and worthy of living (worthy of happiness)—his need of self-esteem is his need of the knowledge that he has succeeded at this task.

■ Since self-esteem *is* a basic psychological need, the failure to achieve it leads to disastrous consequences.

■ Since a man's self-concept is crucially important to his choice of values and goals, the degree of his self-esteem (or lack of it) has a profound impact on every key aspect of his life.

This approach stands in rather sharp contrast to that of most contemporary psychologists and psychiatrists, who tend to see man as a passive, helplessly determined product of his environment and genetic inheritance, and who seem singularly indifferent to the fact that man's biologically distinguishing characteristic, and basic means of survival, is his power of conceptual thought— his ability to reason. They evidently have not discovered that a species' distinctive means of survival, of coping with the environment, has the most profound implications for its behavior.

Insofar as the issue of self-esteem has been dealt with by other writers (and it has been dealt with to an appallingly small extent), the position almost invariably taken is that the child's self-esteem is determined by the treatment he receives from parents and other authority figures. Without denying that parents can influence the development of the child's self-concepts, I chose to deal in *The Psychology of Self-Esteem* with the most ignored (and usually denied) aspect of the human personality: man's power of self-determination.

In *Breaking Free* (Nash Publishing, 1970), I demonstrate a technique, through dramatized case histories, of exploring the childhood origins of adult psychological problems—specifically, negative self-concepts —in terms of early child-parent interactions. Here, the issue of self-esteem is approached from the perspective of the family environment, and what is investigated is the benevolent or harmful influence on the child's growing self-concept that can be exercised by parents.

The investigations presented in *Breaking Free* led to a growing interest in the childhood repression of pain, fear, frustration and rage, and the impact of such repression on subsequent personality development. This led to continuing experimentation with various techniques and strategies for breaking through the barrier of repression—repression originating either in childhood or in adulthood. During the same period, and related to the foregoing concerns, I became increasingly interested in the problem of self-alienation—a condition in which the individual is out of contact with his own needs, feelings, emotions, frustrations and longings, so that he is largely oblivious to his actual self, and his life is the reflection of an unreal self, of a role he has adopted.

The problem of obliviousness to self, the causes and consequences of such obliviousness, and its treatment psychotherapeutically—is the central theme of this book.

While there are anticipations of the theme of *The Disowned Self* in both my earlier books, at the time of writing them I was not prepared to provide the analysis the subject required. Today, I cannot regard any discussion of self-esteem as complete that does not take cognizance of the issues dealt with in this work.

I include in my presentation some of the techniques or methods I have found especially helpful in working on the problem of derepression. In the case of one of these techniques, the sentence-completion exercise, I provide a detailed explanation of its use and application, for the benefit of other psychotherapists who may wish to experiment with it. However, this is not primarily a book on therapy. Its chief focus is on the problem for which therapy may be required: the problem of self-alienation.

Because of the central importance of the nature of emotions to the present work, I include, as Appendix A, the chapter on emotions from *The Psychology of Self-Esteem,* with annotations. As Appendix B , I present an essay that originally appeared in *The Objectivist Newsletter,* on the psycho-political aspects of alienation, because it discusses relevant features of the problem that are not otherwise covered in this book, and contains an analysis of the attempt to "politicize" the phenomenon of self-alienation.

The present study is self-contained and does not require or presuppose familiarity with my two earlier books. The discussion it offers is not intended to be exhaustive or definitive. Like its predecessors, *The Disowned Self* is "a report on work in progress." I offer it at this time as a necessary supplement to and extension of my earlier work, in the hope that the observations it contains may open doors for others as they have opened doors for me.

Nathaniel Branden

Los Angeles 1971

Chapter 1

Discovering the Unknown Self

One afternoon I was lunching in a small, rather elegant restaurant, when I fell into a conversation with the owner, whom I knew slightly. An attractive man in his late thirties, he projected a restless, buoyant energy, a facile glibness and an aggressively colorful style of dress, all of which seemed clearly intended to fulfill the image of a jet-set playboy. In the midst of a long, nonstop monologue about his recent trip to Las Vegas and his problems with his tailor, interspersed with random references to sex, Vietnam, and a new discotheque in Acapulco, he interrupted himself suddenly to say—with desperate earnestness, and with eyes that were dark holes of screaming pain—"Nathaniel, I've got to talk to you. Let's have lunch one day. I can't stand this hollowness inside of me"—he brought his hand to his chest—"Man, it's killing me—it's one big emptiness inside—nothing here—know what I mean?—I don't know how to describe it—there's nothing there—*no feeling*—listen, we've got to have a talk."

I deliberately let a moment pass—to let him know that I had heard him, and to give him a chance to hear himself—before I answered, "All right." Whereupon,

1

without an instant's pause, he began rattling on again about girls and Acapulco, running some nameless race through a private darkness, driven by forces he dared not pause long enough to admit into his consciousness— as if fearing that to look into the face of those forces would mean to be annihilated.

Later, when I was leaving, he called out cheerfully, "Don't forget. Lunch."

"I won't," I promised—feeling absolutely certain that *he* would.

But there had been that one moment when some unexpected impulse had prompted him to drop the mask of his public personality and to become authentic, even if tortured—and to reveal, behind his words, a person curiously touching and youthful—and I went away thinking something that probably would have astonished him: how much more likeable, how much more attractive, how much more *interesting* was the self he had permitted me to glimpse in that one moment, the self he chose to hide from the world, not because he could not permit the world to see it, but because he could not permit *him* to see it.

I drove back to my office, to meet with twelve men and women in a group therapy session—and to deal with twelve variants of the problem I had just left, differing in form, differing in degree of severity, differing in the particular words with which the sufferer chose to describe his agony—but alike in that feeling of self-alienation and self-impoverishment, sometimes admitted, sometimes denied, that touched them all, alike in each person's need to hide behind a mask, alike in each person's desolate sense of inner emptiness, of a void wrapped in a scream straining to reach past a wall of defenses to the ears of the screamer.

It is a problem that every psychotherapist encounters daily, although there is no simple name to describe it. Sometimes it is experienced as a feeling of self-estrangement; sometimes, as the feeling that one's self is only a dark question mark or a guilty secret; sometimes, as the feeling that one's self floats in a vacuum, disconnected from one's body; sometimes, as the feeling that one has no self. It is present in every neurosis; it is the core of neurosis. I call it: the problem of *the disowned self*.

*

* *

We hear more and more today about the fact that many people suffer from a sense of personal unreality, that they have lost touch with themselves, that too often they do not know what they feel, that they act with numb obliviousness to that which prompts or motivates their actions. The problem is not new, but in recent years it has received an unprecedented amount of discussion and publicity—not only among psychologists and psychiatrists, but among educated people everywhere. Psychotherapists of different schools have developed numerous techniques and methods aimed specifically at bringing people into better touch with themselves and guiding them to experience a more meaningful sense of their own identity.

Unfortunately, however, just as the ordinary man tends to dichotomize thinking and feeling, reason and emotion—often to regard them as antagonists—so do many psychotherapists. The result is that, in their enthusiasm to help men become reconnected with their denied selves, reconnected with their feelings, they sometimes permit themselves orgies of anti-intellectualism—implying or explicitly stating that men cannot feel because they think too much.

Bad biology makes bad psychology. Whoever attacks man's distinctive nature as a biological entity, his ability to reason—whoever attempts to study man psychologically after chopping off his head—is in trouble. In the study of a living species, the biologist is vitally interested in learning the nature of that species' distinctive means of survival, since he recognizes that such information constitutes an indispensible key to the species' behavior. In the case of man, it is clear that *his* distinctive way of dealing with reality, of maintaining his existence, is through the exercise of his conceptual faculty. All of his unique attainments—scientific knowledge, technological and industrial achievements, art, culture, social institu-

tions—proceed from and are made possible by his
ability to think. Whatever the path to mental health and
to a strong sense of self, it cannot be reached through
an abandonment of thinking.

But man is not merely a thinking machine; he is also
a being who feels, who experiences emotions; and he is
also a being who acts. If it is true to say that his life
depends upon his ability to think, then it is equally true
to say that his effective functioning as an organism, the
fulfillment and enjoyment of his life, depends on the
successful *integration* of thought, feeling and action.
When that integration is broken—when thought, feeling and action are split off from one another, to operate
in separate vacuums, so to speak—the result is disaster
to the organism. One of the forms of that disaster is an
impoverished sense of self.

Any normal human faculty is susceptible to a perversion of its proper function by a person wishing to avoid
confrontation with some frightening or painful aspect
of reality. And this applies to thought, feeling and
action.

Thinking can become that form of counterfeit reasoning known as "rationalizing"; or it can become
"intellectualizing," a flight into abstractions that have
no meaningful relevance, or no *experienced* relevance,
to the issues one is considering—which is a perversion
of the purpose of thought. This is manifested, for instance, in the behavior of the "intellectual" who discusses his personal problems as though they belonged
to someone else, in a state of total personal dissociation
in which he does not experience the emotional meaning
of anything he says or hears; who prefers to talk about
psychology in general rather than his agony in particular; and who, in the context of his personal life, engages
in mental activity not for the purpose of expanding his
awareness but for the purpose of avoiding it.

Feeling can become, not a consequence of open-
minded awareness of the full range of one's emotional
experience, but a blind clutching at one or two emotions
on the top layer of consciousness, intended to blot out
not only thought but also knowledge of the rest of one's

emotions—which is a perversion of one's capacity to feel. This is manifested in the behavior of the "emotionalist" who dwells only on his emotion of sadness but refuses to confront the rage beneath it; or who blindly surrenders to his anger while refusing to confront the hurt that motivates it; who talks endlessly about his emotions as a means to avoid knowing what he feels.

Action can become, not a natural expression of integrated thoughts and emotions, not a means to the enjoyment and enhancement of one's life, but merely an anxious flight from contact with one's inner world, with one's thoughts *or* one's feelings—which is a perversion of the function of action. This is manifested in the behavior of the "man of action" who, impatient with thought and scornful of emotions, runs compulsively from one activity to another, dreading to face the question of what his actions are adding up to or what benefit they bring (or fail to bring) to his life—who uses action as a means to avoid facing the meaning and significance of action.

In all such instances, the motive is *avoidance*— avoidance of some aspect of reality. If we look deeper, we discover that, predominantly, the aspect of reality the person wishes to avoid is internal rather than external; what he wishes to avoid, most often, is a feeling he regards as intolerable. Sometimes this is obvious, as when a person is struggling to avoid experiencing pain or anxiety or depression or rage or jealousy. But even when he is struggling to avoid thoughts, or the knowledge of certain facts, he is usually struggling to avoid, not the thoughts or facts as such, but their internal consequences for him, their emotional meaning to him, the things they cause him to feel, such as guilt or helplessness or humiliation or frustration.

To express this another way: the aspect of reality the person wishes to avoid *is his inner experience.*

I do not wish to imply that in any and all circumstances the primary focus of a healthy, well-integrated personality is on what he feels at that moment. There are obviously many times when his focus must be elsewhere. If a person is engaged in a process of problem solving, then his dominant focus is normally cognitive or intellectual; it is turned to an impersonal consideration of specific facts, logical relationships, and so forth. If he is engaged in performing some action, his primary focus is normally on the action.

But whereas a person engaged in problem solving is generally able to describe the thoughts and issues with which he is occupied, and a person engaged in action is able to know and state the nature of the action he is performing, most people do not enjoy any comparable facility in describing the nature and content of their emotional experience. And more: there are many instances in which they clearly have a block against doing so. They are not *real* to themselves, which is to say: there is a solid wall standing between their conscious awareness and their immediate internal psychological state.

To be *real,* in a psychological sense, means to be integrated—integrated in thought, feeling and bodily behavior. For example, when a person professes to be cheerful and carefree but we see that his movements are abrupt and jerky, and his voice and speech betray a current of irritability, we do not necessarily conclude that he is consciously lying, but we say that he is cut off from himself, he is not being authentic, he is not being real, he is cut off from his emotions—he is not integrated.

Emotions are implicit value responses; they reflect subconscious, super-rapid appraisals of "for me or against me," "good for me or harmful," "to be pursued or to be avoided," and so forth. His emotional capacity is man's automatic barometer of what is for him or against him, within the context of his knowledge, beliefs, values and past experience. Emotions reflect the value-meaning that different aspects of reality have for the perceiver. To cease to know what one feels is to cease to *experience* what things mean to one—which is to be cut off from one's own context.

This last point must be stressed. Man is not a disembodied intellect, and he is not merely a mind who happens to inhabit a body. Man is an organism—a living entity—who is conscious; which is to say, *he is a person.* And he can relate to the world effectively only as a person, only as an integrated unity. One of the greatest acts of self-delusion is for an individual to imagine that he can preserve the clarity of his thinking after he has become disconnected from his own person, from the reality of his emotional experience.

I discuss this issue briefly in *The Psychology of Self-Esteem,* in my analysis of emotions and the subconscious. In *The Psychology of Self-Esteem,* however, the dominant emphasis is on the fact that a default on the responsibility of reason, an abdication of thought, results in disaster in the *emotional* sphere—including an impoverishment of one's sense of identity. In the present context I wish to emphasize the fact—which I shall illustrate through examples taken from my work as a therapist—that a denial or repression of feeling, a subversion of the emotional capacity, results in disaster in the *intellectual* sphere—as well as an impoverishment of one's sense of identity.

*

*   *

But first let us consider the question: How does a person arrive at the state of being disconnected from his own emotional experience, of being unable to feel what things mean to him?

To begin with, many parents *teach* children to repress their feelings. A little boy falls and hurts himself and is told sternly by his father, "Men don't cry." A little girl expresses anger at her brother, or perhaps shows dislike toward an older relative, and is told by her mother, "It's terrible to feel that way. You don't really feel it." A child bursts into the house, full of joy and excitement, and is told by an irritated parent, "What's wrong with you? Why do you make so much noise?" Emotionally remote and inhibited parents tend to produce emotionally remote and inhibited children—not only by the parent's overt communications but also by the example they set; their own behavior announces to the child what is "proper," "appropriate," "socially acceptable." Parents who accept the teachings of religion are very likely to infect their children with the disastrous notion that there are such things as "evil thoughts" or "evil emotions"—and thus fill the child with moral terror of his inner life.

Thus a child can be led to the conclusion that his feelings are potentially dangerous, that sometimes it is advisable to deny them, that they must be "controlled."

What the effort at such "control" amounts to practically is that a child learns to *disown* his feelings, which means: he ceases to experience them. Just as emotions are a psychosomatic experience, a mental and physical state, so the assault on emotions occurs on two levels. On the psychological level, a child ceases to acknowledge or recognize undesired feelings; he super-rapidly deflects his awareness away from them. On the physical level, he tenses his body, he induces muscular tensions, which have the effect of partially anesthetizing him, of making him numb, so that he is no longer readily able to feel his own inner state—as in the case of a child who tenses the muscles of his face and chest, and curtails his breathing, so as to wipe out the knowledge that he is hurt. Needless to say, this process does not take place by conscious, calculated decision; to some extent it is subconscious. But the process of self-alienation has begun; in denying his feelings, in nullifying his own judgments and evaluations; in repudiating his own experience, the child has learned to disown parts of his personality. (It must be understood that the process of learning to regulate behavior in a rational manner is a different issue entirely. Here we are concerned with *the censoring and denying of inner experience.*)

There is more, however, to the story of how emotional repression develops.

For the majority of children, the early years of life contain many frightening and painful experiences. Perhaps a child has parents who never respond to his need to be touched, held and caressed; or who constantly scream at him or at each other; or who deliberately invoke fear and guilt in him as a means of exercising control; or who swing between over-solicitude and callous remoteness; or who subject him to lies and mockery; or who are neglectful and indifferent; or who continually criticize and rebuke him; or who overwhelm him with bewildering and contradictory injunctions; or who present him with expectations and demands that take no cognizance of his knowledge, needs or interests; or who subject him to physical violence; or who consistently discourage his efforts at spontaneity and self-assertiveness.

A child does not have a conceptual knowledge of his own needs nor does he have sufficient knowledge to comprehend the behavior of his parents. But at times his fear and pain may be experienced as overwhelming and incapacitating. And so, in order to protect himself, in order to remain able to function—in order to survive, it may seem to him—he often feels, wordlessly and helplessly, that he must escape from his inner state, that contact with his emotions has become intolerable. And so he denies his feelings. The fear and the pain are not permitted to be experienced, expressed and thus discharged; they are frozen into his body, barricaded behind walls of muscular and physiological tension, and a pattern of reaction is inaugurated that will tend to recur again and again when he is threatened by a feeling he does not wish to experience.

It is not only negative feelings that become blocked. The repression extends to more and more of his emotional capacity. When one is given an anesthetic in preparation for surgery, it is not merely the capacity to experience pain that is suspended; the capacity to experience pleasure goes also—because what is blocked is the capacity to experience *feeling*. The same principle applies to the repression of emotions.

It must be recognized, of course, that emotional repression is a matter of degree; in some individuals it is far more profound and pervasive than in others. But what remains true for everyone is that to diminish one's capacity to experience pain is to diminish also one's capacity to experience pleasure.

*

*   *

It is not difficult to establish that the average person carries within him the burden of an enormous quantity of unacknowledged and undischarged pain—not only pain originating in the present, but pain originating in the early years of his life.

One evening, discussing this phenomenon with some colleagues, I was challenged by a young psychiatrist who felt I was exaggerating the magnitude of the problem in the general population. I asked him if he would be willing to cooperate in a demonstration. He was an intelligent but somewhat diffident person; he spoke quietly, almost reticently, as though he doubted that anyone present could really be interested in his opinion. He said he would be glad to volunteer, but he warned me that if I were proposing to explore his childhood I might be disappointed and defeat my purpose, even if my general thesis was correct, because he had had an exceptionally happy childhood. His parents, he said, had always been marvelously responsive to his needs, so perhaps he was not a good subject for my demonstration and it might be better to ask for another volunteer. I replied that I would like to work with him; he laughed and invited me to proceed.

I explained that I wanted him to do an exercise that I had developed for use with my clients in therapy. I asked him to sit back in his chair, relax his body, let his arms rest at his sides, and close his eyes.

"Now," I said, "I want you to accept the following situation. You are lying on a bed in a hospital and you are dying. You are your present age. You are not in physical pain, but you are aware of the fact that in a few hours your life will end. Now, in your imagination, look up and see your mother standing at the side of the bed. Look at her face. There is so much unsaid between you. Feel the presence of all the unsaid between you— all the things you have never told her, all the thoughts and feelings you have never expressed. If ever you would be able to reach your mother, it is now. If ever she would hear you, it is now. Talk to her. Tell her."

As I was speaking, the young man's hands clenched into fists, blood rushed to his face, and one could see the muscular tension around his eyes and forehead that was aimed at suppressing tears. When he spoke, it was a younger voice and much more intense, and his words were a rising moan, as he said: "When I spoke to you, *why didn't you ever listen to me? . . . Why didn't you ever listen?*"

At that point, I stopped him from continuing, although it was obvious he had much more to say. I did not wish to carry the demonstration further because to do so would have meant invading his privacy. This was not the occasion to do psychotherapy and I had not been requested to do it; but it would have been interesting to point out to him the possible relationship between the frustration of his need to be listened to as a child and his over-reserved personality as an adult. After a moment he opened his eyes, shook his head, looked astonished and a bit sheepish, and glanced at me with an expression that conceded the point.

Let me mention that the full use of this technique involves having the subject or client confront *both* of his parents, one after the other. Sometimes, in addition, he is requested to imagine the presence of an ideal mother or father, in contrast with his actual parents, and to ask that ideal mother or father for whatever he wants. This can be very helpful in putting a person in touch with early frustrated needs that have been denied and repressed. (Further, the exercise is usually conducted with the person lying on the floor, legs uncrossed and arms spread wide, because it has been found that when a person lies in a position of physical defenselessness there is a tendency for psychological defenses to weaken.)

Returning to the young psychiatrist, I want to draw attention to the fact that there was no question of his consciously lying about his childhood. It was obvious that he had been speaking sincerely when he spoke of it as happy; but in repressing his early pain, he was disowning certain of his own legitimate needs, disowning important feelings, therefore disowning a part of himself. The consequence for him as an adult was not only an emotional impairment but also a thinking impairment, since any attempt he might have made to relate his past to his present, or to understand his reticent personality, would be hampered by distorted judgments; and further, distorted judgments necessarily obstruct his present effectiveness in human relationships.

In repressing significant memories, evaluations, feelings, frustrations, longings and needs, a person denies himself access to crucial data; in attempting to think about his life and his problems he is sentenced to struggle in the dark—because key items of information are missing. Further, the need to *protect* his repression, to *maintain* his defenses, operates subconsciously to keep his mind away from "dangerous" avenues of thought—avenues of thought that might lead to a "stirring up" or a re-activating of submerged and feared material. Distortion and rationalization are virtually inevitable.

Sometimes a client exhibits considerable resistance in working with this exercise; he fears to enter into it completely. But observing the particular form of a client's resistance can itself be illuminating.

I recall an occasion when I was invited to demonstrate this technique at a group therapy session conducted by a colleague. At first the woman with whom I was working addressed her father in a detached, impersonal voice; she was quite cut off from the emotional meaning of her own words. Gradually this defense began to dissolve, as I pressed her with such questions as, "But how does a five-year-old girl *feel* when her daddy treats her like this?" Then as she descended deeper into her emotions, she began to cry; one could see the hurt and anger on her face. However, just when she seemed prepared to let go completely, she abruptly pulled back to a more impersonal manner, obviously frightened by what she was experiencing, and said in a tone of self-reproach, "But actually it's silly of me to blame you—you couldn't help it—you had your own problems and you just didn't know how to handle children." When I explained that no issue of "blame" was involved, that all that mattered was for us to know what had happened and what she had felt about it, she seemed reassured and began again to descend into her emotions, and she spoke more forcefully about what had happened to her and what she had been made to feel; but always, just when she seemed about to explode with anger, it was as though some cut-off mechanism was activated, her impersonal voice returned and she again offered "excuses" to justify the treatment she had received. She was not yet ready to let go of her defenses.

To permit herself fully to experience her anger would have been unbearably threatening. It would have made her feel guilty to harbor such rage against her parents. It would have caused her to feel that if they somehow learned of her feelings, she would lose them forever. And further, if she permitted herself to follow her anger down to the bottom of her emotions, she would have had to face the enormity of the hurt and frustration lying there—and she was not yet prepared to face that, not only because the pain was so excruciating, but also because she would then have to confront the full reality of her *aloneness,* the full reality of the fact that the little girl who had been herself had not had, and now would never have, the parents she wanted and needed.

I can recall another instance when a client's block, at a certain point in the exercise, was as eloquent as anything that could have been revealed. The event took place about a month after the client—a man in his middle twenties—entered group therapy. He was one of the most physically tense and rigid persons with whom I have ever worked. His chief complaint was his utter incapacity to feel, or to know what he wanted out of life, or to know what career he wished to pursue. He informed me that he was incapable of crying. As we began the exercise, he spoke of his father in a soft, timid voice, describing the fear he had always felt at his father's remoteness and unyielding severity. Then I suggested that perhaps at times a young boy would feel rage toward a parent who treated him so cruelly. Then his whole body shuddered, and he shouted, "I can't talk about that!" "What would happen," I asked, "if you told him about your anger?" Tears suddenly streaming down his face, he screamed, "I'm afraid of him! I'm afraid of what he'll do to me! He'll kill me!"

His father had died nearly twenty years ago, when my client was six years old.

During the weeks that followed, I did not call upon him to perform this particular exercise again. Predominantly, I merely let him watch while I worked with others in his group. But now he cried at nearly every session, as he watched one client after another reconfront early traumatic experiences. He became more and more able to remember and talk about events in his childhood, and to do so with emotional involvement. As the weeks went by, one could observe the growing relaxation of his body, the gradual dissolving of tensions, and the reawakening of his capacity to feel. As he permitted himself to experience his formerly disowned needs and frustrations, he discovered within himself desires, responses and aspirations of which he had had no knowledge. Within a few months his passion for a particular career, which he had repressed long ago, was reborn.

The particular exercise I have described is only one of a number that have proved useful in helping to dissolve emotional blocks, to restore repressed memories and to expand the capacity to feel. In releasing the buried pain of the past, such exercises help release a person's capacity to experience emotion in the present, and thus to be in better touch with his needs, desires and values, and thereby to *think* more clearly and effectively.

*

*   *

If an adult lets down his defenses and permits himself to experience all of his feelings, he opens the door to whatever pain he denied or repressed in the past—which for many people is terrifying. When a psychotherapist uses techniques aimed at helping an adult to experience his present emotions, it is very common for a rush of childhood memories—sometimes excruciatingly painful ones—suddenly and explosively to flow into conscious awareness.

The following case, which I shall describe in some detail, illustrates many of the principles I have been discussing.

The client was a man of thirty-four, a dedicated and ambitious lawyer, who had had many relationships with women but who, until a few months before coming to see me, had never been in love. In former affairs, he had always enjoyed a strong sense of "control"—derived from the knowledge that the women were far more deeply involved than he was. At times he wondered if his inability to fall in love indicated some deficiency, but he tended to push such thoughts aside. He told himself that what he primarily wanted from women was "physical sex" and that passion was to be reserved for his work. He described himself, in his dealings with women, as honest and considerate; he was never intentionally cruel; if he sometimes found himself lapsing into callousness, he regretted it and reproached himself for it.

A few months prior to our first meeting, he met a woman to whom he was strongly attracted and whom he admired more than any he had ever met. He felt that he was falling in love with her. Yet during the first month of their affair, he twice slept with other women —for no reason he could explain to himself; he felt himself suddenly hit by what he described as "an absolutely insane impulse." He told the woman he loved of his actions and, though hurt, she forgave him; she told him she was convinced that he loved her.

It was her reaction, he thought, that had somehow precipitated him into his present emotional crisis. Her stated confidence in him and in their relationship, her willingness to admit that she was hurt and the fact that she did not become cold and withdraw from him, were perceived by him as astounding, inspiring and challenging. He felt that he must somehow find a way to equal her self-confident honesty, trust, and emotional openness. Whereas before he had always been reluctant to speak of his feelings, beyond stating that he loved her, he now felt compelled to communicate the depth of her meaning to him. He was appalled at the difficulty he encountered; his mind seemed frozen, the words would not come. What shocked him far more, however, was that when he did at least begin to speak of his feelings, he found himself struggling not to break down in tears. This happened again and again, to his intense embarrassment and humiliation.

He began working late at his law office, finding excuses to see her less frequently. Sometimes, when they were together, he felt numb and remote, and told himself that he was no longer in love. On other occasions he felt passionately in love; but when he tried to express it, he was stopped by the burning sensation of tears. He was utterly bewildered by the strange process by which the most ecstatic feelings of love seemed to draw in their wake an oppressive torment—a torment that wiped out his sense of manhood and left him feeling helpless.

Returning home from her apartment after an unusually happy evening together, he "found himself" (that is how he described it: "found himself") walking to the telephone, calling a former girl friend and inviting her over to spend the night. In the morning, after the girl had left, he felt sick—not with anxiety or guilt, he said, but with an inability to feel anything other than a strange sense of tension. He was unable to confess his action to the woman he loved; he felt certain that this time she would leave him. He decided to seek psychotherapy.

By the time he had finished telling me his story— which I have condensed considerably—I had formed a hypothesis that would account for his behavior. But I prefer to lead a client to the understanding of his own motivation in a manner that will be maximally meaningful and convincing to him, which means: allowing him to confront his motive on the level of direct inner experience, rather than through abstract discussion.

The session from which I am about to quote was tape-recorded and subsequently transcribed. But before

I proceed, I must say a word or two about the technique employed. I have developed a list of phrases, the beginning parts of sentences, which are to be finished by the client with the first words entering his mind that constitute a completion of the sentence. I have found these particular phrases to be highly productive of significant material. They are not necessarily presented in any particular order nor are they necessarily all used at any given interview. (The method and its uses will be discussed further in Chapter 4.) As soon as the client gives a response that I wish I to explore further, I temporarily leave the pre-selected phrases on the list, and begin improvising new items that will illicit illuminating material. After following a given trail for the length of a few exchanges, I go back to the list, until new material emerges that I wish to pursue.

When my client expressed willingness to cooperate in this particular exercise, I explained the procedure as follows: "I will say the first part of a series of incomplete sentences. As quickly and spontaneously as possible, you will reply with the first grammatical completion of the sentence that occurs to you. Try to avoid editing, censoring, or worrying about the rightness or appropriateness of your responses. There are no "right" or "wrong" completions. We're simply interested in the first response that occurs to you. Never mind if the responses sound foolish, illogical, ridiculous or to the exact opposite of your beliefs. I suggest that you make yourself comfortable, let your hands rest at your sides, close your eyes, take a deep breath and let your body relax. Don't try to *make* anything happen. Don't try to analyze. Just let what happens happen of its own accord."

The client was then given a deliberately innocuous phrase, in order to test his understanding of what was wanted: "When I look at the ocean—" and he immediately responded "—I see water." Now we were ready to begin.

Therapist: When I wake up in the morning—
Client: —I wonder what I have to do today.

T: All my life—
C: —I wanted to succeed.
T: Sometimes I feel—
C: —what's it all about?
T: As a man—
C: —I sometimes don't know what that means.
T: I don't understand myself because—
C: —I'm losing control.
T: "Control" to me means—
C: —being on top of things.
T: "Being on top of things" means—
C: —not letting my feelings overpower me.
T: Why do I always—
C: —run away. I don't run away; this is ridiculous; I don't know what I'm saying.
T: Don't try to evaluate now. Just let the responses come to you. Whenever I try—
C: —I usually succeed.
T: I want—
C: —I want—I don't know what I want.
T: I can't tolerate—
C: —weakness.
T: "Weakness" to me means—
C: —giving in to my feelings.
T: If I give in to my feelings—
C: —I'll be helpless.
T: Sometimes I want to cry out—
C: —I'm tired of the pressure!
T: When people look at me—
C: —let them look.
T: Why do people so often—
C: —expect things of me.
T: Right now I am feeling—
C: —anxious.
T: If I sink deeper into my anxiety—
C: —I feel that something unpleasant is going to happen.
T: When I look in the mirror—
C: —I wonder: Is that me?
T: Ever since I was a child—
C: —I felt tense.
T: Sexually, I—

C: —feel safe.

T: I feel safe because—

C: —because . . . I don't know. I feel like I'm blocking.

T: Never mind, let's continue. Mother was always—

C: —suffering.

T: She always seemed to expect—

C: —me to do something about it. I don't know what. I never did.

T: She never—

C: —could pull herself together. She was always leaning on me.

T: That made me feel—

C: —lousy, suffocated, inadequate.

T: And it also made me feel—

C: —angry.

T: Father was always—

C: —there. Expecting things. Looking at me.

T: He never—

C: —would explain anything.

T: He always seemed to expect—

C: —me to understand everything without being told.

T: He seemed to want—

C: —me to never make a mistake.

T: When I did make a mistake—

C: —he looked at me with contempt.

T: That made me feel—

C: —guilty.

T: And it also made me feel—

C: —that I must never make a mistake.

T: When I'm in bed with a woman, I feel safe because—

C: —I'm close, but there's no involvement.

T: Women to me are—

C: —emotional.

T: Men to me are—

C: —they should be strong and in control.

T: Women always seem to want—

C: —me to feel things.

T: That makes me—

C: Freeze.

T: I can remember—

C: —Mother, God damn it!

T: A woman's body–

C: –is a challenge. Am I man enough?

T: Pleasure to me is–

C: –being free.

T: "Freedom" to me means–

C: –being out of reach.

T: "Being out of reach" means–

C: –you can't get hurt that way.

T: If I ever let out my anger–

C: –God help somebody!

T: I don't dare show my anger because–

C: –I show it sometimes.

T: If I ever let it all out–

C: –I'd be wiped out.

T: I'd be wiped out because–

C: –that son-of-a-bitch would kill me!

T: When I was with father–

C: –I tried to stay cool. I tried to stay out of his way.

T: Sometimes I push my thoughts away because–

C: –I don't want to know.

T: When I think that I am my parents' child–

C: –I don't think of it.

T: Sometimes I feel guilty–

C: –because I know there's something wrong with me.

T: Sometimes I want to cry out–

C: –I'm tired!

T: The thing I'm most tired of is–

C: –I don't know.

T: Right now, I'm feeling–

C: –pain . . . tension at the back of my neck.

T: If I sink deeper into the tension at the back of my neck–

C: –I can feel how tense I am.

T: I make myself tense because–

C: –how should I know? Do I make myself tense deliberately?

T: Sometimes I push my feelings away because–

C: –I'm afraid of what I'll find.

T: If I were more emotionally open–

C: –I might feel better, but I don't believe it.

T: It's hard to be emotionally open because–

C: —I can be hurt.

T: "Being hurt" means—

C: —really needing somebody.

T: If I ever admitted I really needed another person—

C: —I need Jennifer.

T: When I admit that I need Jennifer—

C: —it feels very strange.

T: When I was first unfaithful to her—

C: —I had to prove that I didn't need her.

T: When I was driving home from her apartment last week before I called my old girl friend—

C: —I was feeling great.

T: But later I began to feel—

C: —tense.

T: And then I began to feel—

C: —cut off from everything.

T: I cut myself off from everything because—

C: —I had to get away. I couldn't stand it.

T: I was frightened because—

C: —I'm really in love.

T: When I admit that I'm in love—

C: —the pain inside is killing me.

T: Right now I am feeling—

C: —to cry.

T: I can remember—

C: —wanting my father to love me.

T: Father—

C: —didn't love anybody.

T: Thinking of him now I feel—

C: —rage.

T: If I sink deeper into my rage I feel—

C: —hurt.

T: I want to call out to him—

C: —look at me!

T: At the thought of running away from Jennifer—

C: —I feel like I'm saying goodbye to my last chance.

T: I tense the muscles in the back of my neck in order—

C: —to stop myself from feeling anything. Jesus! That's true!

T: Right now I am feeling—

C: —I'm beginning to relax.

T: When I begin to tell Jennifer what I feel for her, I want to cry because—

C: —I've never felt it before.

T: And also because—

C: —all the pain starts coming back to me.

T: The pain began when—

C: —a long time ago.

T: I can remember—

C: —the time I wanted to sit on the arm of my father's chair.

T: Father was—

C: —impatient.

T: Right now I am feeling—

C: —better. But I don't know why.

T: The most important thing I've learned today is—

C: —I'm afraid to commit myself.

T: "Committing myself" means—

C: —letting myself really care for another person, and letting the other person know how much I care.

T: I can't do that because—

C: —it feels too threatening.

T: If I didn't always have to protect myself—

C: —I could let myself be happy. I could live.

T: Basically, I—

C: —feel unreal. Or usually, anyway. Right now, I feel real. What's happening to me?

At this point, I terminated the exercise and invited my client to discuss his reactions. Very little "interpretation" on my part was necessary. My client was able to perform the synthesis himself, especially after replaying the tape recording two or three times during the following week. One of the advantages of the method is the extent to which the material virtually speaks for itself, in a manner more convincing to the client than any therapist's "analysis."

This case was selected because it so eloquently illustrates the process by which a person can come to deny and disown certain of his own needs and desires, and thus cripple his personality, out of a misguided effort to attain a sense of control, efficacy and personal worth;

and because it dramatizes the destructive impact of emotional repression on a person's cognitive contact with reality: in the handling of his personal life, this highly intelligent man was utterly helpless intellectually. So long as he was cut off from his fear of being hurt, and the fear of emotional intimacy to which it led, his own responses and behavior—including their strangely compulsive character—would be incomprehensible to him.

When a person denies his real needs, the inevitable outcome is the creation of an unreal self—the personality he presents to the world. In this case, that personality consisted, in effect, of a work-machine and a sex-machine, not a human being. For many persons who have a strong desire for efficacy, but a neurotic fear of emotional intimacy, sex can become their one bridge to other human beings, their one acceptable form of reaching out; and the more intolerable their inner state, the more anxiously unbearable their unacknowledge loneliness, the more erratically compulsive their sexual behavior is likely to be. Sex without personal involvement is often called upon to perform that same psychological function which is performed, for persons of a different psychology, by prayer or alcohol or tranquilizers.

His mother's extreme dependency and emotionalism and his father's remote sternness both contributed to this client's animosity towards emotions—the mother's example encouraging him to associate emotions with weakness, the father's behavior and the hurt it produced in the son encouraging him to associate emotions with vulnerability, pain and rejection.

But if a person spends years repressing his emotions and denying his loneliness, if he blocks the knowledge of his need to love and to be loved, if he numbs himself to the pain of his frustrations, but then partially overcomes his fear of being hurt, enough to fall in love, he finds himself trapped in an anxiety-provoking dilemma: that love, which should signal the end of his loneliness and the fulfillment of his happiness, becomes instead a formidable threat. In order fully to experience the love and the potential happiness it offers him, he has to be willing to confront his past pain, the pain he had never permitted himself to acknowledge. In order fully to experience the meaning of the present, he must be able to experience the meaning of his past—including his loneliness, frustration, and feelings of rejection—which constitutes his *particular psychological context*.

Fear of such a confrontation was a major factor incapacitating this man. As soon as he began to experience and to make real his feelings for the woman, the past rose up like a terrifying specter, announcing itself by the onset of incomprehensible tears. In reverting to a state of emotional dissociation and turning to senseless infidelities, he was clearly seeking to deny the importance of the first serious relationship he had ever had with a woman. Paradoxically and tragically, his infidelity—seen in this light—was a twisted form of tribute to her.

Still another element involved in his infidelity, which became much more apparent in a subsequent session, was his fear of being hurt in the present, a fear whose origins obviously extended back to his childhood. This fear was as powerful a factor in his motivation as his dread of confronting his past suffering.

Every person who dreads emotional intimacy does so because he lives with the expectation that, in any relationship, sooner or later he will be rejected. So sometimes he "protects" himself by rejecting before he can be rejected, or by acting in such a way as to imply that the relationship is less important than it actually is. Such behavior often results in bringing about the very rejection and loss he had feared, which, of course, merely intensifies his fear of future rejection and loss. This is one of the commonest forms of self-destruction men and women practice.

*
*   *

Few of the irrationalities people commit—the destructive behavior they unleash against themselves and against others—would be possible to them if they did not first cut themselves off from their own deepest feelings. Paradoxically, the person we sometimes describe as "ruled by his feelings"—the irresponsible, impulsive "whim-worshipper"—is as dissociated from his inner emotional life as the most inhibited "intellectualizer." The difference in personality is more of form than of essence.

To take an extreme example: a pathological murderer is not a man guided by his intellect, but neither is he a man in good, integrated contact with his emotions. Indeed, it is the brutal repression of feeling, specifically feelings of hurt, anger and rage, that sometimes leads to sudden, unexpected and seemingly uncontainable explosions of violence. A tension generated by denied feelings becomes so unbearable that it finally erupts in physically destructive behavior.

When people complain—as so many complain today —of a bewilderingly diminished capacity to feel, pain is the primary underlying emotion they have repressed. In many people, an enormous quantity of unacknowledged and undischarged pain is so close to the surface of awareness that often it only takes the right word at the right moment to unleash a torrent of agonized self-awareness.

Once, during a group therapy session, a man was discussing the effects on him of marijuana and LSD which, prior to therapy, he took with compulsive regularity. He regretted relinquishing the use of such drugs, he said wistfully, because under their influence all his cares seemed to fade away and he was able to enjoy his own feelings. "You mean," I said, "when you take drugs you're able to experience something besides screaming pain." He looked astonished and agitated, and I added, "That's what it's all about, isn't it? Don't you know that pain is what you otherwise feel—and *all* you otherwise feel—twenty-four hours a day?" He nodded his head several times, he looked like a man slowly emerging from a trance, and he began to cry; the mere fact of my naming his pain seemed to dissolve his defenses and the pain began flooding his body and emotions. What was especially interesting was that I looked around the room and saw that five other members of the group, none of whom were or had been on drugs, were also crying: it had taken only the sound of a human voice identifying the "open secret" of their lives—the mere mention of "screaming pain"—to bring their denied feelings to the surface.

As to the matter of drugs, I do not think one can understand the attraction they have for many people if one does not recognize that, in the absence of drugs, they see life as offering them two possibilities: bad days, on which they feel pain and dread, and "good" days, *on which they feel nothing.*

The repression of emotions, which begins in childhood with the denial of pain, frustration, fear and rage, extends in later years to more and more areas of one's emotional life, resulting in a progressively deepening sense of self-estrangement.

A person denies his need to find human beings he can respect, admire and love—and then superimposes on himself the unreal personality of a cynic. A person denies his loneliness—and then withdraws from people behind an artificial front of indifferent remoteness. A person denies his need of self-esteem—and then proceeds to seek it in the bodies of an endless procession of women. A person denies his longing for beauty —and then affects a vulgarity aimed at proving his "practicality" and "realism." A person denies his pain— and then loses his sensitivity and buries his perceptiveness beneath a brutal blindness to the pain of others, including those he professes to love. A person denies his anxiety—and then finds himself locked in a self-made tomb of passive rigidity. A person makes himself thoroughly invisible—and then agonizes over the fact that no one sees or understands him. A person extinguishes one part of his personality after another— and then feels horror when he looks inward and finds only a sterile void.

*

*   *

In approaching this problem, what is needed—first— is an understanding of the meaning of emotions and their place in human psychology.

An emotion is the psychosomatic form in which a person experiences his estimate of the beneficial or harmful relationship of some aspect of reality to himself.

An emotion is a value-response. It is the automatic psychological result (involving both mental and somatic features) of a super-rapid, subconscious appraisal. Emotions are psychosomatic embodiments of value judgments. (For a more detailed discussion of emotions, see Chapter 5 of *The Psychology of Self-Esteem,* reprinted in Appendix A with annotations.)

Since emotions are the product of complex integrations of ideas, beliefs and experiences, they cannot be *commanded* in or out of existence, neither by an act of will nor by repression. It is a disastrous error to imagine that an emotion—merely because it is judged undesirable—can be dismissed or repressed with impunity.

With the acquisition and integration of new understanding, one can change the content of future emotions. But, at any given moment, once an emotion exists, it exists; it is a fact of reality—the reality of one's own person.

Once an emotion arises in a human organism, it tends to follow a natural course of its own: it is experienced, it is expressed in some form of bodily behavior, and it is discharged. That is the normal progression. When that process is blocked by denial or repression, unresolved tensions remain in the body—the emotion is "dammed up," as it were—even if conscious awareness of the emotion has been extinguished, or was never permitted to occur.

This does not mean that every emotion need be acted on; every emotion carries within it the impulse to perform some particular action—but emotion and action are two different and distinct categories, and such impulses need not be obeyed blindly and uncritically. What the organism does require for its well-being, however—especially in the case of emotions that are more than superficial and momentary—is that they be *experienced* and *acknowledged*.

Whether a person's values and value judgments in any given situation are correct or mistaken, and whether it is appropriate and possible to act on his feelings or not—his emotions reflect the meaning that reality has for him at that point in time. *They are to be treated seriously.* They are not to be dismissed as inconsequential or irrelevant. One does not destroy an emotion by refusing to feel it or acknowledge it; one merely disowns a part of one's self.

If the essence of rationality is respect for the facts of reality, then that must include the facts of one's own psychological state. That, too, is part of reality. Yet that is the aspect of reality men are most inclined to avoid. The exercise of reason does not pertain only to awareness of the external world; it includes the internal world of consciousness as well—meaning: the world of one's inner experience. It is here however, that—in the lives of most men—the default on reason is most tragic.

If a person is to function effectively and to achieve that state of psychological integration which mental health requires, he must learn to function on two levels: to preserve contact with external reality *and* with internal reality—with the objective requirements of any given situation *and* with its emotional meaning to him; with the facts *and* with his appraisal of the facts; with what he must do *and* with what he feels about what he must do.

When a man in effect decides to disregard external reality in order to lose himself in his feelings, the only feeling usually left to him is anxiety. When a man in effect decides to cut off contact with his emotions in order to function effectively in reality, he sabotages his ability to think.

Let me stress that to treat one's emotions with respect, in the manner I am suggesting, does not mean to regard emotions, of and by themselves, as suitable guides to action; clearly they are not. But we must recognize that our emotions reflect *"where we are at"* at this moment of our life. The voice of our emotions can be silenced by repression; but that does not cancel out the message they contain nor the necessity to deal with it. And it cannot be dealt with effectively if it is not experienced.

It is generally easier for people to understand and accept the necessity of experiencing emotions they regard as desirable: love, joy, pleasure and so forth. But it is no less imperative that one permit oneself to experience emotions one regards as undesirable. And it does not matter whether one regards them as undesirable because they are painful or because one is convinced they reflect mistaken values and value judgments.

There is a difference between *experiencing* an emotion and merely *naming* it to oneself. Suppose, for instance, a client comes to therapy, his therapist inquires, "How are you?" and the client answers, in a tense, distracted manner, "Rotten." Then the therapist says sympathetically, "I see that you are really feeling depressed." Then the client sighs, the tension begins to flow from his body, and in an altogether different tone of voice—the voice of a person who is now real to himself—he acknowledges, "Yes, I'm miserable. I'm really miserable." When, with his whole body tensed to resist the experience of his own feelings, he had answered, "Rotten," he was denying his emotion at the same time that he was verbally acknowledging it. The therapist's response encouraged him to *experience* it.

Now why is that so important? That question lies at the heart of the issue we are considering.

By way of approaching the answer, I should like to quote a passage from Dr. Haim Ginott's book, *Between Parent and Teenager* (Macmillan, 1969). The art and challenge of child raising is to educate a child, to provide him with guidance and instruction, but without doing violence to his psychology in the process. No one has spoken more eloquently and helpfully than Dr. Ginott on the importance of parents treating with respect the feelings of children, of acknowledging a child's feelings and permitting the child to experience them without fear or guilt.

David, age seventeen, was interviewed for a summer job, but was rejected. He returned home disappointed and depressed. Father felt sympathy for his son and conveyed it effectively.

Father: You really wanted this job, didn't you?

David: I sure did.

Father: And you were so well equipped for it, too.

David: Yeh! a lot of good that did me.

Father: What a disappointment.

David: It sure is, Dad.

Father: Looking forward to a job and having it slip away just when you need it is tough.

David: Yeh, I know.

There was silence for a moment. Then David said, "It's not the end of the world. I'll find another job."

I think we can understand that such an approach on the part of the boy's father would be very effective. But *why* is it effective? I would explain it in the following way.

It is very likely that, at the same time the boy is feeling disappointed and depressed, he is *resisting* the feeling of disappointment and depression; he is tensing his body against it; he is struggling to deny his feeling. By acknowledging the boy's context, by recognizing what the boy would necessarily feel, by naming it in words, and by communicating benevolent acceptance and respect, the father is in effect permitting the boy to experience his emotions fully, to let them become completely real to him—accepted and integrated into conscious awareness. We do not fully explain the healing effect of the father's response if we merely say that the boy feels better because he received sympathy. He feels better because, in being helped fully to experience his feelings, they are expressed and discharged—they do not remain trapped within him. He is able to assimilate the painful experience and therefore move beyond it: his natural, healthy sense of reality is now able to assert itself and bring him to a wider view of his context.

Just as the body contains its own self-repairing powers, so does the mind. But those healing powers must be allowed to work. Repression obstructs the healing—meaning: the integrative—process. One reason why people of high intelligence and great knowledge can be so helpless in the face of personal problems is that, by denying their feelings, by refusing to experience them, they make it impossible for their intelligence and knowledge to "go to work" on the problems—to achieve the new integration necessary to resolve them.

Most parents do not respond to such situations like the father in Dr. Ginott's example; they respond instead in a manner likely to prolong and aggravate the depression. Dr. Ginott gives seven examples of common types of destructive response, perpetrated by parents, which I would like to quote:

"What did you expect? To get the first job you wanted? Life is not like that. You may have to go to five or even ten interviews before you are hired."

"Rome was not built in one day, you know. You are still very young, and your whole life is in front of you. So, chin up. Smile and the world will smile with you. Cry and you will cry alone. I hope it will teach you not to count your chickens before they are hatched."

"When I was your age I went looking for my first job. I shined my shoes, got a haircut, put on clean clothes, and carried the *Wall Street Journal* with me. I knew how to make a good impression."

"I don't see why you should feel so depressed. There is really no good reason for you to be so discouraged. Big deal! One job did not work out. It's not worth even talking about."

"The trouble with you is that you don't know how to talk with people. You always put your foot in your mouth. You lack poise, and you are fidgety. You are too eager, and not patient enough. Besides, you are thin-skinned and easily hurt."

"I am so sorry, dear, I don't know what to tell you. My heart breaks. Life is so much a matter of luck. Other people have all the luck. They know the right people in the right places. We don't know anyone and no one knows us."

"Everything happens for the best. If you miss one bus there will soon be another, perhaps a less crowded one. If you didn't get one job, you'll get another—perhaps even a better one."

Considering these responses in the present context, it is easy to appreciate how unhelpful they are—how destructive they may be. But I should like to draw attention to the fact that this is precisely the sort of destructive nonsense with which people respond to their *own* pain; and the results are no less unfortunate.

Most people tend to deal with their emotions as they learned to do in childhood, which generally means: to deal with them as destructively as their parents did. Their parents' policies become *internalized*.

If we acknowledge and permit ourselves to experience our painful or undesired feelings, without self-pity and without self-condemnation, we facilitate the process of healing integration. But if we ridicule ourselves, lecture ourselves, recite meaningless clichés to ourselves, or wallow in tragic thoughts about the futility of life, we do not bring our emotions into constructive contact with our intelligence and our knowledge, and so we needlessly prolong and even worsen our agony.

An understanding of the healing effect of acknowledging and describing emotions, in a noncritical manner, is essential to the practice of effective psychotherapy. A client one day began reproaching herself for feeling anger at her husband over the fact that he was leaving on a two-week business trip. She called herself irrational, she called herself stupid, she told herself it was ridiculous to feel that way—but the anger persisted. *No one has ever talked himself (or anyone else) out of an undesired emotion by hurling insults or by delivering a moral lecture.*

I asked her to try to describe her feeling of anger, to describe where in her body she experienced it and how exactly it felt to her. She expressed annoyance and irritation at the request. "What good would that do?" she wanted to know. "I don't want to feel the anger! I want to get rid of it!" But I persisted, and gradually she began to describe feelings of tension in her chest and a tight knot in her stomach. Then she exclaimed, "I feel indignant, I feel enraged, I feel: how can he do this to me?" Then, to her astonishment, the anger began to dissolve. Another emotion emerged in its place: anxiety. I asked her to describe the anxiety. Again she began to argue and reproach herself. I asked her to go deeper into her feeling of anxiety, to try to experience it more completely, to immerse herself in it, as it were, and to see if, in effect, it would begin to speak to her. "My God!" she cried, "I'm afraid of being left alone." Again she began to rebuke herself: "What am I, a child? Can't I be on my own for two weeks?" I asked her now to sink more deeply into her fear of being left alone. "I'm afraid of what I might do when he's gone," she said suddenly. She added, "You know—other men; I might get involved with another man. I don't trust myself."

By now, the anger was gone, the anxiety had dissolved, the fear of loneliness had faded away. A problem remained that had to be dealt with—but now, since it was admitted into conscious awareness, it was *capable* of being dealt with.

Another example: A young man—a professional singer—was preparing for his first important role in an opera. He complained of intense feelings of stagefright. Even as he described the problem, I could see him tensing his body against his feelings. Naturally, the more he tensed his body, the more tense he felt; the more tense he felt, the more apprehensive he felt; the more apprehensive he felt, the more he made himself still more tense. By fighting his feelings in this manner, he was escalating them into panic. This is a very common pattern.

I suggested to him that, instead of fighting his anxiety, he try to experience it more intensely, to surrender himself to it for the moment, rather than fight it. He looked at me with horror—and it took considerable urging to persuade him to make the attempt. I asked him to describe his feelings, both his emotions and his bodily sensations. After much faltering and hesitancy, he proceeded as follows: "I can feel my heart pounding in my chest . . . going a mile a minute. My chest is tight, it feels like it's being pulled in two opposite directions . . . my breathing is shallow, my breath keeps jerking in and out in little spurts . . . my throat feels tight, feels constricted, I feel like I'm choking. I'm aware of tension in my legs, my thigh muscles feel strained. My

arms are shaking . . . I just had a flash of myself on the
stage and now I feel myself beginning to perspire . . .
At the thought of all those people looking at me, I feel
terrified." I asked him, "Would you say, very loudly,
'I feel terrified'?" He gasped and shouted, "I feel
terrified!" I asked him to shout it again; he did so.
"How are you feeling now?" I inquired. He paused for
a moment and then looked astonished. "Better," he said.
"I'm beginning to feel relaxed."

One more example: A woman in her mid-twenties
came to group one evening, feeling nervous and depressed. A few weeks earlier, she explained, she had
met a man at a party to whom she was strongly attracted and who evidently returned her feeling. After
several meetings, they began an affair. The next morning, in answer to some casual question about her past
life, she volunteered the information that she had once
been married; the truth was that she had been married
and divorced twice. It was a petty lie, she felt acutely
embarrassed about it, and recognized that it had been
prompted by a momentary fear that he would lose
respect for her at the knowledge that she had been twice
divorced at so young an age. She felt too humiliated to
confess the truth. What made matters worse, she went
on, was the fact that she felt happier with this man than
with any man she had ever known; for the first time in
her life she felt visible to and appreciated by another
human being. She said she could not decide what to
do.

At this point, one member of the group began to lecture her on the sin of dishonesty; another interrupted to
offer the warning that sooner or later the man would
find out the truth, anyway, so it was better to act now
rather than face a worse predicament in the future;
another suggested that her reaction of depression was
exaggerated and that the situation did not warrant it.
The girl listened and became more and more depressed,
more and more remote, and more and more helplessly
bewildered.

I was convinced that this girl had all the knowledge
necessary to arrive at a reasonable decision—and that

lecturing her on morality or belittling her feelings or deepening her guilt would merely aggravate her condition and solve nothing. To persuade her of the importance of honesty in human relationships, or the self-defeating nature of her behavior, was not what needed to be done; the most important task was to enable her to discover that she already knew it, and that it could have personal meaning to her.

I therefore asked her to imagine confessing the truth to the man, to visualize the scene as clearly as possible, and to let herself experience—and then describe aloud —her feelings of humiliation. She did so. She then remarked, "I'm always expecting to be rejected." I asked her to immerse herself as deeply as possible in her feeling of anticipated rejection—and to describe it. She did so. Then I asked her to describe the unique quality of the happiness she had found in her relationship with this man—to describe it in as much detail as she could. She did so—and as she talked, as the relationship became emotionally real to her, everyone in the room could see her body relaxing, could see her tension dissolving, and I doubt that anyone was surprised when she suddenly smiled and said, "Oh, this is ridiculous. Of course I'm going to tell him the truth. It's the only thing to do. I can't imagine what I was thinking of."

I asked her to describe what she was feeling now. "Happy," she answered. "What else?" I asked. "As though I suddenly have more self-esteem," she replied. "Can you say anything more about that?" I inquired. "Yes," she said, "It's not just because I've decided to tell him the truth. It's because for the past twenty minutes I've been treating myself with respect —taking myself seriously—treating myself and my emotions as real—not brushing myself aside like garbage."

In Chapter 3 we shall discuss, in some detail, *why* the method described in these three examples works as effectively as it does, and we shall consider the wider psychological implications involved.

In the practice of therapy I find it necessary to devote a good deal of time to teaching clients the art of describing their own emotions. Virtually everyone encounters considerable difficulty in the initial attempts. They comment on their emotions, they "explain" their emotions, they "apologize" for their emotions, they speculate as to the historical origins of their emotions—and, of course, they *reproach* themselves for their emotions—but they find it extraordinarily difficult simply to let themselves *feel* their emotions and then describe what they experience. They have to overcome years of defenses erected to protect them against their inner emotional life.

When the emotions with which they are struggling to make contact are unpleasant or painful, the almost universal impulse is to resist them, to convulse one's body against them—which frequently serves only to intensify them. Just as the driver of a skidding car must resist his impulse to turn the wheel against the skid and instead turn the wheel into the skid, in order to regain control, so the person hit by a disturbing emotion must learn the art of going "with" the emotion, not "against" it, in order eventually to dissolve it. (We shall explore this further in Chapter 3.)

If no one ever achieved emotional fulfillment by following his feelings impulsively and uncritically, it must also be realized that no one ever won a battle against his emotions by declaring war on them. "Nature, to be commanded, must be obeyed," and if men are to achieve an integrated harmony of mind and emotion, they must appreciate the laws of emotional functioning, and respond accordingly. *That* is the application of reason to the sphere of emotion.

Chapter 2

Childhood and Neurosis

In recent years a number of psychologists and psychiatrists have proposed that the concepts of "mental health" and "mental illness" be discarded. Dr. Thomas Szasz, for example, in his book *The Myth of Mental Illness* (Hoeber-Harper, 1961), argues that such designations are inapplicable to psychological states and are dangerously misleading. Among the various reasons offered by Dr. Szasz and others for this position are the following. "Illness" or "disease" originally referred to a *physical* condition of the organism, and still retain that connotation. The use of the "medical model" conveys a picture of the psychologically troubled individual as a passive, non-self-responsible victim who somehow has been "hit" or "struck" by an affliction; this obscures the role of volition and of self-destructive ideas in mental, emotional and behavioral disorder. Further, "mental illness" is often used merely to brand nonconformist or "socially deviant" behavior, by psychologists and psychiatrists who have failed to provide an *objective* standard of mental health that is free of cultural bias.

That there are radical differences between physical illness and that which we call mental illness, is indisputable. Mental illness is not a condition one can

37

"catch," nor is it a condition one can "give" to someone else. It cannot be corrected, like a broken arm or
the measles, by passively surrendering oneself to the
ministrations of a doctor. The process of correcting it
has virtually nothing in common with the medical treatment; rather, the process is one of *education*. And, like
every form of education, success requires volitional
participation and intellectual initiative on the part of
the person who is being educated.

Nothwithstanding these considerations, there are
powerful reasons in favor of retaining the concept of
"mental health" and "mental illness"—and there is, I
submit, a method of establishing the standard by which
these respective conditions are to be judged that is independent of cultural or social bias.

To quote from my discussion of this issue in *The
Psychology of Self-Esteem*:

The key to the problem of defining the concepts of
health and disease, as they pertain to man's mind, consists
of placing the issue in a biological context—of remember-
ing that man is a living organism, and that the concepts
of health and disease are inextricably linked to the basic
alternative confronting all organisms: the issue of life and
death.

In the sphere of *physical* health and disease, this fact is
clearly recognized. A healthy body is one whose organs
function efficiently in maintaining the life of the organism;
a disease of any part of man's body is judged by the
standard of how well or poorly it performs its survival-
function. *Life* is the standard of judgement.

No other rational standard is possible. It is only the
alternative of life or death that makes the concept of
health or of disease meaningful or possible. An inanimate
object can be neither well nor ill; the concepts are not
applicable. Without life as the standard, the concepts of
health and disease are not intelligible.

Just as medical science evaluates a man's body by the
standard of whether or not his body is functioning as
man's life requires, so the science of psychology must
employ the same standard in appraising the health or
disease of a man's mind. The health of a man's mind

must be judged by how well that mind performs its biological function.

The basic function of man's consciousness is *awareness*—and, collaterally, the regulation of behavior.

If man is to act effectively, if he is to maintain and further his life, he requires a knowledge of his environment and of his own state—of external reality and of internal reality—of the world and of self.

His faculty of awareness is indispensible to his survival. In order to function successfully, man needs to be in contact with the universe in which he acts—and with his own needs, feelings, desires, frustrations, capabilities and goals. To the extent that his awareness is blocked, to the extent that he is blind to facts about the world or about himself which, in the absence of his blocks, would be available to him, his life and well-being are impaired.

When his mind is unblocked and unobstructed, a person tends to maintain a free, natural, spontaneous flow of awareness back and forth, between the outer world and the inner, as circumstances require. A person's needs, interests, goals and general context, at any given time, determine the aspects of external reality that will be drawn into the forefront of awareness.

A blindness concerning important aspects of self leads to a blindness concerning important aspects of the environment. For instance, a person who denies the presence of a need will be oblivious to opportunities to satisfy that need. A person who denies the reality of his pain will be blind to the source of the pain and will continually reexpose himself to new hurt. A person who guiltily disowns certain of his own desires may, via the mechanism of projection, falsely attribute them to others. Thus we are led to a profoundly important law of psychological functioning: awareness moves freely in both directions—or it moves freely in neither.

A person is mentally healthy to the extent that the functioning of his consciousness is unimpeded by blocks; he is mentally unhealthy to the extent that blocks obstruct the functioning of his consciousness.

This formulation may be characterized, not as the "medical model," but—more fundamentally—as the *biological model*. It exemplifies the biocentric approach to psychology which I discussed in *The Psychology of Self-Esteem*. In retaining the designation of health and illness for psychological states, one focuses and stresses the *survival-function* of consciousness—the fact that the issue of awareness and unawareness is the issue of life and death. Until and unless alternative terms can be found that convey this biological orientation, "mental health" and "mental illness" remain immensely useful and desirable, notwithstanding the other medical connotations from which they need to be thoroughly disassociated.[1]

The foregoing discussion is offered not as an exhaustive analysis of this very complex issue, but only as a general characterization of my own views insofar as they are relevant to this study. I hope to deal with the issue in detail in a future work.

The goal of psychotherapy can be stated very simply: to remove obstructions to awareness, and thereby to the integrative power of the mind.

*   *

A child does not begin by repressing awareness of some aspect of the external world; he begins by repressing awareness of some aspect of the internal world— the world of feeling. ("Feeling" is used here in a very general way, to cover both emotions and the sensory awareness of bodily states.)

Repression begins as a flight from inner experience— a flight from feelings of pains, fear, frustration, helplessness, rage. A child discovers very early, often wordlessly and subconsciously, that he can deflect his awareness away from undesired feelings and, further, that by tensing his body and constricting his breathing

[1] While I do not agree with Szasz' view that mental illness is a "myth," I think he has made an invaluable contribution in drawing attention to the appalling victimization of mental patients in our psychiatric hospitals, in emphasizing the evils of confining people to mental hospitals involuntarily, and warning of the dangerous political implication of "community psychiatry."

he can partially numb himself to his own state. The process soon becomes involuntary. Later, repression extends to thoughts and memories, as well as to perceptions of the external world, that tend to evoke undesired feelings.

Repression grows and becomes pathological if and to the extent that a child's biological and psychological needs are persistently and traumatically frustrated—and if and to the extent that, as he grows older, he is unable to assimilate his disturbing experiences on a conscious level. Repression may become, more and more, an automatized response to threatening emotions, thoughts and perceptions—in which case it operates as the effective motor of neurosis.

Repression is an *involuntary, subconscious avoidance reaction.*

A person's thoughts, memories, emotions, evaluations and perceptions are expressions and/or actions of his *self.* In disowning them, he diminishes his sense of self and induces feelings of self-alienation. Yet a child may experience so intensely painful a sense of pressure from a bewildering, frightening and seemingly hostile environment, that repression becomes virtually inevitable; he feels he has no alternative. There is a respect in which the defense mechanism of repression is very "natural" to a child, in that the desire to escape pain and feelings of helplessness is "natural." In the face of an environment that is experienced as threatening and frustrating, a child's susceptibility to repression stems from the fact that he lacks the intellectual weapons to understand his situation and to protect himself, and from the fact that he cannot yet function and survive as an independent entity—he is chained to his tormentors.

The extent of his repression and of subsequent psychological damage depends on many factors, such as the magnitude of the pain and frustration to which he is subjected, the nature and extent of any counteracting benevolent factors in his environment, and very importantly, the degree of his will to think, to grow, to develop his powers, to transcend his adversity. A child with a strong commitment to remaining in good contact

with reality (and there are great differences among
children in this regard) will better withstand the impact of a destructive environment than the child whose
commitment to reality is more fragile. (This issue is
discussed at length in *The Psychology of Self-Esteem*.)
But *some* degree of repression in children seems universal.

There are psychologists and psychiatrists who regard
repression, as well as a host of other defenses, as in-
dispensable and desirable not only for children but
for all adults. They principally object to defenses only
when they "break down," which thereby permits an
eruption of anxiety. They see one of the purposes of
psychotherapy as being "to strengthen the patient's
defenses"—which means (in fact, although not in their
explicit statement): to help prevent the individual from
ever becoming fully integrated, fully real.

This is a view to which I am unreservedly opposed.
Such an approach to psychotherapy produces not psychologically healthier individuals, but individuals who
are more "socially acceptable"—at the cost of deepening their neuroses. In a culture such as ours, in which
human relationships are permeated by unreality on the
part of all participants and conformity to socially acceptable madness is the norm, the psychotherapist is or
should be the most passionate guardian of personal
integrity and personal authenticity. His job is to guide
men through the fog of unreality back to their real
selves.

A *defense* (or defense mechanism) is a subconsciously adopted technique whereby a person makes and
keeps himself unaware of impulses, feelings, ideas and
memories which are unacceptable and intolerable to his
conscious mind. If the goal of psychotherapy is to remove obstructions to the individual's awareness, then
this entails helping him to *discard* his defenses, helping
him to understand that they are unnecessary. It is his
defenses that keep him alienated from reality and from
himself.

A great many methods and techniques have been
developed by psychologists and psychiatrists for the pur-

pose of breaking through defenses and thereby bringing denied aspects of the self into conscious awareness. Some of these methods, relating back to the work of Wilhelm Reich, who first identified the role of muscular tension ("armoring") in repression, attack the problem of blocked feeling on a somatic level—by means of various physical exercises and other body-oriented techniques, such as are used in the Bioenergetic Therapy of neo-Reichian Alexander Lowen. On a more purely psychological level, some of the most brilliantly imaginative techniques for developing self-awareness have been originated by Frederick S. Perls, founder of Gestalt Therapy.

Among the many psychotherapists working in this area there are, of course, profound differences of theoretical orientation—differences in their view of man and of the nature and source of mental illness. But one can appreciate the effectiveness of some of the techniques they have developed, without necessarily subscribing to the wider theoretical premises that lie behind their work.

The question is sometimes debated: in the treatment of psychological problems, can the psychotherapist achieve desired results by dealing only with the client's present life, or is it necessary to explore and uncover the childhood origins of his defenses and negative self-concepts?

There are therapists who are interested only in the present and are disdainful of explorations of childhood; and there are therapists who are contemptuous of a concern with the present, which they regard as "superficial," and concentrate their focus primarily on the early years of the client's life. Psychotherapy is beset by many artificial dichotomies and the past/present dispute is one of them. There are highly specific and localized complaints, such as, for example, migraine headaches, that often respond well to direct treatment, without the necessity for childhood exploration; hypnosis, to name only one form of such direct treatment, can be remarkably effective in such cases. But in the overwhelming majority of complaints, the investigation of childhood traumas is essential—not *instead* of a concern with the present, but *in addition* to it. The most effective psychotherapy involves a fairly constant shift of concern, back and forth, between the past and the present—on the one hand guiding the client to reexperience and recognize the meaning of traumatic childhood events, and on the other hand guiding him to an awareness of the neurotic blocks and defenses that cripple him as an adult—thereby assisting him to achieve a better integration of his life experiences.

In working in the area of childhood, however, it has been found that the best results are obtained when the past is "converted" into present. This principle is exemplified in an exercise described in Chapter 1, where the client is asked to imagine himself lying on his deathbed and, in that context, to talk with his mother. Observe that he is not asked to tell "about" his childhood relationship with his mother, but to talk to her now, in the present. Or consider this example taken from *Breaking Free*. I ask a client, "Are you able to say what you felt for your father when you were a little boy?" The client answers, "I loved him, I suppose." Then I say, "Imagine you're in the house and your father hasn't come home yet. Now you hear his footsteps. He's coming come. What do you feel?" And now, through imagination, the client's mental focus shifts from present to the past and the past becomes the present, as he says, "What kind of mood will he be in? I hope he'll be cheerful. Sometimes he is. Sometimes he's in a bad mood and he yells at me. I feel fear. I never know what to expect. I never know what will make him angry. I don't know why he has to yell so much. . . . Oh Christ . . ." And the client begins to cry.

One converts the past into the present and also one converts the general into the specific—as the same examples illustrate. To describe his childhood relationship with his parents in terms of abstractions and generalities permits the client to remain remote from them, to leave the meaning of his own experiences unintegrated and unassimilated. But to guide the client to a confrontation with the meaning of that relationship, in the present and in terms of concretes and specifics, is to make the past real to him, now, so that his adult knowledge and intelligence can deal with it in a wider context than was available to him as a child. Only after this has been done can conceptual analysis and summation of the meaning of his experiences be therapeutically productive.

Only the present exists; the past and the future are abstractions. Only particulars exist; concepts or abstractions are a code or "shorthand" by means of which man is able to identify, retain and systematize his knowledge. That only the present and the particular are real is the philosophical principle at the root of this therapeutic method.

Nowhere is this rule more applicable than in the de-repression of childhood pain. To know, in a general sort of way, that one suffered or was frustrated a great deal as a child is almost useless therapeutically—although an astonishing number of clients lack even this vague memory.

It is traumatic childhood pain (and "pain," as used here, includes feelings of fear, frustration and helplessness)—pain with which the individual felt powerless to deal—that marks the beginning of the neurotic defense system and the individual's consequent self-alienation. Clinical observation makes this conclusion inescapable.

The mechanism of repression—in conjunction with other such defenses as rationalization, projection, intellectualizing, dissociation, etc.—serves, as we have seen, to keep a person out of touch with certain of his needs, feelings, preferences, frustrations and longings; which in turn results in cognitive distortions and blindness. The policy of denying one's inner experience began in childhood; to solve the problems generated by that policy one usually must return to "the scene of the crime."

This was not always my view. At one time it seemed reasonable to believe that, by working with the psychological problems originating in a client's adult life and helping him to become aware of the blocks and defenses that forbade him to solve those problems, one could

complete the therapeutic task—limited only by the dedication and perseverence of the client and the knowledge and skill of the therapist.

But in attempting to work more or less exclusively
with problems of the client's adult life, I found that one
of two things happened. Either we were led irresistibly
back into the past, down through layers of blocks and
defenses to the traumas of early childhood; or, at a
certain point, therapy reached an impasse, progress and
improvement were arrested and could proceed no further, and there was the dark sense of some impenetrable
barrier mocking our efforts.

I found that there was only one way that barrier
could be penetrated: by finding the defenses behind the
defenses, the blocks behind the blocks, the fear behind
the fear, the terror whose only relationship to the
present was symbolical, and whose origins lay in the
client's childhood—a terror that had never been unmasked, never been dealt with, and that continued
to act as the elusive but devastatingly potent saboteur
of the individual's growth.

The pain against which a child may feel driven to
defend himself by repression is occasioned by the frustration of basic needs. The particular needs in question
are ones which depend for their satisfaction on the behavior of the child's parents (or parent surrogates) and
which, therefore, parents have the power to frustrate.
(A child has other needs which he must satisfy himself.)
These parent-dependent needs include, but are not
limited to, the following: the need to be cared for and
protected physically; to be touched, held and caressed;
to be respected, loved, treated as a value; to receive
interest, understanding and concern; to love and admire;
to be free to explore one's environment and move toward increasing physical and mental mastery; to express
oneself physically, emotionally and intellectually and
receive an appropriate response; to be dealt with reasonably, justly and intelligibly. They are characterized as
"needs" because their satisfaction has a demonstrably
enhancing effect on the child's psychological growth and

development, and because their frustration has a demonstrably impeding effect.

I do not wish to suggest that the child's fate is determined solely or primarily by how his parents deal with these particular needs; other factors are crucially important, which are discussed in *The Psychology of Self-Esteem*. A human being normally plays a profoundly significant role, creatively or destructively, in determining the course of his own psychological development. Since I explore that subject at length in *The Psychology of Self-Esteem*, I shall not repeat my views here; I wish instead to focus on aspects of the individual's development not covered in that earlier book.

What I wish to draw attention to here is the long-range devastation that can result from a child's repression of these needs and of the pain associated with their traumatic frustration.

So long as, in later years, that repression remains intact and unrescinded, so long as there are aspects of an individual's life (past or present) he dreads to confront, so long as he continues to repudiate certain of his needs, so long as there are long-buried emotions he is terrified to face and experience, in profoundly important respects he remains cut off from himself and a stranger to his own person—regardless of what advances he may otherwise make toward increased self-awareness.

So long as there are large areas of institutionalized avoidance built into his psychology, the habit and policy of defensive avoidance reactions persists tenaciously. If one defense is unmasked, another quickly tends to take its place—like that mythological many-headed monster who grows another head as soon as one is chopped off.

The traumas of childhood, and the child's method of coping with them, are responsible for more than the *start* of the neurotic defense system; they play an active and virulent role in *maintaining* that defense system in later years. In support of this statement, I offer the following observations:

1. A number of psychologists and psychiatrists, developing further the work begun by Wilhelm Reich

(*Character Analysis,* Farrar, Straus and Giroux, 1949), have demonstrated that repressed childhood conflicts and traumas have an enduring impact on the muscular and postural condition of the body, and that these physical alterations, if uncorrected, tend to block or inhibit the free flow of feeling, of inner experience, so that they have the effect of reinforcing the defensive apparatus.

2. Once a person institutes the policy of responding to undesired feelings with a defensive avoidance reaction, that policy tends to feel more and more "natural," more and more "instinctive," and tends to become a habitual or characteristic method of psycho-epistemological functioning in new situations experienced as threatening.

3. When thoughts, memories, emotions and the awareness of needs have been represented, there is a strong tendency for the individual to experience anxiety —the sense of being threatened, endangered or overwhelmed—if such repressed material begins to rise to the surface of awareness. Therefore defenses are activated in the adult which are aimed at blocking awareness of perceptions or feelings that might stimulate the emergence of previously repressed material.

An incident that took place in one of my group therapy sessions provides an interesting illustration of this last point.

One member of the group, a boy of nineteen, was describing his reactions to another member, a young woman. When he looked at her, he said, he felt the urge to cry—because she seemed to be the warmest person he had ever encountered; if he spoke, she would listen and understand; if he reached out to her, she would not turn away; that is how he perceived her. He began to describe, simply and un-self-pityingly, the loneliness and isolation of his childhood, the remote indifference of his parents, his desperate longing for someone to talk to, his terror of his mother's bewildering religious fanaticism and of the physical beatings he received from his father, his sense of being trapped in a world with which he could not deal.

At some point, without my fully noticing it, my attention shifted to the rigidly crossed arms of one of the men in the group; it took me a moment to grasp what had arrested my interest: his arms were rising and falling, in rhythm with his breathing, at a tempo that made it unmistakably evident that he was experiencing anxiety; yet his face, as he stared indifferently at the opposite wall, was closed, expressionless, empty. Then I noticed that of the twelve group participants, almost none were looking at the boy who was speaking; some were looking at the ceiling, some were looking at the rug, some had their eyes closed; the faces of all were frozen into immobility. I glanced at my watch, then at the chests of the various members of the group. A normally relaxed person, not engaged in physical exertion, breathes about thirteen to seventeen times a minute; some members of the group were breathing close to thirty times a minute; everyone was breathing more rapidly than normal, which meant that everyone present was experiencing a good deal of tension and anxiety.

When the boy finished, I inquired as to the group's reactions. Not one person mentioned feeling anxious; their responses tended to be stilted, strained, remote. In the most casual manner possible, I pointed out the significance of the rapid breathing—and within a moment three or four people began to cry. "I tried to screen him out," one girl said. "I tried not to hear him. It was too close to home. It hurts too much to remember." "I wanted to run out of here," said another member. "I suddenly felt myself growing numb," said a third. "I felt if I didn't tune out I'd explode," said a fourth.

Everyone present had been reached by the boy's statements, everyone had begun to experience painful feelings erupting from a distant past—and everyone had struggled to escape his perceptions in the present in order to avoid hearing the long-denied screams of the child who had been himself now struggling, from some unspeakable depth, to reach the surface of awareness.

To quote a relevant passage from *Breaking Free,* where I describe another occasion on which the members of a therapy group find themselves hit by frightening and painful emotions originating in a sudden explosion of childhood memories:

I encouraged them to pay attention to the emotions they were feeling and to let themselves experience those emotions fully—not to block them or inhibit them or repress them. I explained that it was healthy and desirable to release those feelings, to bring them into full conscious awareness. These were emotions they had not permitted themselves to experience as children; they had repressed them out of fear or confusion or guilt or the desire to remain "in control." I explained that repressed, stored-up pain always represents an unsolved problem . . . and that only by feeling the pain now, only by admitting and experiencing its full reality, could one solve the problem buried in that pain. I explained that no pain was so destructive as the pain one refuses to face—and no suffering so enduring as the suffering one refuses to acknowledge.

When a person undergoes an experience that occasions profound suffering, his psychological well-being requires that he assimilate that experience, intellectually and emotionally, that he integrate it, that he deal with it consciously and rationally, so that he is not scarred by long-range harmful effects—such as the explicit or implicit conclusion that life is inherently tragic, that frustration and defeat are inevitable, that intimacy or fulfillment in human relationships is impossible, that happiness and self-esteem are unobtainable, that he is helpless or stupid or ineffectual or evil by nature. In repressing the pain occasioned by some shattering experience, a person forbids himself to know the meaning and significance that that experience has for him: the experience cannot be dealt with consciously and conceptually; it cannot be assimilated rationally and integrated non-selfdestructively.

Implicit in the repression of pain is the conclusion: here is a problem with which I am helpless to deal. This conclusion paves the way for other devastating inferences, such as I have indicated above.

A child may not have any alternative but to repress, at least some of the time, under conditions of extreme shock and deprivation. But then the adult, who has the advantage of experience and knowledge must, in effect, go back in time and rescue the child within him, setting him free of his pain, thereby allowing the process of maturity to become complete. To assist the adult in this undertaking is one of the central tasks of psychotherapy.

At this point let me hasten to correct one possible misunderstanding. I am not maintaining that it is desirable, necessary or possible to resurrect and thoroughly resolve every incident of repressed childhood pain or shock. To attempt such an undertaking might come very close to a lifetime endeavor, at least in some cases. I am suggesting rather that *major* areas of childhood repression need to be unearthed and confronted on the conscious, adult level. How far one should persist in this work is a matter of individual clinical judgment. If a client exhibits evidence that he is unobstructed, or reasonably unobstructed, in his ability to be self-aware in the present, and is able to function effectively in the key spheres of life—work, love, human relationships—then the therapist does not persist in childhood "excavating" for its own sake.

In working with the problem of the derepression of childhood experiences, one frequently encounters a paradoxical attitude in one's clients. On the one hand, many clients are eager to blame external circumstances, and most particularly their parents, for their plight, thereby absolving themselves of personal responsibility. To see themselves as helpless victims provides them with a justification for their passivity. In denouncing their parents they find a bitterly satisfying sanction for the continuation of their own destructive behavior. (Needless to say, the therapist must oppose this "blaming" tendency by every means possible to him—since it only serves to confirm the client's feelings of helplessness and passivity.) On the other hand, however, when one inquires into the nature of a client's childhood suffering, one frequently encounters the most ferocious resistance. Clients tend to talk in vague generalities, while avoiding any real confrontation with painful childhood incidents or with a personal meaning of those incidents to themselves.

Some clients, of course, cannot bear to reproach their parents; they pour every sort of blame on themselves; and continue to do nothing to change the quality of their lives.

The "deathbed situation" is an extremely helpful exercise in leading a client to an emotionally meaningful confrontation with painful and significant early experiences. The following example illustrates its use in some detail, and helps to illuminate the connections between childhood repression and later neurotic systoms.

The client—I will call her Jane—was an attractive girl of twenty-six. She came to therapy, she explained, because of anxiety associated with a current sexual relationship. She was having an affair with a man some years older than herself, a colonel in the air force; he had recently persuaded her to accept the presence in bed of another girl during their lovemaking. She acquiesced, in spite of considerable misgivings, primarily out of fear of losing him.

To her shock and dismay, Jane found herself actively enjoying the sexual participation of the other girl, and felt herself stirred by unwanted yearnings toward the girl. Occasionally they kissed or embraced, but their sexual intimacy did not extend beyond that.

Jane now felt very strongly, she said, that this three-way relationship was "sick." She had lost all respect for the man, and she felt helplessly bewildered by her inability to break with him or to understand her strange sense of gratification at the physical proximity of the other girl when she was having sex with the man. She wondered if she was "really a homosexual" or "just a very neurotic girl" or perhaps merely "stupid" and "unsophisticated" to feel that anything whatever was wrong with her present situation—this last being the position expressed by the man.

What especially struck me, while listening to Jane, was the childlike air of innocence she projected—an innocence that almost left one feeling she was talking about someone else, as if none of the events really concerned her. It was obvious that she was keeping her anxiety within manageable limits by utilizing the defense of dissociation, thereby preventing herself from fully experiencing the events of her own life—cutting herself in two, so that the self who performed the actions she was describing was, in effect, a different self than that of the girl facing me in my office.

On the basis of intensive questioning, the following facts seemed clearly established: Jane experienced strong feelings of attraction to the opposite sex; women generally did not sexually attract her; except under the very special conditions operating in her three-way relationship, a woman had no sexual meaning to her; she felt freer to enjoy sex with the man, uninhibitedly and guiltlessly, when the other girl was present than when she was absent; at the same time, made anxious by her own desire for physical affection from the other girl, as well as by a general sense that the three-way relationship was unhealthy, she strongly would have preferred a relationship consisting exclusively of the man and herself, and seemed sincerely to regret that the other girl had ever entered the picture.

Jane's personality was characterized by a strong desire to be pleasing to others and by chronic, painful doubts about her own judgment and worth.

The foregoing is the essence of what was learned during the first interview. Several weeks later, at a group therapy session, I proposed that we work together on the "deathbed situation."

I explained the premise of the exercise (as described in Chapter 1); I suggested that she see her mother standing at her bedside, and that she talk to her. I chose to begin with her mother because, on the basis of the facts she had revealed, it seemed likely that her mother rather than her father was the significant figure at the root of her problem. This hypothesis proved to be correct.

"I don't want to talk to her," she said. "Mother never listens to me anyway." I replied, "From now on, speak only to your mother. Don't converse with me during this exercise." But it took several more exchanges before she would even begin. When, finally, she did speak to her mother, her voice was flat, unemotional and uninvolved.

"Well, here we are. It doesn't make any difference, does it? You've never cared—why should you care now?" Then Jane turned her head to me and said, "I've got nothing else to say." Again I had to remind her to stay with her mother and not attempt to communicate with me. After a moment, she said, "You would never pick me up. You would never hold me. What kind of mother is that? Don't you know that mothers are supposed to hold their children? Why wouldn't you ever hold me? Why did you have me in the first place? Just because that's what women are 'supposed' to do, I'll bet. God, I hate you." There was a long silence. Then she said, "And the way you treated Daddy was no better. You treated him like a worm. Men were so disgusting to you. That hurt me. Made me ashamed of caring for Daddy, which I did sometimes, but not often, because he was so weak, he never stood up to you. I hated him for that, I wanted to respect him and I couldn't."

I said to her, "You're five years old. She's your mother. What is it like to be the daughter of this woman? Tell her about that."

After a long moment, she took a deep breath and the first tears flowed into her eyes. "I was so lonely. I'm still lonely. Why won't you see me? Why won't you ever see me?" Then she let out a piercing scream, *"Why won't you look at me?"* Then she began to sob convulsively. After a while, she continued, "You always made me feel I was so bad! . . . The time I was playing with myself . . . You didn't have to scream at me, you didn't have to make me feel so dirty, you didn't have to make me feel like some terrible monster! . . . And . . . and . . . whenever I'd tell you where I had been, you'd always look at me as if I were lying. *Why did you do that?* Why couldn't I ever just be your daughter? Didn't you know how frightened I was?"

Gradually, as if descending deeper into a hypnotic state (and hypnotic age-regression sometimes does occur spontaneously in this exercise), she began to speak in a younger voice, the voice of a child, beseeching her mother, reproaching her, recounting various painful incidents of her early years, begging her mother for a loving response she had never received—until at last, panting with exhaustion, Jane whispered, "I can't talk to you anymore now. Please go away. You have nothing to give, anyway. You're all dried out and miserable yourself."

Then I asked her to fantasize not her actual mother but the mother she had never had and always wanted, and to ask that ideal mother for what she needed.

"Just let me enjoy being me and being alive," she said. I asked, "And how can your mother help you do that?" "Let me sit on your lap," she said. "Tell me that everything is all right. Tell me I'm clean . . . and good . . . and that I'm not evil . . . and that what I feel matters to you . . . really matters . . . and that I can love somebody without you looking down at me with contempt and . . . " Here she stopped. "Can you finish that?" I asked. In the voice not of a little girl but of a grown woman, she whispered, "Let me love a man."

Then I said, "Take two or three deep breaths now, and let your body relax, and let the meaning of everything you've been saying come into your mind, naturally and easily, without effort, let it all be there where you can see it. And when you feel ready, you can open your eyes and talk about this experience. Don't rush yourself."

When she opened her eyes and looked around her, her body was entirely relaxed and her smile was radiant and she exclaimed, "Holy cow!" Then she added, "If you had asked me yesterday what I thought about Mother or what she meant to me, I would have shrugged and said, 'Who cares?' I would have said I was indifferent. Wow!"

Then she laughed. "Did I scare you?" "No," I answered, "I knew you were having a good time."

She said, "It feels so good to get all that out." She yawned and stretched. "I feel marvelous. It's funny—I was so frightened of getting into this. In advance it seemed terrifying. And there's nothing to it." I answered,

"It wasn't the adult Jane who was terrified. It was Jane the little girl, the girl who originally repressed this material. It was she who felt she couldn't handle it. And it was her perspective, still operating in your subconscious, that made it so hard for you to break through."

Looking at her, I suddenly noticed that her usual state of semidissociation was absent; she was, at least for the moment, natural, authentic, real. This prompted me to say, "And what does a little girl feel when her mother treats her that way?"

"She feels lonely and hurt."

"And what else does she feel?"

"As though there's something wrong with her, something bad about her."

"And what else does she feel?"

"Angry."

"And what does she do with all those feelings? How does she handle them?"

"She . . . they just get cut off . . . she cuts them off . . . I don't know how to describe it . . . I just take myself someplace else."

"And leave the feelings behind?"

"Yes."

"Now can you speak in the first person and take responsibility for what you do? Can you say it—acknowledging that it's you who's doing what you're doing?" "When *I* feel threatened by my feelings, *I* run away, *I* cut myself from them, *I* don't let them be real, don't let them into my head."

"I'm wondering," I said to Jane, "if you can see any relationship between the things you've been talking about and your sexual problems."

She was thoughtful for a moment. Then she said decisively, "I really like men. I really do. I *am not* a homosexual."

"I never thought you were."

"Mother always made me feel that sex was sinful and I was evil—whatever I wanted was evil . . ."

"Go on."

"I wouldn't let myself know how much Mother

still mattered to me—how much I still wanted something from her."

"What?"

"Approval. Understanding. Acceptance. I've been repressing how much I wanted that. Wouldn't admit it to myself. It's too humiliating. And it hurts too much."

"What are your feelings for that other girl, if you think of her now?"

"She just seems . . . irrelevant. She can't . . . she can't give me what I want . . ."

"Ah, that's becoming clear to you? . . ."

"Something . . . I don't know how to say it . . . something insane is coming into my head . . . Well, you're going to think this is . . . I don't know what you're going to think, but, anyway . . . it's just . . . that's right, she—the things she makes me feel—how can I say it? . . . It's like . . . she's a substitute, yes, that's it, she's a substitute."

"A substitute . . ."

"Are you ready for this? My God! A substitute for my mother! . . ."

"I'm ready for it. Are you certain?"

"I wanted a woman's love. I wanted . . . that's what I wanted . . . a woman who would make me feel . . . protected . . . cared for . . . Oh, God . . . that's what it is, that's what I wanted, isn't it insane?"

"Often, when a person represses and denies his childhood needs, later he tries to satisfy them symbolically—because the pressure of the frustration is still there."

"It's Mother's love I've got to get."

"No. It's too late for that. You're not that little girl anymore. It's she who needed it—not you."

"That hurts. That's painful. Where do I go from here? How do I accept . . . never having it? How do I—?"

"We'll talk about that another time. Let's stay with the sexual problem now."

"I don't know what to think about that, beyond what I've said."

"Imagine yourself making love to your man friend—with the girl looking on. What does it make you feel?"

"Like . . . it's all right, somehow."

"As though the act is being morally sanctioned."

"Yes! My God! It's . . . it's my mother telling me it's all right to sleep with a man!"

"Looks that way, doesn't it?"

"That's fantastic!"

"You'd be surprised how common this pattern is. When a young person is traumatically starved for affection and love from the parent of the same sex, years later, as I said, he often seeks the gratification of that frustrated need—symbolically, through another person. And sometimes the longing is so intense that it takes a sexual form. Even in a person who is basically heterosexual. Not understanding his own feelings, that can be very mystifying and frightening. He may feel he wants that other person sexually, but it isn't sex he's after; it's physical contact signifying love. There are many, many people in the world who perhaps have never acted on these feelings, never actually practiced any physical intimacy with a person of the same sex, yet who are aware of yearnings in that direction and are tortured with the fear that they are homosexual. And that isn't the problem at all. I call this phenomenon 'pseudo-homosexuality.' "

"You can't imagine how good I feel! Like I'm flying!"

"We'll be going through all this again. Next time we do the exercise, I'm sure we'll get into other interesting material. But that's enough for today." She had brought a tape recorder, as I encourage my clients to do, and the entire exercise as well as the conversation following it had been recorded. "Play it several times before our next meeting. I think you will find more and more in it. For your first time with this exercise, you did well—better than well."

Two days later, Jane informed her man friend that under no circumstances did she wish to see the other girl again. The man accepted her decision. Three weeks later, entirely of her own volition and desire, she terminated her relationship with the man.

At no time did I or anyone else in the group offer her practical advice concerning what to do; it was not necessary. She remained in group, to work on other problems; but she was not troubled again by fear of homosexuality.

*

*   *

Included in a person's "experience" of some event is the way that event or aspect of reality is perceived by the person; the way it is judged, evaluated or interpreted, and how it is responded to emotionally and physically.

While we have a great deal yet to learn about the way in which the brain stores and "files" memories, there is significant evidence to support the conclusion that all of a person's experiences are permanently recorded in his brain. (See, for example, Wilder Penfield, "Memory Mechanisms," *A. M. A. Archives of Neurology and Psychiatry,* 67 (1952):178-198.) We can, by a process of abstraction, differentiate perception, evaluation and response, but it seems that the brain records these elements as an integrated unity, as part of one experience. This fact helps us to understand why the repression of an emotion so often extends to the event that evoked it; and why the derepression of painful childhood emotions so often triggers a release of repressed memories.

Through the utilization of the exercise I have described above, or the exploratory techniques presented in *Breaking Free,* or hypnosis, or a number of other possible methods, one is able to penetrate the barrier of childhood "amnesia," to dissolve repressive blocks and to trace the origins of an individual's negative self-concepts.

The younger a person is, the more helpless and lacking in knowledge, the fewer are his resources in coping with stress and shock—and, as a consequence, the more vulnerable he is to experiences of intense fear and pain. That is why the defenses which protect repressed childhood traumas are generally the most formidable and difficult to dissolve. But once these defenses have been penetrated, it is generally far easier to deal therapeutically with defenses and blocks origi-

nating in adulthood: the worst has already been faced
by the client and his strongest point of resistance overcome.

After the pain of childhood traumas has been confronted, after repressed memories have been released,
after the client has grasped significant connections between his past and his present—what then?

Does the now-experienced pain of his childhood
frustrations disappear? Sometimes it does—it tends gradually to fade away—if the pain is experienced fully, if
the client is able to make peace with his past, to accept
that which cannot be changed and to move forward as
a self-responsible adult.

But not every client *wants* to be rid of his pain. There
are persons who cling to their pain as to a precious
possession, refusing to relinquish it, nurturing it like
some sacred fire. Many times I have observed clients
who project an attitude which, if translated into words,
amounts to the declaration: "My needs were not satisfied by my parents when I was five years old—and I
am not moving on—I refuse to grow older—until they
or *somebody* gives me the things I want."

The fact that a person has experienced his formerly
repressed pain does not guarantee that he will now
wish to assume responsibility for his own existence.
That is a separate step that he may or may not choose
to take.

By way of illustrating this point, I shall quote at some
length from a tape-recorded therapy session in which
I work with a young man of twenty four—I will call
him Alan—who reveals his motivation in a very illuminating way. Alan's chief complaint on entering therapy
concerned his passivity, lack of ambition, and general
feelings of worthlessness. He had considerable previous
experience with psychotherapy. On two occasions, he
said, he had been suicidal. Investigation revealed that
his childhood had been inordinately frustrating, frightening and painful; the details do not matter in this context.
The following discussion took place a few months after
he began working with me.

Alan: Why is it that . . . I'm trying to think of something . . . When I hear people make positive remarks about me, I never accept it. It doesn't mean anything, because I'm not looking for that. But anytime I hear something negative or I think people are thinking something negative, I really absorb that. It's like I'm a machine programmed only for negative stimuli, and anything that's positive that might get in and do me some good, to start reversing the way I feel about myself, doesn't have a chance to get in, because it's thrown out right away. And everything that's negative, that I imagine or is real, just keeps pouring in. It's almost like I go out of my way looking for things. I'm deliberately trying to get hurt. But then I turn around and I want to hurt other people the way they've hurt me. That's one thing I really detest about myself, I guess. I don't feel anything for other people except hatred, bitterness and anger and jealousy . . . Maybe deep inside I don't want to be the way I am; I want to be different. But the me that wants to be different isn't in control. He doesn't have anything to say about the situation. So when you are talking to me, you're talking to the other me, the guy that's in power, you know, the evil part of me. Whenever you try to help me, he's going to say, "No!" So how is anything that happens here in group going to get down to the other part of me, the part that wants to change?

Therapist: Let's borrow a technique from Gestalt Therapy. I would like you to have an imaginary dialogue between the good you and the evil you.

A: All right. (He leans back and closes his eyes.)

T: Begin talking as the evil you and then let the good you answer. Go back and forth until I ask you to do something else, please.

A: Start with who? The bad guy?

T: Yes.

A: Just talk about anything?

T: About how the bad guy is looking at your situation.

A: Oh, he's laughing.

T: Go ahead, be the bad guy.

A: Well, he's laughing. It's—

T: No, you're talking to me. I want the bad guy to talk to the good guy in you.

A: I'm laughing because I know I'm in control. I'm pulling the strings. I'm manipulating you—we—us. I'm torturing myself. I'm sort of playing games. Because I really enjoy torturing myself, making the other me—you—suffer. I really get a kick out of that. Yeah, I really get satisfaction.

T: Now let the good you respond.

A: Wait a minute. I've got to find him . . . Okay. I I can't understand why you do that. Why do you want to make me suffer? What have I done?

T: Now let the bad guy answer.

A: You are an inferior . . . an inferior being. You are not up to my standards. You don't deserve to be happy. And you . . . Oh, I'm getting very dizzy.

T: Try to stay with it.

A: The room's spinning around. I feel like I'm going to pass out.

T: Are you willing to continue?

A: I can't breathe. Oh God, it feels terrible.

T: Are you willing to continue?

A: I feel like I'm getting flushed all over. I can't breathe. My face feels like it's on fire.

T: Are you willing to continue?

A: I don't feel worthy. I don't feel that I'm worthy of being happy and having the things I should have.

T: Tell the good you why he's not worthy.

A: I know it sounds silly, but I feel the main reason he's inferior is because he's not good-looking enough. Even to me that sounds stupid. When people say that they like me and that I'm halfway decent-looking, I don't understand it . . . I don't want to be liked. I want to be unhappy. It's like I'm deliberately forcing myself to be unhappy. And deliberately torturing myself. And deliberately keeping myself from any opportunity to be happy. All I want to hear about myself is bad things. I feel that's the easy way out. It's much easier than to fight back, you know . . . than to really try. I feel this is so important.

T: Now become the good you and respond.

A: I don't deserve . . . I don't deserve that. I should have a chance to be happy. It's not fair that I feel only bad things.

T: Now we're going to do something a bit different, Alan. I'm going to become your bad self. You be the good self. Okay?

A: All right.

T: What do you mean it's not fair? What right have you got to be happy? You know why you can't be happy.

A: I should be happy. Why should—

T: No, you shouldn't be happy, and you know why.

A: I don't care. I don't care if I deserve to be happy or not. Why don't I deserve to be happy?

T: You deserve to suffer every day and I'm going to keep you that way.

A: No. Why?

T: You know why. You know why.

A: No.

T: Yes.

A: I don't want to talk to you anymore.

T: I'm not going to let you go.

A: Why the hell don't you get out of my life and leave me alone?

T: What would you do if I did?

A: I could . . . I could . . . I could live.

T: Could you live? What would you do?

A: I don't know, but I could do something. I could . . . I could get out of this prison . . . (sobbing)

T: Well, why don't you fight your way out instead of asking for permission? I don't give permissions.

A: (sobbing) You're too strong. I can't fight you. I can't—

T: What makes me so strong?

A: You're so big. You step on me all the time. Every time I want to do something, you say, "No!" You say, "You can't do that. You're not able to do that. You're not good enough to do that."

T: And what do I mean when I say that?

A: (sobbing) You don't want me to do it. Because you hate me.

T: Who am I?

A: I don't know.

T: Who am I?

A: I honestly don't know. My grandmother? My mother?

T: What's the worst thing I ever did to you?

A: You made me a coward. You made me afraid to face things. You made me want to run.

T: How did I do that?

A: I don't want to talk. I don't want to talk anymore.

T: You're stuck with me.

A: I could say it was my father—because he wasn't there, because he died.

T: One less person to make you unhappy.

A: The worst thing you ever did to me . . .

T: Yes?

A: I don't know what the worst thing you ever did to me was.

T: Well then answer this. What's the worst thing that could happen to you now, if you ever solve your problems, if you ever make something of yourself?

A: I couldn't feel sorry for myself anymore. I'd have no reason to feel sorry for myself.

T: So.

A: And then—

T: And then?

A: Then I'd have . . . then I'd have to do something.

T: You're eager to feel sorry for yourself?

A: It takes me off the hook.

T: It takes you off the hook.

A: I don't even know what the hell I'm talking about.

T: Don't try to judge now.

A: I just hate myself so much. That's why I hate myself . . .

T: Ah . . .

A: Part of the reason, anyway. Part of the reason why I dislike myself. I know I'm taking the easy way out. I know I'm being a coward by not fighting.

T: And if you don't fight . . .

A: Somebody will take care of me, or somebody will say, "All right, you poor boy, you had a terrible experience, you had a terrible childhood. You're not able to take responsibility for your actions." And I can just sink into that and not have to think anymore and not have to do anything. I can just sit there and live in my dreams of what I might have been or what could have been . . . and block out the whole world and everybody in it. But I'm never able to succeed in doing it. I'm never able to block out everything.

T: Yeah . . .

A: I really think I tried to be psychotic. I really think I wanted to block out everything and lose all contact with reality, but I was never able to do it. And it's been getting harder and harder.

T: Especially as you get to understand more.

A: Yeah. Because everybody expects me . . . The older you get, the more people expect you to take responsibility for yourself and . . .

T: I'll bet that makes you furious.

A: Yeah, it does. Yeah . . . Or does it? I don't know. It just makes me feel people don't understand. They don't feel sorry enough for me.

T: And if they won't feel sorry enough for you . . .

A: I'll make up for it.

T: Nobody ever really understood how bad your condition was, how much you suffered.

A: They didn't. God, they didn't. Everybody looked the other way.

T: Nobody ever really cared.

A: Everybody looked the other way.

T: So you're going to make up for all that. You'll suffer and suffer and suffer—until they look.

A: You better believe it.

T: And if you have to destroy yourself in the process —so what?

A: Yeah, that doesn't seem to be the most important thing to me. My happiness is not the most important thing . . .

T: No.

A: I think the most important thing is to make people realize that I suffered, that I'm still suffering.

T: They've got to do something.

A: Right! Who are you? You're not the bad me anymore. What am I saying? What am I talking about?

T: No, I stopped being the bad you a few minutes ago. I became myself again.

A: Well, anyway, that's why I hate myself.

T: Uh-huh.

A: Well, I can't have what I want, anyway, so it seems to me . . .

T: What do you want that you can't have?

A: If you're going to ask questions like that, I won't even answer you.

T: What do you want that you can't have?

A: I can't have immediate success at whatever I try to do. Everything takes time. Everything is so hard . . .

T: Nobody has it any different.

A: Well, I don't give a damn whether anybody else has it different or not. What do I care? What do I care about anybody else?

T: What we're talking about is the nature of reality.

A: Well, I don't give a damn about reality. You talk to me about this reality shit. So what? Why do I have to give a damn about it? I don't want anything to do with reality. If reality means that I have to accept myself as just a human being . . . with wants and desires and having to feel pain and all that shit, I don't want it. I don't want anything to do with it. And you can't force me to accept that either. You can't make me!

T: I'm not going to try to make you. You have to make your own choices and take the consequences.

A: Who the hell is this talking? This can't be me. All I want is to climb into some box and shut out the lights and say, "I don't want anything anymore." I think I really enjoy being unhappy. I really do. I really don't think I want to be happy. Oh, God, is this me talking?

T: You can't be sorry for yourself if you're happy and successful.

A: Maybe that's the main reason that I'm unhappy . . . the main reason I'm not accomplishing anything . . . I don't really want to.

T: When you were a boy . . .

A: That's how it got started. But now . . .

T: Now you're carrying on the family tradition, telling yourself you're no good, telling yourself you can't possibly succeed, just the way your mother and grandmother did.

A: I don't want anything. I don't want to do anything.

T: So what's the problem? Just earn enough to feed yourself and let it go at that.

A: If it was that easy, yeah.

T: It isn't that easy, is it?

A: No. Because it hurts me so much when I see other people, you know, accomplishing things.

T: Because then you know you're being a traitor to your own life and to your own potentiality.

A: Yeah.

T: You know you've sold out.

A: Yeah.

T: If we betray ourselves, that's the real guilt.

A: Yeah. I hate myself for so many goddamned reasons. I'm rotten.

T: That's self-indulgence, too. One more excuse to remain passive. "I'm no good, I'm worthless—don't expect anything of me."

A: Oh, God, I live . . . I feed off that. It's my source of life. It's my source of energy. Negativeness. Self-contempt.

T: If anyone took that away from you, where would you be?

A: I would cease to exist. I would be an inanimate object. Oh, this is all so goddamn silly. Sitting here talking like this. I'm afraid to open my eyes and look at anybody.

T: It doesn't sound silly to me. To me, it sounds like one word of wisdom after another.

A: You know, after last week, I signed up for that course. Now, I'm afraid. I have to make an effort. I really don't want to. I would rather sit around and feel sorry for myself and be miserable. I want to make everybody goddamn sorry for me. I really feel like I've been gypped. I just stay awake at night just thinking of ways to get back at everybody, to deliberately hurt people. Then, sometimes, I feel awful because of feeling that way. I'm so disgusting. I think the thing I'm really most ashamed of is that I know I'm not really trying. All I want is for people to feel sorry and say, "Oh, wow, this guy really has had it bad. I can understand why he does the things he does."

T: Do you want to open your eyes now?

A: I can't believe I've actually been saying all these things. (He opens his eyes.) You sure got me mad at you. You can be very perverse.

T: Well, that was the idea. I thought it might be helpful, might get us somewhere. It did.

When other members of the group began to express their reactions to Alan's revelations, he received as big a shock as any he had experienced that day: a number of them expressed the feeling that, to varying extents, he had been speaking for and about them.

It would be an error to conclude from the above transcript that Alan's problem is simply one of malingering, and that all that is now necessary is for him to "snap out of it." It is true that he need not take as passive and unthinking an attitude toward his problems as he does. But it is also true that pathological forces operate within him, on a subconscious level, to make his behavior feel "plausible" to him, at least at times. While the discovery of those forces will not release him from the responsibility of making a volitional effort, will not spare him the obligation of thought and struggle, it is the necessary next step in the therapeutic process.

As for the reaction of the other clients in the group, what they recognized in his statements and could relate to themselves was the attitude of *waiting*—waiting for someone to respond to their plight and to *do something*. To "do something" means: to provide a solution to the pain of childhood frustrations. This is the element of the child still persisting within them: their reluctance to assume full responsibility for their own existence and thus move forward to authentic autonomy.

It might be argued that in the case of such individuals there are still unexplored areas of repressed childhood pain which need to be brought to awareness. So long as an individual is unable or unwilling to break free from the prison of childhood, it is always possible to speculate about unknown areas of repressed experience that act to subvert his growth. But it is a gratuitous assumption—and unsupported by the evidence—to assert that derepression is all that the solution of psychological problems requires. Granted it is essential; but it does not guarantee automatic results.

Problems do not continue to exist in adults merely because of childhood traumas. They continue to exist because they are *actively sustained* in the present. And no part of psychotherapy is more important than making the client aware of the actions by which he keeps his problems alive and flourishing.

As a being of volitional consciousness, a being who is psychologically free to think or not to think, to focus his conscious mind or to avoid the effort and responsibility of doing so, man can strive to expand the range of his awareness or he can, in effect, cooperate with his subconscious resistance to awareness—and thereby tacitly participate in the sabotaging of his mental health. (Man's freedom to think or not to think, to focus his awareness or to suspend it, is discussed in detail in *The Psychology of Self-Esteem.*)

Here, then, we have a theme to which we will have occasion to return: that of an individual's willful alienation from the possibilities of his own growth—for the sake of clinging to a childhood irredeemably behind him.

Chapter 3

Self-Acceptance
and Self-Awareness

Self-esteem has two interrelated aspects: a sense of personal efficacy and a sense of personal worth. It is the conviction that one is competent to live and worthy of living.

The conviction that one is *competent* to live means: confidence in the functioning of one's mind; confidence in one's ability to understand and judge the facts of reality (within the sphere of one's interests and needs); intellectual self-reliance. The conviction that one is *worthy* of living means: an affirmative attitude toward one's right to live and to be happy; a self-respect derived from the conviction that one practices the virtues one's life and happiness require.

Self-esteem is a basic need of man, a cardinal requirement of his mental health and psychological well-being. There is no value judgment more important to man than the estimate he passes on himself.

This estimate is ordinarily experienced by him, not in the form of a conscious, verbalized judgment, but in the form of a feeling, a feeling that can be hard to isolate and identify because he experiences it constantly: it is part of every other feeling, it is involved in his every emotional response.

An emotion is the product of an evaluation; it reflects an appraisal of the beneficial or harmful relationship of some aspect of reality to oneself. Thus, a man's view of himself is necessarily implicit in all his value-responses. Any judgment entailing the issue, "Is this for me or against me?"—entails a view of the *"me"* involved. His self-evaluation is an omnipresent factor in man's psychology.

The nature of his self-evaluation has profound effects on a man's thinking processes, emotions, desires, values and goals. It is the single most eloquent key to his behavior. *(The Psychology of Self-Esteem)*

One of the tragedies of human development is that many of a person's most self-destructive acts are prompted by a blind, misguided (and subconscious) attempt to protect his sense of self—to preserve or strengthen his self-esteem.

When a person represses certain of his thoughts and memories, because he regards them as immoral or humiliating, he disowns a part of himself—in the name of protecting his self-esteem.

When a person represses certain of his emotions, because they threaten his sense of control or conflict with his notion of "strength" or "maturity" or "sophistication," he disowns a part of himself—in the name of protecting his self-esteem.

When a person represses certain of his desires, because he cannot tolerate the anxiety of wondering whether or not he will attain them, an anxiety that makes him feel helpless and ineffectual, he disowns a part of himself—in the name of protecting his self-esteem.

When a person represses certain aspects of his personality which seem incompatible with the standards of his "significant others," because he has tied his sense of personal worth to the approval of those "others," he disowns a part of himself—in the name of protecting his self-esteem.

When a person represses certain of his legitimate

needs, because their frustration leaves him feeling impotent and defeated, he disowns a part of himself—in the name of protecting his self-esteem.

When a person represses his capacity for spontaneity and self-assertiveness, because he wants to be certain that his responses always conform to the "moral ideals" laid down by his particular authorities, he disowns a part of himself—in the name of protecting his self-esteem.

Do such attempts succeed? They do not. Self-esteem cannot be built on a foundation of self-alienation. The consequence of such attempts is the sabotaging of one's ability to enjoy life, the inner sense of some nameless fraudulence and self-betrayal, the anxious need always to be on guard against dark, frightening forces which might erupt from the limbo of one's denied self to threaten the structure of one's existence—and the subversion of one's self-esteem.

In attempting to deal with the problem of self-alienation, one must understand the subconscious purpose directing the individual's behavior; one must understand the manner in which he is striving to satisfy his needs and, in particular, his need of self-esteem.

When a young child represses a pain that he experiences as intolerable, he does so not only because pain is intrinsically a disvalue, but also because it threatens his sense of control, it causes him to feel impotent and incapable of functioning; it nullifies his sense of efficacy. In later years, his block against reconfronting that pain serves the same purpose as in childhood: to maintain his equilibrium, to protect his sense of efficacy, of control, of self-esteem.

Men destroy themselves every day—in the name of assuring their survival. Neurosis might almost be defined as the attempt to protect one's self-esteem and assure one's survival by self-destructive (reality-avoiding) means.

Psychosomatic illness, for example—the development of physical symptoms whose ultimate causes are psychological—is often the result of the sustained internal stresses to which the body is subjected when powerful but unacceptable emotions—fear, rage, hurt, despair, etc.—are blocked, repressed, denied awareness and expression, and thereby imprisoned within the physical system. (The phenomenon of psychosomatic ailments, incidentally, is one of the factors that supports the characterization of psychological disorders as a form of "illness"; the life of the organism itself may be placed in direct jeopardy—by psychological policies aimed at protecting the organism.)

The following examples, excerpted from transcripts of group therapy sessions, illustrate some of the foregoing observations.

In the middle of a session, a young woman suddenly complains that she has a violent headache. The sentence-completion technique is used:

Therapist: When I wake up in the morning–
Client: –I feel tired.
T: Ever since I was a child–
C: –I've been bored.
T: Perhaps I wouldn't be bored if–
C: –I could feel strongly about something.
T: I might be able to feel strongly about something if–
C: –if . . . if I found . . . I don't know.
T: I can remember–
C: –wondering why Mother never laughed or cried or got angry or showed any feeling of any kind.
T: That made me feel–
C: –that that was the way to be. Always calm and in control. Maybe then she would care for me.
T: Today, in group, my headache began when–
C: –Jack began talking about his problems at work. Yeah . . .
T: I found myself thinking–
C: –why is he always wasting our time on trivia?
T: If he hadn't been talking about his problems–
C: –I could have talked.
T: The thing I wanted to talk about involved–
C: –I don't know, but I haven't talked in group in a long time, and I felt I should.

T: When I am talking in group—
C: —I feel I am doing something about my problems.
T: When I don't know what to say—
C: —I start talking anyway, fumble around and hope you'll help out.
T: As I sat listening to Jack, I found myself feeling—
C: —furious.
T: I told myself—
C: —that I was being unfair and unreasonable and ridiculous and stupid.
T: And then—
C: —I told myself not to feel angry.
T: And then—
C: —the anger went away.
T: And then—
C: —I got a headache. That's right, that's what happened. Yeah. I . . . it seems to be lifting now.
T: If I had expressed my anger in group—
C: —that would be irrational.
T: If I raise the issue of my anger as a problem to be discussed—
C: —people would think I was irrational.
T: If people think I'm irrational—
C: —probably I'll think so too.
T: "Being irrational" means—
C: —showing emotions.
T: "Showing emotions" means—
C: —getting hurt. Being childish.

A man in his thirties complains of his inability to assert himself or to express his own opinions or even to know what his opinions are:

T: At the thought of expressing my desire—
C: —I don't know what I want.
C: I might know what I want if only—
C: —I could be sure.
T: The thing I want to be sure of is—
C: —that it's right to want it.
T: If I want something that's wrong—

C: —that means there is something the matter with me. I'm immoral.

T: When it comes to expressing my opinions—

C: —it never seems worthwhile.

T: It would be worthwhile if—

C: —I didn't feel so empty.

T: I feel empty, perhaps, because—

C: —I make myself empty. It's saf—

T: Say it.

C: —It's safer.

T: It's safer because—

C: —I never have to decide.

T: Making decisions frightens me because—

C: —what if I'm wrong?

T: If I express an opinion my friends disagree with—

C: —I feel anxious.

T: I avoid feeling anxious by—

C: —I wish I knew how to.

T: I *try* to protect myself from anxiety by—

C: —being very careful about what I say.

T: To me, "spontaneity" means—

C: —being self-confident. But how do you do it?

T: I cover up my lack of confidence by—

C: —being silent and looking wise.

A business executive complains that he too-often loses his temper with his wife:

T: Basically I—

C: —feel happiest when I am working.

T: When I'm with my wife—

C: —I often feel cut off.

T: When I feel that way—

C: —I wish I knew what to do.

T: Sometimes I want to cry out to her—

C: —"Can't you help me!"

T: The help I need involves—

C: —understanding me, seeing that I don't want to be remote, seeing that I don't know what to do, finding a way to get through to me.

T: If she responded that way—

C: —I'd probably go blank.

T: If I see that she's upset—

C: —I become upset and irritable.

T: I become upset and irritable—

C: —because I feel helpless.

T: I feel helpless because—

C: —there should be something I can do, but I don't know what it is. It feels like it's my responsibility.

T: When I feel that responsibility—

C: —sometimes it's a burden.

T: "Feeling helpless" means—

C: —being worthless.

T: Yesterday, just before I exploded at her—

C: —I was feeling very nervous.

T: I was feeling nervous because—

C: —I don't know, she was just making me nervous.

T: I became nervous when I noticed that—

C: —*she* was feeling unhappy and anxious.

T: Seeing her distressed—

C: —made me aware of my own feelings, my pain.

T: When I became aware of my feelings—

C: —I wanted to get away from them.

T: I got away from them by—

C: —snapping at her, becoming impatient.

T: Afterwards, I felt—

C: —a little guilty.

T: If I could admit to my feelings of helplessness and anxiety—

C: —what a relief!

T: It's hard to do that because—

C: —that's not my idea of a man.

T: I tell myself I have to be strong because—

C: —I don't want to know what's inside of me. I have to admit that. That's the truth, no doubt about it.

T: I don't want to know what's inside of me because—

C: —it's too much, it would wipe me out, it would devastate me.

T: Thinking of that now—

C: —I don't like that image of myself. Personal problems are for somebody else to have, not me.

The ease with which such material can be elicited by the sentence-completion technique should not obscure the fact that a good deal of what is said and revealed during the exercise was previously blocked from the client's awareness. It is very common for clients to be astonished by the things they hear themselves saying; or to be astonished later, when they hear the tape-recorded playback.

It is not enough to prove to a client that his self-esteem is not served by the policy of avoiding self-awareness. It is necessary for him to confront the reasons why he feels such avoidance is necessary. Such avoidance practices are not performed capriciously; however irrational they may be, they are experienced by the client as serving a vital purpose.

Consider the case of Alan, described at the conclusion of the previous chapter. That his passivity and willful surrender to self-pity are self-destructive is obvious— and obvious to him. Prior to the session I reported, Alan avoided self-awareness assiduously. He clung to his pain as to his sole possession of value. He wallowed in feelings of rage against the world. He described himself as indifferent to the requirements of "reality."

I was impressed by the number of group participants who responded with empathy to one or another feature of his story. Contrary to Alan's expectations, they had not been horrified by his statements, although everyone was inclined to agree that Alan's expressed attitudes were reprehensible.

Two weeks after that session with Alan, I said to the group, "I would like to try an experiment. Let us try to build a defense of Alan's attitudes. After all, it might be argued, no one can really *want*—in the full sense— to let his life go down the drain. No one can fully want to be filled with resentment and hatred. No one can really enjoy wallowing in pain. If these attitudes are experienced by Alan as necessary, if they are helping to protect him in some way, how are they performing that function? Perhaps some of you will be willing to try, in effect, to testify in Alan's defense, to offer argu-

ments in support of his feelings. Let's see where they
might lead us."

It is doubtless apparent that I was inviting the group
members to speak—implicitly—about themselves, since
they were required to consult their feelings of empathy.

"What's the point of trying to accomplish anything?"
said one member of the group, speaking on Alan's
behalf. "You feel unreal and invisible to people all your
life, ever since you were a child. No one sees, no one
cares, no one ever has—so why should they start now?
What makes you think they'll start now? Even if you
do something right. Even if you accomplish something.
Trying to accomplish something now is just opening
yourself to a new hurt. Just a new defeat, another blow.
You'll end up feeling more futile and impotent than
ever. Your sense of yourself will just go down a few
notches more."

"If pain is the only emotion you've ever felt," said
another, "if every other emotion has been repressed or
maybe never existed in the first place, giving up your
pain is giving up your last hold on feeling anything—
giving up your last hold on being alive. Pain is all you've
got, maybe. Pain means you're there, means you're able
to feel something, means you're not dead. Saying goodbye to pain is saying goodbye to yourself, to your one
tiny feeling of having an identity."

Other members of the group assented especially
vigorously to the statement about pain.

"He's never felt real to anyone," said someone else.
"That's why all he can think about is somebody feeling
sorry for him. He can't imagine himself being real to
anyone in any other way; all he can hope to be is an object of pity."

Alan nodded several times.

"Giving up his pain," said someone else, "feels to him
like giving up his knowledge that there was something
terribly wrong with the world into which he was born—
I mean, his family, the way they acted, their craziness,
their cruelty and all that. He can't absorb it, he can't
digest it or understand it, but giving up his pain feels
like he would be resigning himself. That's how it feels to

me, anyway. Like I would be accepting something I can't accept and forgiving something I can't forgive. That would be just one more blow to absorb."

"He has no self-esteem of his own," said someone else, "no self-confidence. So he needs other people's response to him, other people's pity or sympathy or caring or something to make him feel he has value, to make him feel he's worth something—so he'll have the strength to make an effort. I feel that way sometimes."

"All that stuff about hating people," said someone else, "I know what that's about. When you know you're not making anything of yourself, not doing anything with your life, stagnating, everything inside you turns sour, like you're rotting away or dying, and anything that was once decent or good in you turns to rage— don't ask me why, but it does—and then you hate yourself for feeling that way because you know it's wrong. You feel so helpless."

Alan nodded vehemently.

"Reality," said someone else—"Alan doesn't know what reality is or means. It's other people he's talking about, the things they expect him to do. Everybody always wants you to do things you don't want to do. From the beginning of your life. Get good grades to impress the neighbors, play the violin for Aunt Mary, excel at sports, pretend to be glad to see your grandparents even if you can't stand them—pretend, pretend, pretend—you've got to make yourself something you're not—never mind what you want, need or feel—that doesn't matter—whatever you are isn't good enough— whatever you want isn't right—you've got to adjust yourself to anybody and everybody else—that's what reality means to Alan. Maybe that's his problem—that that's what he thinks reality means. Anyway, that's what he's trying to defend himself against. He doesn't know how to fight for anything. He has nothing to fight for, maybe, but he doesn't want to give in—so he just says 'No!' to anybody and everything. That's his only self-assertiveness. If he gives that up, what's he got left?"

"So what's the solution?" I asked the group.

"This is all bullshit," said someone, "even if it's true.

You've still got to get off your ass and do something with your life. Why should what other people see or think or expect or want matter that much, anyway, one way or the other?"

"True," I said. "But there's a little more to it than that. What do you think, Alan?"

"I'm feeling pretty good," he replied. "Everything being said hits me right. That's the way it is. This is amazing."

"So I guess your situation is hopeless."

"Yeah, that's right. No, is it? That doesn't sound so good. Why should it be? This is all crazy. I'm enrolled in that training course and I'm feeling a little better about it."

"But the basic lethargy is still there."

"Yeah."

Several members of the group reported that they felt elated. They did not feel that they had found or been given a justification for passivity, but the exact opposite: as if verbalizing the attitudes they had verbalized, bringing them into the open, giving them full acknowledged reality, had made the problem shrink in importance and had liberated some source of energy within them. I turned back to Alan:

T: If I really commit myself to succeeding—
C: —I might . . . I don't know.
T: If I never really try—
C: —I can dream all I want.
T: I can dream about—
C: —how great I can be, if my life hadn't been wretched.
T: I began to tell myself that I was great—
C: —when I was a kid.
T: When I told myself that—
C: —it made me feel better.
T: The thing I felt better about was—
C: —how miserable I was, always being told I was no good and a disappointment and all that.
T: Sometimes I felt I was great because—
C: —sometimes Mother would tell me good things about myself, or somebody would tell me I was bril-

liant, and even a couple of my teachers told me I was very smart.

T: As things stand now—

C: —I'll never find out.

T: I'll never find out—

C: —what I am.

T: That makes me feel—

C: —miserable, but also good.

T: It makes me feel miserable because—

C: —it means my life is a failure.

T: It makes me feel good because—

C: —suppose I couldn't accomplish that much, anyway? Suppose I'm not so special?

I said to him, "If you never really commit yourself to struggling for a career and a real life for yourself, you'll never have to find out just what your potentiality is."

"I'll never have to find out," said Alan, "that maybe I'm not so great."

"So, to protect your self-esteem, to avoid finding out what you can or cannot accomplish, you do nothing, you just drift—and then loathe yourself for your passivity."

"Yeah. Well, maybe I could do something. You know, I mean, it's not impossible . . ."

I said, "It will be interesting to see what you choose to do."

"That's your way of reminding me that it's my responsibility."

"That's my way of reminding you that it's your responsibility."

"I don't like that. It makes me feel uncomfortable."

"I hear you saying that you want me to do something."

"Yeah."

"I can't. It's your move."

*

*   *

Self-esteem is the psychological result of a sustained policy of *commitment to awareness,* by which is meant:

a will to understand the facts of reality, as they relate to one's life, actions and needs; a respect for facts and a refusal to seek escape from facts, including the facts of one's inner experience; a policy of being guided by one's awareness of reality when one acts, so that one does not take actions or pursue goals that require or entail the subversion of consciousness, the restriction or evasion of awareness, the betrayal of knowledge, reason or honest conviction.

The "self" one is esteeming is one's mind—one's mind and its characteristic method of functioning, of dealing with reality (one's psycho-epistomology). All life is a process of interaction between organism and environment, and successful life for man is that which has awareness as the cutting edge of his motion through the world.

This way of relating to reality produces that sense of efficacy, power and worth which is the meaning of self-esteem. And contained in the experience of self-esteem is the sense of living at the vital center of one's existence—of being the active cause of one's responses, the generator of one's goals, the power that directs the flow of one's energy and the direction of one's life.

To assist the client in becoming more aware, to make him sensitive to the ways in which he obstructs the activity of his consciousness, to disclose to his sight the reality from which he has estranged himself, to liberate his mind's ability to function—and thus to encourage the growth of his self-esteem—is the purpose and goal of the various therapeutic techniques I describe in the course of this book.

To the extent that the therapeutic undertaking is successful, the client learns, not to "assume" responsibility for his life, but rather to *recognize* that he *is* responsibile for his life.

We often speak of a person learning to assume, or refusing to assume, responsibility for his life; however, this language is not fully exact when applied to the psychological sphere. It is only in the financial or material sphere that one can accurately speak of a person assuming responsibility for his life, as when he ceases to be supported by someone else and proceeds to support himself. On the psychological level, man does not have this option; by his nature, he is necessarily self-responsible; his option is only whether or not he will choose to be aware of that fact and to accept its consequences.

Contrary to the words of the famous poem, there are important respects in which each man *is* an island unto himself. This is implicit in the fact that the unit of life is the single organism; every organism is a separate entity that lives or dies as such. There is no collective life, just as there is no collective consciousness. But men have destroyed their minds, wrecked their lives, practiced unspeakable cruelties against one another, established social systems which have resulted in the slaughter of millions—to escape awareness of these facts.

Man cannot escape the responsibility of choice. If he chooses to do nothing, that is *his choice,* and it will have consquences for his life. If he chooses to surrender his mind to the authority of others and to follow them blindly, that is *his* decision and he will pay the price of it. A retreat from life is fully as much a decision as a commitment to life, and fully as much the responsibility of the person who decides.

When a person clings to the pain and frustration of childhood, refusing to see or move beyond it, he avoids awareness of the present, he refuses to integrate the reality of his present context, he rejects the fact that he is not a child any longer. When a person passively waits for the arrival of "someone" who will do "something" about his suffering, he makes himself unaware of the fact that his life and happiness are in his own hands and can be in no one else's. In so doing, he contributes to the deterioration of his self-esteem. If and when he reverses this policy and permits himself fully to be aware of the inescapable reality of his condition as a human being—including the fact of his unchangeable basic aloneness and self-responsibility—that is the first step toward the rebuilding of his self-esteem.

The more a person grows in self-awareness, the more he is prepared to acknowledge responsibility for his actions, responses and psychological state. The "responsibility" to which I refer does not carry any necessary implication of moral blame; the issue of moral blame may be entirely irrelevant; a person may behave self-harmfully because he does not know any better or cannot imagine an alternative; but the fact remains that it is *he* who is behaving, not some external agent.

It can be an exhilarating experience to confront the fact that one suffers not through the malevolence of some impersonal fate, but rather because one has chosen to nurture one's pain—and that one has the power to stop doing so. There are clients who resist this awareness; but there are others who welcome it eagerly.

There are profoundly important transitions in the course of psychotherapy when a client learns to switch his perspective on himself, to move from the view of himself as a helpless victim to the view of himself as the active agent of his own fulfillment or defeat. The more self-aware he becomes, the more readily he can accept this shift of perspective. When it takes place, that is the single most important event in the process of therapy.

Thus, a client learns to say, not "Why am I so passive?" but rather, "Why and how do I make myself so passive? What do I tell myself to keep myself so passive?" ("Why," in this context, means: for what purpose?)

Instead of saying, "Why can't I care about anything?" he learns to say, "Why and how do I prevent myself from experiencing strong feelings about anything?"

Instead of saying, "Why do I frequently have headaches?" he learns to say, "Why and how do I frequently give myself headaches?" (The answer might be: "I tense the muscles at the back of my neck and head, or I tense the muscles in my face, to hold back tears or to hold back anger.")

Instead of saying, "Why does the back of my neck become painfully tense?" he learns to say, "What feelings am I trying to avoid experiencing by tensing my neck muscles?"

Instead of saying, "Why do people so often take

advantage of me?" he learns to say, "Why and how do I encourage or invite people to take advantage of me?"

Instead of saying, "Why do people never understand me?" he learns to say, "Why and how do I make it difficult for people to understand me?"

Instead of saying, "Why do women always turn away from me?" he learns to say, "Why and how do I cause women to turn away from me?"

Instead of saying, "Why do I always fail at whatever I attempt?" he learns to say, "Why and how do I always cause myself to fail at whatever I attempt?"

I do not mean to imply that a person never suffers through accident or through the fault of others. But psychotherapy is primarily concerned with the suffering that a person brings on himself.

It would be a mistake to assume that this way of looking at oneself tends to increase guilt. Quite the contrary: it tends to produce a sense of power and liberation. Experiencing responsibility can be intoxicating.

*

* *

The essence of morality—if man's life and happiness are the standard and purpose of virtue—is (a) a dedication to awareness; and (b) a policy of acting in accordance with one's awareness. Awareness is the basic good that makes all other goods possible.

It is possible, however, to hold beliefs that actively obstruct or constrict awareness. In the effort to become more conscious, more self-aware, and to reintegrate disowned elements of one's personality, many persons are hampered by an especially formidable notion: the belief that there are such things as "evil thoughts" and "evil emotions"—that is, thoughts and emotions which, simply by virtue of their presence, constitute evidence of one's immorality, sinfulness or depravity.

In the Western World, the single historical force most responsible for the dissemination of this doctrine is Christianity.

One of the cardinal teachings of Jesus, as reported in the most authoritative source available, the synoptic

Gospels, is that people must "believe in me"—which evidently means, believe "that Jesus is the anointed," that "he is the son of God," believe in and accept his claims to divinity or semi-divinity. He does not offer any justification for this demand nor for any of his other precepts, beyond announcing "that the kingdom of heaven is at hand," and that those who "believe" in him and obey his precepts will be rewarded in heaven, while those who disbelieve and disobey will be condemned to suffer, will have "weeping and gnashing of teeth." What are offered are not rational arguments, but threats and promises.

This approach to morality, so highly subversive of reason, permeates Christian teaching. Holding that disbelief in Jesus and his teachings is a most profound sin, that infidels should be *forced* to believe, that heresy should not be tolerated, Thomas Aquinas maintained that heretics who revert to the "true doctrine" and relapse again should be received into penitence and then killed (*Summa Theologica,* 2-2. 1-16).

A legacy of this doctrine, in the present age, is that beliefs can be *commanded* in and out of existence, by an act of will—which, realistically, can only mean: by a psychological process resembling self-hypnosis, whereby one focuses on certain beliefs until one's brain "accepts" them—and that the presence or absence of certain beliefs are, per se, evidence of one's moral status.

Thoughts as such cannot be immoral; they can only be correct or mistaken. However, to accept beliefs without regard for reason, knowledge, evidence, probability, or respect for facts, *is* immoral. But this is what Christianity demands.

Reason and man's psychological well-being require that a person be free to consider, evaluate and accept or reject *any* idea, in accordance with his understanding of the facts. But this is what Christianity forbids.

Closely related to Jesus' pronouncements concerning sinful beliefs are his statements concerning sinful emotions. For example, at one point he says, "Ye have heard it said by men of old time, Thou shalt not kill . . .

But I say unto you, That whosoever is angry with his brother without a cause shall be in danger of the judgment." Elsewhere he utters his famous statement to the effect that not only is the act of adultery evil, but that adulterous *desires* are evil.

Desires and emotions as such are involuntary; they are not subject to direct and immediate volitional control; they are the automatic result of subconscious integrations. (See Appendix A). It is impossible to compute the magnitude of the disaster, the wreckage of human lives, produced by the belief that desires and emotions can be commanded in and out of existence by an act of will.

To those who accept the validity of Jesus' pronouncements, and their wider implications for undesired or "immoral" emotions in general, his teachings are clearly an injunction to practice repression. Whether or not by intention, that is their effect.

It should be mentioned that these two doctrines are not incidental to Christianity, but lie at the heart of Jesus' teachings. (For an excellent discussion and critique, see Richard Robinson, *An Atheist's Values,* Oxford University Press, 1964, pp. 113-157.) I do not mean to imply that the notion of "evil thoughts" and "evil emotions" was originated by Christianity; doubtless it is as old as the belief that there are supernatural beings who have the power to read men's minds and hearts—and may take offense at what they find there. But in the Western world Christianity has been the chief germ-carrier.

Today, with or without a belief in religion and the supernatural, the notion of "evil thoughts" and "evil emotions" is overpoweringly pervasive in our culture. Its impact on mental health is devastating. On the one hand, it generates guilt; on the other, it sabotages men's efforts at self-awareness. One cannot pursue self-investigation with a gun aimed at one's head.

Self-awareness requires an ability to approach the content of one's inner experience as a noncritical observer, an observer interested in noting and describing facts, not in pronouncing moral judgments. This is not a counsel to abandon morality but to recognize its destructive misuse in this context. To approach an investigation of one's inner experience with the question, "What does it signify about my moral worth if I have such-and-such thoughts or such-and-such emotions?" is to make the censorship of one's perceptions a foregone conclusion.

Further, implicit in this moralistic approach so inhibiting to psychological growth is a view of the self that is dangerously mistaken and must be rejected: the notion that the self is some sort of "essence" within a person that is basically good or bad—and that a moral appraisal of a person's thoughts and feelings will determine into which category his "essence" falls. The origin of this view may lie in religion, but it is by no means confined to those who consider themselves religious; it is widely prevalent in our culture. In the practice of psychotherapy I encounter this attitude constantly among clients who have repudiated religion and proclaim themselves atheists, but who have converted their moral convictions into a noose that strangles the life out of their personalities. They approach self-investigation with a powerful if unstated negative bias, and attitude of anticipatory self-repudiation, expecting to discover that their "essential" self is "bad."

First of all, moral appraisal, realistically understood applies to a person's volitional choices and actions, *not* to his thoughts and feelings.

Second, the self is not a static, finished entity, but a continually evolving creation, an unfolding of one's potentialities, expressed in one's thoughts, judgments, choices, decisions, responses and actions. If a person's choices and actions characteristically or typically are consistent with his standards, he tends to feel proud of himself. If his choices and actions are incompatible with his standards (however he may have arrived at those standards), he tends to feel guilt and self-disapproval. But the fact that yesterday's choices and actions conform to his standards does not guarantee that tomorrow's necessarily will. And the fact that yesterday's choices and actions violated his standards does not guarantee that tomorrow's necessarily will. That is up to him. The matter is constantly open to change. In this sense, man is engaged in a continual process of self-creation. To view one's self as basically and unalterably good or bad—independent of one's future manner of functioning—is to avoid the fact of freedom, self-determination and self-responsibility.

It should be added that for some persons, self-condemnation, the characterization of oneself as worthless or evil, can be very tempting: if one is bad by nature, why struggle? Neurotic guilt and self-castigation are often a means of avoiding responsibility.

So long as an individual cannot accept the fact of what he is, cannot permit himself fully to be aware of it, cannot fully admit the truth into his consciousness, he cannot move beyond that point: if he denies the reality of his condition, he cannot proceed to alter it, cannot achieve healthy changes in his personality. This thought is expressed in Gestalt Therapy as "the paradoxical law of change," which states that a person begins to change only when he accepts what he is.

The attitude of self-acceptance is essential to the achieving of unobstructed self-awareness. But what does it mean to "accept what one is?"

*

* *

Stated negatively, to accept one's self, to accept what one is, is to refuse to disown any part of one's experience—one's thoughts, feelings, emotions, desires, aversions, actions. The simplest form of disowning is to make one's self unaware of unwanted elements of one's experience, to refuse to perceive them. But there are other forms of disowning, less readily recognized.

A person notes one of his feelings or reactions and tells himself, "That's wrong! That can't possibly be my attitude!" In this case, he begins to be aware, but aborts the process, and proceeds to convince himself that he is mistaken, and the awareness surrenders and vanishes. (Parents specialize in teaching their children this type of disowning. "You can't possibly hate Johnny! He's your brother!")

A person contemplates some action he has taken and tells himself, "That wasn't me, not the *real* me!" In effect, he tells himself that certain aspects of his behavior "don't count," belong to an inferior order of reality, and thus the meaning of his behavior is prevented from being integrated into consciousness; it remains as a foreign body, an intruder within his system, to be banished from memory at the earliest opportunity. (An action taken by a person impulsively, that is in conflict with his conscious values, is still an action *he* has performed, and expresses something important about his state at the time of performing it.)

A person becomes aware of an emotion to which he reacts with shame or embarrassment, and he apologizes to himself or to others, saying, "I know this is silly" or "I know this is awful." Here he is eager to put as much psychological distance between himself and his feeling as possible, aggressively forbidding integration of the fact that, at a given point in time, this particular feeling was his way of experiencing some aspect of his existence. (I do not mean to imply that one should never acknowledge one's recognition that a given response clashes with one's view of what is rational or appropriate; obviously sometimes this is necessary. What I wish to draw attention to is the device of self-insult as a means of undercutting the reality of an unwanted experience.)

A person becomes aware of an emotion that is painful or threatening, and he proceeds to intellectualize, saying, "Now this is an interesting phenomenon! I wonder what causes a person to have such an experience? It really makes one feel dreadful." By a flight into impersonality, by inducing a state of dissociation, he seeks escape from the awareness that the emotion he is experiencing *is his own,* that it says something about *him* and *his* condition, and he strives to keep it unreal, meaning: unintegrated into awareness.

Stated positively, to accept one's self, to accept what one is, is to let oneself be fully aware, without censorship and without interfering self-criticism, of one's thoughts, feelings, emotions, desires, aversions, actions —to let them be fully real—to accept responsibility for them—to acknowledge them as one's own—to accept the fact that they are all expressions of one's self *at the time they occur*.

This attitude is not possible so long as one is more preoccupied with moral evaluation than with the desire to understand. "Accepting what one is" requires that one approach the contemplation of one's experience neither with approval nor disapproval but rather with an attitude that makes such concepts irrelevant: the desire to be aware.

Suppose a deeply frustrated and unhappy person has feelings of resentment and rage against anyone who appears successful, confident or happy. To accept his feelings means simply to permit himself to experience them, without the interference generated by self-criticism and self-rebuke. His attitude should be, in effect, "Oh, so this is how I'm feeling now. This is how I am experiencing my relationship to other people at this moment. These are my impulses." There is in such "self-acceptance" no implication that he does not desire to feel differently, merely the acknowledgement that they are there and that they are what they are.

He does not need to tell himself, or be told by anyone else, that it would be wrong to unleash in action his destructive feelings; he knows it; that is one of the reasons why he resists awareness of his feeling in the first place. If he forbids himself to experience and acknowledge them, he merely blocks their entry into conscious awareness; he does not wipe them out of existence; and then his destructive impulses emerge in disguised and unrecognized forms. If, on the other hand, he permits himself to experience his feelings, if he acknowledges and accepts them, he is free to discover their origin, to discover the frustrated needs he is blindly and neurotically struggling to satisfy, and thereby to move toward an authentic dissolution of these unwanted feelings. I have illustrated this process earlier in the book and will return to it again.

There is a more profound meaning to the concept of self-acceptance than I have yet indicated. Without an understanding of it, the full significance of the foregoing discussion cannot be appreciated. I am speaking of an attitude toward one's self that is deeper even than self-esteem, and that is a precondition of the attainment of self-esteem; perhaps it is more precise to say: it is the root or beginning of self-esteem.

Self-acceptance, in the sense I am endeavouring to describe, refers to a person's basic attitude toward himself, an attitude of self-value and self-commitment, that derives from the fact that he is alive and conscious and himself—a prerational, premoral act of self-affirmation—a kind of primitive egoism that is the birthright of every conscious organism—and yet which man has the power to act against, to repudiate, to nullify.

It is this attitude of self-acceptance that an effective psychotherapist appeals to or strives to awaken in a person of even the most appallingly low self-esteem—an attitude which, hopefully, will inspire a person to face whatever he most dreads to encounter within himself and not collapse into self-hatred, not repudiate the value of his person, not surrender his will to live, to grow, to rise out of his despair, to preserve his sense of membership in the human race, to struggle for the attainment of his human potential.

It is an attitude, I might mention, that is entirely incompatible with the most vicious of all religious notions: the doctrine of Original Sin and of man's inherent unworthiness.

It is an attitude that reflects the fact that the root of all values, of man's ability to value, is *self-value*—and that, so long as man lives, to repudiate the value of his own person is to commit the ultimate act of treason.

*

*   *

In dealing with the self-alienated individual, an effective psychotherapist seeks to establish a context that facilitates the process of self-acceptance.

This requires that he treat the client, not with "love," but with *respect*—respect for his needs; respect for his thoughts, desires and feelings; respect for his right to think and feel as an independent entity; respect for his ability to manage his own life (an ability he may be all too eager to deny); respect for that basic autonomy which is his by virtue of being human.

Required also is an attitude of *acceptance,* but a special kind of acceptance, the nature of which needs to be clarified.

For example, when Carl Rogers writes of having an "accepting" attitude toward his clients, he defines this as an attitude of "unconditional positive regard." *(On becoming a Person,* Houghton Mifflin, Sentry Edition, 1961, p. 62.) If Rogers intends his statement to be taken literally, this is not the view I am advocating. To have "positive regard" for a person means: to value him, to respond to qualities that have a positive meaning to oneself. To have *"unconditional* positive regard" means: to value him whether or not one finds anything in him to value, to value him whether or not any of his distinctive qualities are positively meaningful to oneself. To have "unconditional positive regard" for him means to experience him as a value to oneself regardless of anything he is or does. If such an attitude were possible, which it is not, it would give the client an appallingly unrealistic view of the nature of human relationships; it would not be helpful but harmful.

To treat the client with respect, to make him feel free to describe his thoughts, feelings and actions without fear of the therapist's moral censure, to communicate a belief in his potential as a human being, to value him on the grounds of his struggle to solve his problems—is *not* to project "unconditional positive regard" for him. It is, however, to provide him with that which he may rationally expect to receive from a psychotherapist. To offer him more is to insult his dignity as an autonomous human being: he does not require the all-embracing "unconditional" love of a mother for her newborn child, and he should not be encouraged to believe he does.

To face the client with an attitude of acceptance, in the sense I mean, is *to accept and respect his right to self-acceptance.*

*

*   *

When I endeavor to communicate the concept of self-acceptance to clients, I am sometimes met with the protests, "But I don't *like* the way I am. I want to be different."

The client will say, for example, "I don't like to be afraid of what people think of me. I hate that part of myself. I wish I could get rid of it." Or, "I'm ashamed of the fact that I feel I can't say 'no' to any man who wants to sleep with me. I loathe myself for being that way. Am I supposed to approve of it?" Or, "I see people I admire—people who are strong, self-confident, self-assertive. That's the way *I* want to be. Why should I accept being a nonentity?"

Two of the fallacious assumptions implicit in these statements have already been discussed: to accept that one is what one is, is not to approve of every aspect of one's personality; and to accept oneself is not to forbid the possibility of change; on the contrary, it is the precondition of change. Let us clarify this matter further.

Earlier in the book I observed that repression obstructs the integrative function of the mind, thereby keeping the organism in a perpetual state of conflict and tension. More precisely, *the person* keeps himself in the state of conflict and tension by blocking awareness of his inner experience—and, at the same time, producing a sense of self-alienation. If he permits himself to experience and acknowledge his denied feelings, he reestablishes contact with himself, he makes it possible for unwanted feelings to be discharged, and he unblocks the integrative process by means of which his internal well-being is preserved.

During a workshop I once conducted, a young woman complained that she was unable to speak freely because she was too eager to win my approval. I asked her to look at me and to tell me, clearly and firmly, that she urgently desired my approval, and to repeat that thought several times. She did so. After five or six repetitions, she was relaxed and smiling. I asked her to describe what she was now experiencing. She said, "I feel calm and clear-headed. I don't care what you think of me. There are certain things I want to say and now I am going to say them. I feel free and good."

Her difficulty in speaking openly was caused, not by her desire for my approval as such, *but by her resistance to that desire,* by the self-induced tension produced by her effort to by-pass her desire rather than to experience and discharge it. The result was a kind of mental clogging or short-circuiting, which she corrected by permitting herself to experience and acknowledge her feeling, letting it be fully real. This process was facilitated by the act of expressing her desire aloud and to the person to whom it was directed. The act of discharging her feeling released her mind, permitting her to be aware of her wider context and of her other needs, and to authentically experience—rather than merely to know abstractly—that her most important need in that particular situation was to say the things she wanted to say rather than to gain my approval.

Another example: A client complained that she was unable to profit from a speed-and-comprehension reading course she was taking, because she felt so anxious that she could not grasp or retain the material her instructor presented. I suggested that, driving to her next lesson, she spend her time describing to herself her various feelings and emotions, while letting herself experience them as fully as possible, even if they were painful and distressing. I suggested further that when her instructor presented her with a task, she request a moment or two to "go into herself," sink into her feelings, and describe them to herself silently. This is her report of what subsequently happened: "Driving there, I was petrified. I could feel my body shaking, but I went on describing all of my feelings and bodily reactions. When I looked at the assignment I wanted to cry. I felt so unsure of myself, so scared. So I cried. I sank into my feelings and described everything I could. After a minute or two, I said I was ready and I did the assignment. I got an almost perfect score. My brain was clicking along beautifully—really functioning."

I asked her if she could describe what changed for her as a consequence of experiencing and acknowledging her feelings. She replied, "My perception of the whole situation became different. Aside from feeling less tense, I felt more in contact with what I had to do, because the obstruction was gone, the obstruction of worrying about whether or not I would do well and fighting my worry at the same time. So I felt that I was there, fully there. I felt more real to myself. And my sense of what was most important shifted. What was most important was not to worry about what might happen but, instead, to understand the assignment. There was a shift in my priorities. It was like gears moving inside my head, bringing the reality of the immediate situation into clearer focus."

What is important to notice, in both of these examples, is that desired change was produced not by resisting awareness of the individual's immediate experience, but by the exact opposite course: by becoming open to that experience. But this approach is not successful if performed ritualistically or mechanically. It is not a matter of reciting certain words while remaining inwardly remote; if one performs the exercise in a mechanical way, nothing will change. The individual must authentically immerse himself in his experience, must be willing to "go with" his feelings, must listen to the messages his body and emotions are sending, must be aware of his own being in the here and now. (Gestalt Therapy has developed many ingenious exercises to assist the individual in cultivating consciousness of the "here and now." It characterizes the changes that result as a form of "organismic self-regulation." See F.S. Perls, R.F. Hefferline, P. Goodman, *Gestalt Therapy*, Julian Press, 1951.)

The following example further illustrates how internal "self-healing" adjustments take place, when denied feelings are admitted into awareness, expressed and discharged.

A man complained that he had lost all sexual desire for his wife, while at the same time insisting that he loved her deeply; he professed to be utterly bewildered by his sexual indifference. I was inclined to believe him. Knowing that a damming up of sexual feeling is often a consequence of the repression of anger and hurt, I suggested that—without attacking or denouncing *her,* but speaking only of his own feelings and reactions —he face her, (she was present at the interview), and utter some sentences beginning with the words "I get angry when . . ." He did so, and very shortly an unexpected (to him) torrent of outraged feelings began to pour forth. It soon became evident that the anger was covering a good deal of unacknowledged pain. I suggested that he utter some sentences beginning with the words "I am hurt that . . ." He did so, and waves of previously unacknowledged pain began flowing into his awareness.

Whenever he attempted to shift from describing his own feelings to making statements about his wife's imagined motives, psychology and so forth, he was asked to abstain from doing so and to confine his statements to descriptions of his own feelings, and to descriptions of the grossly observable *facts* to which his feelings were experienced as a response (facts available to his sight and hearing, rather than "facts" he imagined to be taking place inside her consciousness). One of the most prevalent forms of seeking to escape from one's inner experience is to switch one's focus to another person, and proceed to make statements about that person's presumed intentions, feelings, moral worth, or whatever. If, for instance, a person does not wish to face his own hurt—perhaps because he experiences it as humiliating or an indication of weakness—he may seek to escape from it by attacking the character of the person he regards as responsible and dealing with that person's *imagined* psychology rather than his own *actual* psychology.

Within a few hours after the couple left my office, my client's sexual feeling for his wife returned in full intensity—as he reported at our next session.

In forbidding himself to experience and confront his anger and hurt, he had effectively cut off *all* his feelings toward her—he had anesthetized himself emotionally—which is, unfortunately, an extremely common pattern between partners in a marital relationship.

Further, on the subconscious level, his wife had become too associated with pain and resentment; as a consequence, his sexual capacity "went on strike." Whenever a person complains of lack of sexual feeling for his partner, a valuable line of inquiry is to look for unexpressed anger, resentment and hurt. Contrary to the "don't-rock-the-boat" theory of marriage, the communication of angry or hurt feelings—when *not* accompanied by an attack on the worth of the other party—is one of the most effective means of reestablishing intimacy as well as of releasing and strengthening sexual passion.

Let me stress once more that it is not unwanted feelings as such that sabotage healthy functioning, but the *denial* of those feelings, the unwillingness to experience and acknowledge them. It is the act of blocking that obstructs the free flow of awareness and disrupts the normal balance among one's actual needs and values—*thereby giving rise to a different set of responses than would occur were one in good contact with one's inner experience.*

The emotions most frequently repressed are pain, rage and fear. Healthy growth, development and change are thereby prevented from taking place, or significantly obstructed. A person who does not permit himself to know what hurts him, cannot permit himself to know what he wants—cannot permit himself to know and/or experience the importance of the desires and needs that are frustrated, and therefore cannot take effective steps toward their fulfillment. A person who does not permit himself to know when he feels assaulted and mistreated, condemns himself to feelings of helplessness and impotence—condemns himself to a state where self-assertiveness is impossible. A person who does not permit himself to know when he is afraid, cannot be aware of the defenses he establishes to protect himself that have the effect of restricting and inhibiting his growth and development—and he cannnot take action to correct the situation. Healthy change necessarily begins with self-awareness—which in turn requires an attitude of self-acceptance.

Unfortunately, many persons desiring to change begin by repudiating what they are—in the name of their "ideals" of what they seek to become. Sometimes, the very nature of their ideals makes this necessary; there are "ideals" that run totally counter to man's nature and thus make self-repudiation mandatory. But even when this is not the case, even when a person's ideals are valid, even when the qualities to which he aspires are rationally desirable, he cannot move toward them successfully by pronouncing himself a nonvalue in his present state and disowning that which he is. The person who accepts himself, whatever his real or imagined shortcomings, is capable of moving from self-awareness to the attainment of new understanding and new integrations, to the attainment of a superior manner of being and of functioning. The man who repudiates himself is not; he has no base from which to move.

Before concluding this discussion, let us clarify one last point. I have mentioned that one of the most frequently repressed emotions is pain. However, when I encourage clients to permit themselves to experience their pain, they sometimes suggest that what I am advocating is self-pity. What is the distinction?

To face one's painful emotions, to experience them fully, to acknowledge them, to listen to the message they contain concerning one's frustrations, and perhaps to describe in words what one is feeling, requires courage and honesty; it is not an exercise in self-indulgence. To be self-pitying is to make no effort to deal with one's suffering or to understand it, to complain of it while seeking to avoid confronting it, and to indulge in thoughts or utterances about the cruelty of life, the futility of struggle, the hopelessness of one's predicament, the unfairness of fate, and so forth. To say, "*Right now* I am feeling hopeless," is not self-pity; to say, "My situation *is* hopeless," *is* (usually) self-pity. In the first instance, one is describing a feeling; in the second, one is making a statement of alleged fact. Descriptions of feelings, however painful, can be therapeutic; statements of alleged facts about life or the world, motivated solely by one's painful emotions of the moment, generally are self-destructive. In the first case, one takes responsibility—the responsibility of awareness; in the second case, one abandons responsibility and surrenders to passivity. This is a distinction of the most vital importance.

*

*   *

In discussing the self-healing and growth-inducing value of self-awareness, I have made repeated reference to integration and the integrative function of the mind.

The concept of integration is central to every aspect of the life process. An organism is a complex integrate of hierarchically organized structures and functions. It sustains itself physically by taking materials from the environment, reorganizing them and achieving a new integration which converts these materials into the organism's means of survival. We can observe an analogous phenomenon in the process by which a consciousness apprehends reality. Just as integration is the cardinal principle of life, so it is the cardinal principle of mind. This principle is operative when, in the brains of men or animals, disparate sensations are automatically retained and integrated (by nature's "programming") in such a way as to produce a perceptual awareness of entities—an awareness which men and animals require for their survival. Integration is essential to the process of concept formation and abstract thought—to that process of gaining knowledge on which distinctively *human* survival depends.

To integrate is to bring together into a nonconflicting, noncontradictory unity those elements which are being integrated, in accordance with a goal, need, purpose or standard that operates as the unifying or organizing principle. The ultimate *biological* principle of integration is: that which is required for the life of the organism.

To quote from *The Psychology of Self-Esteem:*

The basic function of consciousness—in animals and in man—is *awareness*, the maintenance of sensory and/or conceptual contact with reality. On the plane of awareness that man shares with animals, the sensory-perceptual plane, the integrative process is automatic, i.e., "wired in" to the nervous system. In the brain of a normal human being, sensations (primary sensory inputs) are automatically integrated into perceptions. On the sensory-perceptual level, *awareness* is the controlling and regulating goal of the integrative process—by nature's "programming."

This is *not* true of the conceptual level of consciousness. Here, the regulation is not automatic, not "wired in" to the system. Conceptual awareness as the *controlling goal* of man's mental activity, is necessary for his proper survival, *but it is not implanted by nature.* Man has to provide it. He has to select that purpose. He has to direct his mental effort and integrate his mental activity to the goal of conceptual awareness—by choice. The capacity of conceptual functioning is innate; but the exercise of this capacity is volitional.

It must be understood that conceptual integrations do not require man's conscious regulation every step of the way, countless integrations occur without separate, accompanying acts of rational deliberation. Man's primary conscious responsibility is *to set the goal:* awareness—to monitor the process of integration, insofar as its workings are consciously available to him— and to test the results against observable reality.

The integration of his life experiences in such a way as to protect his well-being falls within the domain of man's volitional responsibility—from the time that he has matured sufficiently to be conceptually self-aware and is able to reflect on the meaning of his own responses. The function of reason and purposeful awareness is to guide and facilitate the integrative process in the realm of knowledge, judgment and the assimilation of experience.

Let us pause for a moment to clarify the relationship of the concept "awareness" to the concept "reason." *Awareness* is the most general term to characterize the biological function of mind: awareness of internal reality and external reality, awareness of immediate sensory experience and of relationships among phenomena which can be grasped only conceptually.

Reason is the conceptual instrument of awareness; reason is the power of integration made explicit and self-conscious; it is the faculty by means of which man apprehends logical relationships and organizes the contents of his awareness into systematic classifications. *Awareness*, then, is a wider term than *reason* and in the case of man, includes it.

Reason is the monitor and guide of conceptual integration. When the exercise of reason is suspended, what frequently takes place may be described as *pseudo*-integration, an unassimilated absorption of experience, or a chaotic "organization" of experience, that tends to produce psychological indigestion—or worse.

The proper exercise of reason does not entail the conceptual analysis of every experience—an undertaking which is neither possible nor necessary. Sometimes, all that is necessary for integration to take place is that a person be aware of what he is experiencing; integration then occurs spontaneously. Often, however, a person "senses" the presence of significant relationships he cannot immediately grasp, or the presence of some dissonance among the signals he is receiving from the external world or from within himself—in which case it becomes the task of reason to guide the process of integration on an explicit and self-conscious plane.

In seeking to dissolve conflicts within himself, man often needs to reflect conceptually on the meaning of his feelings, responses and actions, to engage in a sustained process of reason. But sometimes what is needed is not, predominantly, sustained thought or analysis, but merely the bringing of some aspect of his experience into awareness; and when the latter course is indicated, the attempt to "analyze" becomes a mistake which obstructs rather than serves the process of integration. However, reason remains the ultimate arbiter, since only reason can determine which course of mental action is appropriate to a given set of circumstances.

Evasion and repression are, by their very nature, anti-integrative processes. When evasion and repression have obstructed the integrative process, the task of reason and awareness is to remove those obstructions.

In the course of their work many psychotherapists have been impressed by the frequency with which self-healing and growth-inducing integrations occur when previously avoided material is brought into conscious awareness and is fully experienced—experienced organismically, one might say—rather than merely grasped cerebrally. The self-repairing process observable on the physical level of man's being appears to have an analogous process on the psychological level—evidenced by the phenomenon of spontaneous integrations. This self-repairing tendency is not infallible, neither in body nor in mind, but its existence on the psychological level seems indisputable—and the challenge for psychotherapy becomes how to employ it creatively.

Since so much of denied and avoided material consists of repressed emotions, and since the derepression of emotions often leads to dramatically successful results there is a growing emphasis on the liberation of feeling as a cardinal therapeutic goal. While this emphasis is understandable, and has much to commend it, it also has its dangers, if and when it becomes the therapist's primary concern. These dangers include: anti-intellectualism, indifference to reason and self-indulgent subjectivism. (Perhaps the extreme of this trend is represented by the Primal Therapy of Arthur Janov. But even in Gestalt Therapy, this tendency seems detectable, although I do not believe it is essential to the Gestalt position and is doubtless absent among many Gestalt practitioners. But see, for example, Frederick S. Perls, *Gestalt Therapy Verbatim*, Real People Press, 1969.)

A person oriented exclusively to the external world and disconnected from the internal world of his own experience, is a robot. But a person oriented exclusively to the internal world of his own experience, disconnected from the external world, is a schizophrenic. Neither condition is desirable for a human being. Neither condition represents a state of mental health.

Psychological well-being and effective functioning

entail the ability to be aware of the facts and requirements of external reality without sacrificing awareness of inner experience—and to be aware of inner experience without sacrificing awareness of the facts and requirements of external reality.

Let me offer a simple illustration. Suppose that a person is ill and knows that a surgical operation is necessary. Suppose, further, that he experiences considerable fear at the prospect of this operation. It would obviously be self-destructive to capitulate to the fear and avoid the needed surgery. But it would also be self-destructive to be aware only of the need for surgery and to be oblivious to the fact of the fear. A fear that is experienced and acknowledged can be dealt with; a fear that is denied, in a case such as this, can precipitate a person into shock.

Another example: Suppose that a woman feels enraged at her husband. If that is her condition, it is essential to her well-being—and to the well-being of the relationship—that she be aware of it. Her right to experience her rage is not dependent on whether or not her rage is "justified." But at the same time that she experiences her rage, it is possible—and necessary —for her to be aware that her rage may or may not be an authentic response to her husband's behavior, that it may be the result of unresolved conflicts within herself having little relevance to her husband's behavior. So two different issues are involved, both of which deserve awareness and acknowledgment. One is the fact of her emotional state. The other is the matter of objectivity: what has actually happened in reality between her husband and herself? It would obviously be a mistake for her to assume, ahead of examining the objective reality of the situation, that her rage is entirely "justified." But it is equally a mistake to forbid herself to know that she feels rage until and unless she can "prove" that it is justified. In either case, the mistake involved is essentially the same: avoiding awareness of reality.

If a person believes that objectivity consists of permitting himself to experience only emotions he can "justify," he ends by corrupting his ability to be objective. It happens in the following way. He feels uncomfortable about simply experiencing an emotion and then expressing his feelings, labeling them as such. So he ignores his feelings and sets out to "prove"—he feels driven to "prove"—that the object of his emotional response is "immoral" or "wonderful" or "vile" or "brilliant" or whatever. In other words, he defends himself via the mechanism of projection. Now sometimes it happens that the qualities he projects onto an object are in fact possessed by the object; but that is not the point; the point is that he has made himself incapable of knowing it. By forbidding himself to experience and acknowledge his emotions, he sabotages his awareness of the distinction between consciousness and existence, between experience and external reality, and thus undercuts his ability to make objective judgments. He does so in the name of his misconceived notion of "objectivity."

The foregoing discussion is not intended to imply that in any and all circumstances an individual must announce his emotions aloud, in the presence of other people. What is essential is that he be aware of his emotions, that he experience them, that he acknowledge them to himself. When and under what circumstances he chooses to communicate his feelings to others is a different question. There will be times when it is impractical or undesirable for him to do so. But if he is silent, he should be silent by conscious choice and decision—not because he feels *incapable* of giving expression to his feelings.

Needless to say, it is very easy for a person to deceive himself and to believe that he remains silent by choice when in fact he does so because of repression.

The more an individual becomes aware of his inner experience, and of the ways in which he resists confronting it, the more choices or options become available to him: he becomes free to communicate his inner experience to others or to abstain from doing so; to continue his present manner of functioning or to experiment with alternatives; to reinstitute a policy of self-repudiation with the full knowledge of what this means or to liberate his disowned self and acknowledge ownership and responsibility.

Chapter 4

The Psychotherapy of Alienation

Most schools of psychotherapy share the conviction that the client's *insight* or *understanding* is basic to the process of psychological improvement, symptom removal and personal growth. They differ, however, not only in their wider theories concerning the nature of man and neurosis, but also in (a) the specific meaning they attach to "insight" or "understanding," and (b) the kinds of facts of which they believe the client needs to become aware.

Consider, for instance, the original position set forth by Sigmund Freud:

It is true that in the early days of analytic technique we took an intellectualist view of the situation. We set a high value on the patient's knowledge of what he had forgotten, and in this we made hardly any distinction between our knowledge and his. We thought it a special piece of good luck if we were able to obtain information about the forgotten childhood trauma from other sources . . . as in some cases it was possible to do; and we hastened to convey the information and the proofs of its correctness to the patient, in the certain expectation of bringing the neurosis and the treatment to a rapid end. It was a severe disappointment when the expected success was not forthcoming. How could it be that the patient, who now knew

about his traumatic experience, nevertheless still behaved
as if he knew no more about it than before? ("On Beginning the Treatment." Originally published in 1913, the
article can now be found in S. Freud, *Standard Edition,*
London: The Hogarth Press, 1953, 12:123–44.)

Contrary to what one might assume from the above
passage, Freud did not subsequently shift from this
"intellectualist" position; nor did he question his assumption that presumed traumas "cause" the neurosis.
His modification consisted of "informing" the patient
not only of his early traumatic experiences, but also
of the reasons for the patient's "resistance" to remem-
bering his traumatic experiences ("the analysis of the
resistance") the assumption being that if the patient
were able to *remember* significant childhood experiences, cure would promptly follow. The results
were disappointing, and in the last years of his life
Freud became deeply despairing of the efficacy of psy-
choanalysis as a therapeutic method. ("Analysis Ter-
minable and Interminable." Originally published in
1937, the article can now be found in S. Freud,
Standard Edition, London: The Hogarth Press, 1953,
23:216–53.)

Subsequent psychologists and psychiatrists have challenged not only Freud's theory of neurosis, but also his
assumptions concerning therapeutic technique. Today,
in the context of treatment, there tends to be far less
emphasis on the question of *why* a client became
neurotic than on the question of *what* he does to keep
himself neurotic. And there is a growing appreciation
of the fact that "informational" knowledge concerning
his problems—historical or theoretical knowledge concerning the presumed origins of his problems—is often
of very little practical value to a client, of and by itself.
(A review of the divergent positions on this matter
held by some of the major current schools may be
found in Erwin Singer, *Key Concepts in Psychotherapy,*
Random House, 1965.)

My own views may be summarized as follows:
Understanding, in the context of psychotherapy, re-

fers to a process that is at once cognitive and emotional —that is, *experiential*. Such understanding does not consist of information or abstractions or theories divorced from the client's immediate, first-hand experience—and neither does it consist of "raw feelings" unaccompanied by a conceptual grasp of their meaning (this latter trend being all too fashionable today). Therapeutic understanding represents an integration of intellect and emotion, cognition and experience, thought and feeling—not either/or, but always both together.

The subject matter of such understanding concerns: *what* the client does to sabotage his effective functioning (for example, he freezes mentally when faced with a difficult problem); the *means* by which he does it (for example, he tenses certain muscles to block off his anxiety, he tells himself he is incapable and induces a sense of passivity and helplessness); the *purpose* for which he does it (for example, to avoid the pain of trying and failing); and (sometimes but not always) the *historical context* in which he first practiced self-sabotaging behavior and in which it first felt plausible and/or necessary (for example, when presented with expectations and demands on the part of his parents that he experienced as overwhelming and beyond his abilities).

*

* *

I said in the Preface that this is not primarily a book on psychotherapy, but on the problem for which psychotherapy may be required: self-alienation. However, it is doubtful that there is any context in which the study of self-alienation can be more productive and illuminating than the daily practice of psychotherapy; hence the many case examples I have presented.

I have offered several illustrations of one particular therapeutic tool that I find exceptionally useful: the sentence-completion technique. I wish to elaborate on the use of this technique, in the hope that other professionals may want to investigate its possibilities.

It is an easily demonstrable fact that a person often "knows" more than he "knows" he "knows"—and that, given the right circumstances and the right approach, that which is apparently "unknown" to a client, or "subconscious," can be brought into conscious awareness. The sentence-completion method accomplishes this task with remarkable efficiency.

The idea of providing a client or subject with a series of unfinished sentences and asking him to complete them is not, of course, new. The novelty of the technique consists of: (a) the specific items with which the client is presented; (b) the method of moving back and forth between standard, predesigned items and items improvised on the spot in response to the client's replies; (c) the manner in which the technique is administered; and (d) the immediate therapeutic effect on the client that often results from his involvement in the exercise.

When I began experimenting with the technique, I regarded it primarily as an information-gathering tool; I did not forsee the value it would offer to the client as a means of achieving emotional release and expanded self-awareness and of stimulating psychological integrations. These benefits, however, quickly became evident. While they are not achieved equally in all cases, they are almost always achieved to some extent, sometimes on the first administration of the technique, sometimes on subsequent administrations.

The client is requested to respond to each item, as quickly and spontaneously as possible, with the first completion of the sentence that occurs to him—without editing or censoring or worrying about the "rightness" or "appropriateness" of his responses. He is informed that some of the responses that occur to him might seem foolish, illogical, untrue, but that this need not concern him; no single response is taken at face value or assumed necessarily to represent his actual beliefs or feelings. He is asked to sit in a comfortable position, feet uncrossed and arms at his sides, then to take two or three deep breaths, let his body relax and close his eyes. If the client seems unusually nervous or anxious, additional time is spent on helping him to relax. He is asked, finally, to be as passive as possible, to let whatever happens happen, and not to strive to *make* anything happen. Then the exercise begins.

The list of standard, predesigned items with which I work is in a continual state of revision and expansion, but here is the list as it stands at present:

When I look at the ocean—*(A deliberately innocuous item such as this is introduced first to help put the client at ease and to ascertain whether he understands what is required of him.)*

When I wake up in the morning—
Ever since I was a child—
Basically, I—
Mother was always—
Mother never—
Mother seemed to expect—
That made me feel—*(It is sometimes useful to follow this phrase with several repetitions of: "And it also made me feel—")*
Father was always—
Father never—
Father seemed to expect—
That made me feel—*(These items about "Mother" and "Father" are normally presented in sequence. The other items are random; they can be presented in any order whatever, interspersed with improvised items.)*
All my life—
Why do I always—
When I look in the mirror—
Right now I am feeling—*(This item may be used many times in one session, at strategic intervals.)*
Why do people so often—
I resent—
Whenever I try—
As a man (woman)—
At the thought of facing my frustrations—
Sometimes I want to cry out—
When people look at me—

I dread—

If I were really honest and let myself simply be what I am—

If I make a mistake—

When my parents saw me make a mistake—

Thinking about Mother, I feel—

Thinking about Father, I feel—

Sexually, I—

A man's (woman's) body—

Pleasure to me is—

If I ever let out my anger—

If people knew how much anger I had in me—

I don't dare let out my anger because—

My thinking ability—

At the thought of asserting my own desires—

I can remember—(*It is often useful to present this item more than once, if and when the therapist suspects that the item may elicit material relevant to the client's preceding responses, or when the client appears to be blocking.*)

I am a person who—(*This item may be followed by any number of repetitions of:* "And I am also a person who—.")

When I think that I am my parents' child—

Sometimes I close myself off because—

I feel most like a man (woman) when—

When I look at my body—

When I am with a woman (man) I find sexually attractive—

The child in me—

Sometimes I push my thoughts away because—

Sometimes I push my feelings away because—

At the thought of being seen naked—

At the thought of being held and loved—

I need—

Sometimes I feel proud—

I hate—

If I had my life to live over—

Men are to me—

Women are to me—

If I were freer sexually—

If I really let myself go—
In my relationships with people—
If I really felt loved—
If I were fully myself—
Strength to me means—
Weakness to me means—
A man is—
A woman is—
Masculinity to me means—
Femininity to me means—
Sex appeal to me means—
I can't stomach—
I get tired when—
Right now I am aware—*(This item may be used many
    times in the course of a session.)*
I don't want to know—
If my (headache, stomach pain, anxiety, depression,
    anger, etc.) could speak, it would say—*(The use of
    this item obviously depends on the client having indi-
    cated that he suffers from some distressing symptom
    or feeling.)*
Sometimes I want to cry out to people—
Sometimes I want to cry out to (a significant person in
the client's life)—
When a woman (man) looks at me appraisingly—
I enjoy—
Pain to me is—
My desires—
My sexual desires—
I can't tolerate—
Life to me is—
What I have to do is—
If I face my actual feelings—
A woman's vagina—
A man's penis —
I get hurt when—
I love—
I'm happiest—
At the thought of totally committing myself to a goal—
I become tense when—
I feel under pressure when—

If I could be free to do what I wanted to do—
At the thought of asserting myself—
When I deny my feelings—
At the thought of asserting my opinions—
When someone gets angry at me—
When someone seems afraid of me—
My body—
At the thought of totally committing myself to another person—

It is not necessary to use all of these items during a single exercise; in fact, I cannot recall a single occasion when I have done so. The greater part of this exercise is normally taken up with improvised items. Sometimes the improvised items are in response not to the client's replies, but to his evident mental or emotional state. For example, if the therapist observes that his client's jaw muscles are pulled tight in anger, he might offer the item: "I became angry when—" or: "I am feeling angry because—."

Now *because* is a very sensitive word; the danger is that the use of such a word may cause the client to become "self-conscious" and analytical. I have found that this can usually be avoided by uttering the word in a casual, offhand tone of voice, frequently preceeded by the equally nonchalant "perhaps"—as in, "I become afraid, perhaps, because—."

It is not uncommon for a client to become deeply emotionally involved during the exercise, to weep, to become anxious or agitated or angry or depressed. When this occurs, one can improvise items that will permit the expression and exploration of these feelings.

The full exploitation of this technique requires a good deal of practice and experience; it is very easy to underestimate the complexities involved. These complexities pertain to the therapist's use of improvised items. This obviously cannot be done mechanically; his skill and ingenuity depend on his understanding of mental and emotional processes, and of principles of motivation, as well as on his sensitivity to the particular client with whom he is working.

I wish to conclude this study of the psychology of self-alienation with one case reported in some detail; the sentence-completion technique figures prominently in this presentation and further elaborations of its use are provided.

*

*   *

The client—I will call her Cora—was thirty-four years old. She was a physician specializing in internal medicine; her husband was a surgeon; they had no children. She was a tall, attractive woman who seemed intent on concealing her attractiveness behind an unbecoming hairstyle and an unflattering manner of dress. Her movements were characteristically rigid, overcontrolled and somewhat awkward. Occasionally, however, for a brief instant her "control" would break and her movements would become fluid, animated and spontaneous; then the "control" would reassert itself and her energy and liveliness would again vanish behind a protective armor.

During our first interview she complained of feelings of depression, inability to enjoy her work or her relationship with her husband, disinterest in sex, and diffuse feelings of guilt which she attributed to the emotional hardship she was inflicting on her husband as a consequence of her depressed spirits. She spoke in a quiet, dignified manner, but without personal involvement—in effect, as one "scientist" to another rather than as one human being to another. But at the end of the interview a small incident occurred that subsequently was to prove significant.

I noticed, as the session was drawing to a close, that a smile was struggling to appear on her face, and I asked, "Are you aware of what your face is doing right now?"

She immediately became thoughtful, and I said, "Don't try to think about it. Try to feel what's happening on your face. Try to experience it directly."

The smile became more open and she said, a bit astonished, "I'm smiling."

"What is your smile saying?"

"I don't know."

"Are you aware that you are trying to suppress the smile?"

"Yes."

"Try to feel your way into the smile and see if you can verbalize what the smile is expressing."

After a moment she said, "I feel comfortable with you. I feel relaxed."

"And what is your resistance to the smile saying?"

"Don't show what you're feeling. It won't last anyway."

"Can you say anything further about your feeling of being comfortable and relaxed here?"

"Yes, it's . . . I don't know if you'll understand or if I can say it clearly . . . You can take anything I might say or do or feel . . . It won't be too much for you, it won't frighten you, I couldn't overwhelm you. So I feel safe."

Ten days later, when Cora handed in the written "homework" assignment that I normally give to new clients, another facet of her personality was briefly revealed that also proved to be significant later in therapy. The assignment given to new clients is to write a paper covering (a) the history and development of the client's personal problems from childhood on, as he understands them; (b) what he believes his problems to be at present; and (c) what, specifically, he hopes to achieve through therapy. For the most part her assignment was executed in a dry, factual style, much like a laboratory report; but there were occasional images, metaphors and phrases that struck me as unusually effective literarily. Ordinarily I am very suspicious of assignments that are conspicuously "literary"; they are usually motivated by a desire to impress the therapist. But in this case I was positive that no such motivation was involved; I felt certain that the literary touches sprang forth involuntarily, almost against the intention of the writer.

A short time later, in group therapy, I suggested that we do some work with the "deathbed method." Although she agreed, it was obvious that my suggestion generated considerable tension in her; she had seen others in the group work with this method and it was my impression that the emotional explosions she had witnessed had frightened her. Lying on the floor, preparing to begin, she looked as I imagine a person might look stretched out on a rack, waiting to be tortured: from her face to her legs her muscles were held in tight contraction.

When she began to speak, she kept interrupting herself to clear her throat, revealing the tension in her throat muscles. I asked her to be aware of the tightness in her throat and to consider what it was accomplishing.

After a moment she answered, "I'm choking myself —to hold the words back."

I suggested that she temporarily abandon the attempt to speak and simply experience her resistance, accepting it rather than fighting it.

Cora said, "It's no use. What's the point of talking . . . My throat's relaxing now . . . a little bit, anyway. Let me try to . . . You were always somewhere else, Father. You were always away. Mother couldn't do anything for herself. So I had to be the man." This was said in an uninflected manner, with no evidence of its personal meaning to the speaker.

I asked, "And how does a little girl feel when her father is never there?"

Instead of replying to what I had asked, she began talking to her father about various past incidents between them, recounting those incidents in the matter-of-fact tone of a statistical report; the incidents dealt with occasions when her father had promised to take her somewhere or do something with her and had then reneged on his promise. "So I knew," she said, "that I just couldn't count on you, I could never count on you, I had to stop wanting and hoping. I would just have to do things myself. When you would come home and I would be so glad to see you and I would run to you and shout and try to reach up and throw my arms around you, you looked uncomfortable and embarrassed. Why did you do that?"

I suggested that she now let her father fade out of her mind and talk to her mother, instead.

She smiled and sighed. "Poor Mother," she whispered. "What a life you've had—frightened, frightened, frightened all of the time—scared of everything. Always crying and feeling helpless and looking to me to do something. What was I supposed to do?" Then, with the first sign of feeling in her voice, her face relaxed slightly and she seemed to become younger and she said, "Will I grow up to be like you? I don't want that. No sir, not for me. I want—I don't know what I want . . . I want to live, but I don't know what that means. Oh, I'm so tired . . ."

A tear rolled down her cheek. Then she took a deep breath and she made her body more rigid again, and she said, talking not to her parents but to me, "I'm feeling very uncomfortable. Very ridiculous. Do I have to do this?"

I said, "You don't have to do anything you don't want to do, of course."

I felt it was undesirable to push the matter further that day, so I asked her to take her seat. We spent a few minutes discussing her reaction to the exercise and any possible conclusions she might have derived from it; but her responses were vague. She seemed unusually numb and out of touch with herself, so I let the matter drop without reaching any decisive point. I felt that good had been accomplished, even if only to a small degree, but that it would not become evident until some subsequent session.

During the next several weeks, Cora was relatively silent in group, beyond volunteering an occasional reaction to the work done by other group members. But she did not appear to be oblivious to what was taking place: she watched and listened intently. Slowly, the first signs of a change began to appear; some of the stiffness vanished from her movements, her body motions were a little more fluid, and the tension in her face softened slightly. The effect was that she looked less "controlled" and more openly unhappy—which I regarded as progress: she was in better contact with her condition.

Then, one day in the middle of group, she announced abruptly, "I want to work today. I can't stand the way I feel."

"Will you describe what you are experiencing right now?"

"I'm feeling anxious. My throat is dry. I can feel my heart beating."

"Are you aware of trying to fight your anxiety?"

"Well, of course. I don't enjoy it."

"Are you willing to try an experiment? Let's see what happens if, instead of fighting your anxiety, you surrender to it, immerse yourself in it, go towards it rather than away from it. Do you know what I mean?"

She closed her eyes and appeared to draw into herself, seeking to be aware of what was happening within her body. "It's getting worse," she said.

"Please try and stay with it. Describe what you are experiencing."

"Well . . . well, I'm becoming dizzy, my heart is beating faster, I'm clenching my fists, I—I just feel awful."

"I wonder if you are aware of any other emotion besides anxiety, at this moment?" This question was prompted by the knowledge that anxiety is often a response to the partial emergence of some other feeling that is regarded as dangerous, threatening or catastrophic.

"I . . . I'm not sure . . . I might . . . be feeling . . . just a little bit angry."

"I'd like to try something—if you are willing to follow this further. To do another exercise."

"I'll try anything."

"Come over here and stand in front of the group." She did so. "No, don't look at the ceiling, look at various members of the group—whomever you like, it doesn't matter—but maintain eye contact—stay in the room, stay in reality." A thought that is spoken aloud can have more reality for the speaker than a thought that is uttered silently inside one's head; and a thought that is spoken aloud to another human being can have more reality still, because of the speaker's greater sense of objectivity.

"That seems to make the anxiety worse."

"Are you willing to do it, anyway?"

"Yes."

"Now I'd like you to say aloud—over and over again, until I ask you to do something else—'I'm angry.' Just repeat the words 'I'm angry.' And be aware of what happens inside as you do so. And let it happen. Let your emotions carry you wherever they want. I'm asking you to take a risk—since you don't know what the outcome will be. But it might be valuable." The purpose of this exercise was to help her become aware of the enormity of the rage within her, which she dreaded to face. Exercises of this kind, in which particular sentences are employed as emotion releasers, originated in the theater as a means of training actors, many years before psychologists and psychiatrists began experimenting with their therapeutic possibilities.

"I'm angry," she said. "I'm angry. I'm angry. I'm angry."

"Are you aware of your voice?"

"Yes, I'm just doing this mechanically."

"Are you aware of what you do to make the exercise mechanical?"

"Yes. I tense the muscles in my chest and throat, so no feeling can get through."

"Do you think you can abstain from doing that?"

"I'm angry. I'm angry."

"Try it a bit louder."

"I'm angry!" she shouted.

"Good. Continue."

She began to shout, "I'm angry," over and over again; within a few moments her body was shaking.

She turned to me. "I feel I'm going to shake right out of my skin," she said.

"The emotion of anger is trying to get out—and your muscles are blocking it. That's the shaking—the conflict of intentions—you want out and at the same time you want to keep yourself in."

"Yes, I can feel that."

She was holding her hands clasped tightly behind her back.

"Are you aware of your hands and of what they're doing?" I asked.

"They're holding each other."

"And what are your hands saying?" The question, of course, was metaphorical; it was intended to draw attention to Cora's emotional state by reference to one of the physical consequences or expressions of that state.

"I don't know."

"Well, one way to find out is to change their position and see what happens. Let them hang by your sides."

She did so. "Now I feel dizzy . . . dizzier than before."

"So clasping your hands behind your back helped to control your anxiety, helped to keep certain threatening feelings from entering awareness . . . Be aware of your shoulders. What are they doing?"

"They're pulling back. This is ridiculous, my elbows hurt."

"Try to feel your way into your elbows and arms and shoulders. What are they saying?"

"You have to control yourself. You have to get a grip on yourself."

"Ah, 'get a grip on yourself'—as in clasping hands?"

"Yes, I'm aware of that now. I have to exercise control."

"Or else?"

"I'll do something I shouldn't do."

"I wonder what that might be?"

"Hit somebody?"

"Is that a question?"

"I want to hit someone. I'm afraid of what I might do."

"What's your dominant feeling right now?"

"Dizziness."

"Aside from that."

"My stomach feels funny—I don't know, strange."

"Upset, perhaps?"

"A little."

"Would you walk around now to several different people in the group and do a sentence that begins with

'I can't stomach—' and finish it any way you want? And be aware of what happens."

She walked over to someone and looked at the wall above his head.

I asked, "Are you going to talk to the wall or to the person?"

She dropped her eyes to the person she was facing. "I can't stomach—my life!"

"Now go to someone else."

She walked to another person. As she spoke, she became progressively angrier; her posture became more rebellious and defiant. "I can't stomach—getting up in the morning!" She went to another person. "I can't stomach—my husband!" She went to another person. "I can't stomach—my work!" She went to another person. "I can't stomach—my in-laws!" She went to another person. "I can't stomach—my parents!" She went to another person. "I can't stomach—my friends!"

Now she was enraged. Her posture had entirely changed. Energy seemed to be exploding through her body, vitalizing her features and movements. At the same time she was radiating a subtle quality of feminine sexuality; it was in her eyes and her mouth and the movement of her hips when she walked.

"Pause," I said. "What are you experiencing now?"

"I don't know," she laughed. "I feel marvelous. I think—I think I feel like a hooker."

"If only hookers looked like you!" someone joked.

Then, suddenly, without apparent transition, the life and energy vanished from her face and body, her shoulders dropped, her body sagged and she said, "But this is so unfair. It's not their fault. It's mine. I've got the problem. There's something wrong with me. My thinking isn't right."

"What are you aware of now?"

"The dizziness is gone. I feel exhausted."

"So—when you're asserting your feelings you feel alive; and when you're being what you think is 'fair' and 'reasonable' you feel exhausted."

"I suppose so," she said listlessly.

"Will you take a stand and commit yourself? Is what I am saying true or isn't it?"

"It's true."

"You know that for a certainty?"

"Oh, yes," she said desolately.

"All right," I said, "you may sit down now. I'd like to make a few general remarks—to you and to the group. Here is something I would like everyone to think about. A girl asserts herself, she expresses her feelings without worrying about whether or not they are 'justified'—and the result is that she feels alive, she feels marvelous, she feels sexual, and—"

"I think I really enjoy it," Cora said sheepishly.

"Of course. But then what happens? Your perspective switches and you start being what you imagine is 'fair' and 'reasonable' and you tell yourself there must be something wrong with you, and now you're being a good girl, only there's no life left, no energy inside you, only exhaustion. What does that suggest?"

"That I've got problems," she said wryly.

"Well, yes, but what kind of problems? Should we take it as a foregone conclusion that your notions of 'fair' and 'reasonable' are irreproachably correct—and that the trouble lies in your inability to experience the 'right' emotions? Shall we simply conclude that Cora's neurotic, Cora doesn't know what's good for her, she doesn't know how to lead a rational life?"

"That's what I've always told myself."

"You know, it's my observation that if doing the 'right' thing always leaves us feeling exhausted and dispirited and without enthusiasm for life, it's time to rethink our views concerning what's 'right.' It's possible we've made a mistake. I offer this thought to anyone to whom it might be applicable. That's all I'll say on the subject at present. Perhaps you'll wish to raise it again, Cora. I leave the responsibility to you."

So much of Cora's psychology had become evident in this session that it took considerable restraint not to launch into a "lecture" and offer her my "interpretations" of her conflicts. But it is not desirable to do for a client that which he is capable of doing for himself. So I waited.

For several sessions, nothing eventful occurred, so far as Cora was concerned. Then one day she said, "I would like to report a discovery I've made. When I find myself beginning to get angry, I make myself tired instead, so the anger won't come out."

"Are you aware of how you accomplish that?" I asked.

"I just . . . tense up . . . and it happens."

"What muscles do you tense?"

"My chest . . . my arms . . . the back of my neck . . . and . . . I think . . . my forehead—I'm not sure about that."

"Are you aware of telling yourself anything at that time?"

"I . . . I tell myself . . . 'I'm tired.' Or sometimes . . . 'Be strong.' "

"Anything else?"

"Wait . . . yes . . . sometimes I say . . . 'Don't be unreasonable.' "

"And then?"

"And then all I want to do is sleep."

"So you're saying the anger is too threatening, too frightening."

"Too overwhelming. I think that calling it 'unreasonable' is sometimes just an excuse, a justification for escaping. But not always—I mean, sometimes I feel so bewildered and confused I don't know what to do or where to go."

"I wonder if you would be willing to try an experiment. Not here, but during the week, when you're on your own. You're aware now of what you do to cut off your anger, to make yourself oblivious to it, to prevent it from entering awareness. You've probably followed that pattern all or most of your life. So now the question is: Are you willing to take a risk and try something different? When we become aware of what we are doing, new choices and options open up to us. We can continue doing the same thing—or we can experiment, we can try something new, something different, and find out what happens. In this case, that would mean abstaining from cutting off the anger, letting it happen, letting yourself experience it."

"But if I were talking to my husband—I don't know what I might say!"

"I don't either. Want to find out?"

The following week she reported, "Nothing much happened. The anger just flared up for a moment—I felt my body was going to explode—then it went."

"Then you sent it away."

"I suppose so."

At the following week's session, she announced, "I want to work. But I don't know on what. I just feel that something could happen today."

"What are you aware of now?"

"A sense of tension, not unpleasant, a sense of anticipation. My heart is beating a bit fast, but, strangely, I don't mind it."

"Would you come over here and face the group?" She did so. "Look at whomever you want to in the room. Try the sentence 'I want.' Just do that sentence several times over. Let's see what happens."

"I want!" she cried vigorously. She was panting.

"Again."

"I want! I want! I *want!*" She began to sob convulsively, putting her hands to her face.

"Would you mind letting your hands remain at your sides? And let your eyes remain open. Stay in contact with the room. Don't run away."

Through her tears, she went on, "I want! I want! I want!"

I could see that her tears were turning into rage, so I said, "Now go to 'I am angry.'"

"I am angry! I am angry! I am angry!" Then she shrieked, "God damn you! I *want!* I *want!* I *want!* God damn you! *Why can't I want?*"

"Where are you now?" I asked.

She laughed. "I feel powerful! I want! I want! I want!" Her body had become transformed: she looked more alive than I had ever seen her and more self-assertive; it was conveyed by her posture, the movement of her hands, the line of her shoulders, the intensity of her face.

"Okay," I said. "Stay where you are, let yourself relax a moment, and listen. There is nothing more precious about us, nothing more sacred in life, nothing more valuable, no aspect of ourselves that so needs to be guarded and defended against everything, than our ability to say 'I want.' That's our center. That's the meaning of life. Without that, a human being doesn't exist."

She smiled weakly and happily. "I hear you."

"That's what you've been sitting on, holding down in yourself."

"Yes."

"I'd like to try something else now," I said, "if you're agreeable. I'd like to go to the 'deathbed exercise' now."

When she lay stretched on the floor, I described once more the 'deathbed situation,' and asked her to talk to her mother. She said sharply, "I want my father there too, I want to talk to both of them." For a long moment she was silent. Then she began.

"I'm tired of you. I'm so tired of both of you. I don't want to care what you feel. If you want to suffer, go ahead and suffer. *I don't care* . . . I felt so suffocated, you always made me feel suffocated, both of you. You never knew what to do with me. Why did you always make me feel it was my fault? Why did I always have to feel something was wrong with me? . . . You hated me for being alive, did you know that? So I turned into wood. So you would love me. It makes me sick. I loathe myself."

"You're five years old," I said. "And these are your parents. What's it like?"

"Why do I always have to be so *quiet?* You always have such a long, sour face, Mother. You're always suffering so much! *What am I supposed to do about it?*"

"That's not a five-year-old talking," I said. "Go deeper and go back. You're a little girl. What do you feel?"

"Alone. Alone all the time." Her voice was becoming younger. "There must be something wrong with me. But what's wrong? What's wrong? I'm frightened. Why can't I have parents? Oh, God, I can't breathe. Why can't I breathe? Why do I have to . . . I brought home a report card. All A's. You looked at me. You just looked at me." (Cora had obviously gone to a later age, but I did not interrupt.) "It didn't mean anything to you. You looked frightened. God damn you, why do you look frightened? Why can't you love me? What do I have to do to make you love me? Why are you both so afraid? What are you afraid of? Do I have to be afraid too? Oh what? What? . . . This can't— I couldn't . . . I want to get away—get away from you —but you can't—a little girl can't—so I . . ."

"And what does a little girl do to make her life bearable?" I asked.

"I—" she gasped for breath—"I just—I don't know what I did—I—"

"Yes, you do."

"I'm angry!" she cried. "I'm angry! I'm angry! *I'm angry!*

"And what does a little girl do with her anger?"

"You can't—she can't—I couldn't . . . do anything. You—I ran away, ran out to play—" she was choking for breath—"I won't let you get me, I won't be like you—I'll be strong."

" 'Being strong' means—"

"Acting. *Doing* something. Not being sorry for yourself."

"If I let out my anger—"

"It will be too much for them. They'll leave me. I'll be alone."

The following week, when she appeared in group, I observed that she had changed both her hairstyle and her manner of dress; the effect was to heighten her attractiveness and her femininity. I observed, further, that her movements were more relaxed and she projected a greater air of self-assurance. However, throughout the session she said nothing. I wondered what was taking place within her. I waited for her to tell me.

For six weeks she did not again ask to work; she merely volunteered reactions to the work of others.

Since I hold the conviction that whether or not a client in group works is his responsibility, I did not prompt her; she had to take the initiative.

Then one day she declared, "I want to work. I've got a problem. My indifference to sex is gone—but not my indifference to sex with my husband. I feel much less depressed a lot of the time. And it's never as bad as it used to be. But what do I do now?"

"What do you want to do now?"

"I'd like to be able to enjoy sex with Stan—or learn why I can't. I'd like to . . . not be so bored so often. I've got all this—I've got all this energy inside me—but I, I feel jumpy. What do I do with it?"

"Let's do sentence-completion work," I proposed.

During this session, I had two basic goals: to make explicit and conscious the integrations that evidently had been taking place within her, and to stimulate new understandings and new integrations.

It had become obvious that Cora carried within her the burden of an immense quantity of repressed anger; this, in part, doubtless contributed to her depression. Since childhood she had repressed her self-assertiveness. She was obviously frustrated; yet she did not feel free to look into the reasons of her frustration—and chose instead to blame herself. To become a specialist in internal medicine had clearly required considerable dedication; yet it was obvious that she did not enjoy her work. She was a woman who concealed great energy and life beneath her protective armor; yet she had striven to make herself a robot. She projected, at times, an immensely attractive femininity; yet she seemed in conflict with her own sexuality. As for her relationship with her husband, she had spoken of that very little in group; that was one of the areas I was now preparing to explore.

Therapist: When I look at the ocean—
Cora: —I see blue.
T: When I wake up in the morning—
C: —I feel sad.

(At this point, I could have gone to "I feel sad, per-

haps, because—" but I chose to let this item pass; there are no firm rules for these occasions: to a considerable extent, one is guided by one's "feeling" for the total situation.)

T: When I look in the mirror—

C: —I feel sad.

T: I find myself thinking— *(Now I will let her tell me why.)*

C: —life is passing me by.

T: Why do I always—

C: —deny what I want.

T: Right now I am feeling—

C: —annoyed.

(Here was another opportunity for probing that I chose to let go by; there are almost always more opportunities during these exercises than it is necessary or possible to pursue.)

T: Basically, I—

C: —am very different.

(Now I began to explore her childhood, which I almost always do very early in the exercise.)

T: Mother was always—

C: —suffering.

T: Mother never—

C: —made me feel that life could be happy.

T: Mother seemed to expect—

C: —me to feel sorry for her.

T: That made me feel—

C: —pity.

T: And it also made me feel—

C: —angry.

T: And it also made me feel—

C: —lonely.

T: And it also made me feel—

C: —hurt.

T: Thinking of all that now—

C: —makes me feel pain.

T: Father was always—

C: —passive.

T: Father never—

C: —acted like a man.

T: Father seemed to expect—

C: —I don't know what he expected. Nothing.

T: That made me feel—

C: —I don't know. Sad.

T: And it also made me feel—

C: —enraged.

T: And sometimes I felt—

C: —suffocated.

T: I felt suffocated whenever—

C: —I had to pretend that everything was all right.

T: If I didn't pretend that everything was all right—

C: —things would be awful.

T: Things would be awful, perhaps, because—

C: —they would just be awful.

(There was obviously a block here, which I chose not to challenge, on the assumption that the material would become available at a later point.)

T: All my life—

C: —I've pretended that everything is all right.

T: Right now I am feeling—

C: —like I want to scream.

T: I want to scream that—

C: —let me breathe!

T: I resent—

C: —people who are afraid.

T: When I see people who are afraid of me—

C: —I want to kill.

T: They make me feel—

C: —I . . . I'm blocking on this.

T: Pleasure to me is—

C: —being alone. But I don't want to be alone.

T: When people look at me—

C: —I wonder what they see. I don't know.

T: At the thought of facing my frustrations—

C: —I become apprehensive.

T: If I let myself sink deeper into my feeling of apprehension—*(Here I am using a form of indirect suggestion.)*

C: —I feel my heart beating.

T: If I go deeper and deeper into my anxiety and let myself experience it fully—

C: –I feel my throat tightening.

T: If I don't resist my tension, but accept it–*(Here, again, I am employing indirect suggestion.)*

C: –I feel better.

T: A man's body–

C: –can be beautiful.

T: When I'm with a man I find sexually attractive–

C: –I feel alive.

T: Sometimes I push my thoughts away because–

C: –because what's the use?

T: Sometimes I push my feelings away because–

C: –they could tear me apart.

T: At the thought of being seen naked–

C: –I like it.

T: My feelings might tear me apart because–

C: –what would I do?

T: Sometimes I feel proud–

C: –of my ability to take it.

T: "Taking it" means–

C: –being supportive and helpful.

T: When I am with Stan–

C: –I want to be happy.

T: Sometimes it's hard to be happy with Stan because–

C: he's not there. He's there but he's not there.

T: Sometimes I want to call out to him–

C: –please see me!

T: A man's penis–

C: –is fascinating.

T: Stan's penis–

C: –is afraid of me. Oh, God! *(She began to sob.)*

T: If I were fully myself–

C: –Stan would die.

T: That would mean–

C: –that I would be alone.

T: I want–

C: –not to be alone.

T: I can't stomach–

C: –what I do to myself.

T: I get tired when–

C: –when I do it.

T: Right now I am aware–

C: –that I am afraid to open my eyes.

T: I don't want to know–*(This is suggested by her fear of opening her eyes.)*

C: –where this is leading.

T: If my fear could speak, it would say–

C: –you'll lose everything.

T: Sometimes I want to cry out to Stan–*(I deliberately used this item a second time, feeling that it might elicit a different response than before.)*

C: –please be happy with me!

T: I get hurt when–

C: –Stan turns away from me.

T: He turns away whenever–

C: –I really show my love.

T: I find myself wondering–

C: –is it too much for him?

T: At the thought of totally committing myself to a goal–

C: –if only I knew what I wanted.

T: If I ever let out my anger–

C: –I'd lose everything.

T: If people knew how much anger I had in me–

C: –they'd be shocked.

T: Then they might–

C: –be hurt.

T: And they also might–

C: –push me away.

T: I don't dare let out my anger because–

C: –I don't want to be alone.

T: Sometimes I'm happy when I'm alone because–

C: –I can breathe.

T: If I could be that way all the time–

C: –I don't know.

T: When I think that I am my parents' child–

C: –I don't feel anything.

T: When I look at my body–

C: –I wonder.

T: And I feel–

C: –frustrated.

T: I wonder–

C: what's happening to my life.

T: The child in me—

C: —is afraid of being alone.

T: When I was young—

C: —I wanted a mother and father. But I never had them.

T: Thinking about that now—

C: —I tell myself it's too late.

T: What I need to do is—

C: —be myself.

T: If I could be myself—

C: —maybe I'd give up medicine.

T: And then I might—

C: —I–I–I feel myself freezing up. I don't know. *(This response made me certain that she had another choice of career in mind. So I attempted an historical approach.)*

T: I can remember—

C: —being in school.

T: When I was in school—

C: —sometimes I enjoyed myself.
(Suddenly I had remembered her first written assignment and what had impressed me about it.)

T: My favorite subject—

C: —was English literature and English composition.

T: What I liked most—

C: —was making up stories.

T: Thinking of that now—

C: —I want to cry.

T: If I told Stan about this—*(I was playing a hunch.)*

C: —he'd look at me with a frown on his face and not say anything but think I was crazy.

T: I could be happy with Stan if only—

C: —he wanted *me!*

T: Being myself would mean—

C: —breaking loose. Not being polite to people I can't stand. Getting rid of our boring friends. Telling my parents and Stan's to go to Australia and leave us alone.

T: If I did that—

C: —it would be the end of everything.

T: I think what I'll do is—

C: −right now I'm mad enough to do it anyway!

T: Sexually, I−

C: −have a lot to give.

T: Right now I am feeling−

C: −that nobody wants it.

T: Sometimes I wonder−

C: −if it isn't time to stop pretending. But . . .

There was a long silence and I decided to terminate the exercise. Cora opened her eyes and said nothing. She looked as if a great deal of mental activity were taking place behind her eyes. I asked, "Do you want to say anything?" She did not answer. "Or ask anything?"

Then she said, "Well, I guess I've been . . . I'm a coward, I've acted like a coward, I haven't . . ."

"What are you conscious of experiencing right now?"

"An immense sense of relief. The pleasure of getting a lot of things out. Also, a feeling of sadness. Also a sense of . . . I don't know . . . the feeling my blood is rushing around inside me, very fast . . ."

"What do you want to do right now?"

"I feel like I want to go home, lock myself in a room, and replay the tape of this session about twelve times."

"I hope you will." Then I asked, "Can you say what is the most important thing you learned or experienced today?"

She shook her head. "No."

"Well, *if* you knew—what would your answer be?"

Once a client professed not to know something I was certain he knew, and I said, as a joke, *"If* you knew, what would your answer be?"—and to my astonishment he ignored the humor of the question and provided the answer I was seeking. Since that time I have used the question with successful results many times, even when the client does appreciate the humorous intention. The structure of the question appears to dissolve the client's resistance—not always, of course, but surprisingly often.

The question succeeded now. She laughed. Then her expression became serious and she said, "I'm afraid of being alone. I've sold out for fear of being alone. Fear of being on my own. Fear of not having anyone. Disgusting!"

Two weeks later, in group, she said, "I've been playing that tape. I don't know if I've played it twelve times yet, but I've sure been playing it a lot."

"And?"

"It really says plenty, doesn't it?"

"Could you express that some other way?"

"*I* say plenty."

"Want to talk about it?"

"I can feel myself beginning to block right now."

"Are you aware of what your block is intended to accomplish?"

"To delay my knowing what I already know."

I stood up. "Will you come and sit in my chair?" She did so. "Thank you. Now face the empty chair you just vacated. You're not Cora now, you're Nathaniel Branden. Will you play me? Tell Cora what she said during that sentence completion exercise. Tell her what it means."

"Nathaniel Branden almost never works that way. He waits for the client to tell him," she said, smiling.

"Are you willing to do it?"

She turned to the empty chair. "Well, Cora, it's all pretty obvious, isn't it? You felt unloved and rejected as a child. You felt that your parents wouldn't let you be you. That they didn't want what you were. They wanted something else. You didn't know what. You felt that what you were scared them. You tried to make yourself into something else—something less—to get what you needed from them. You turned yourself off and you've been paying for it ever since." She turned to me. "How am I doing?"

"Please don't stop."

"That's what you're doing with Stan, too," she said, addressing the empty chair. "You feel that you're too much for him. So you repress yourself—and then resent him. Maybe you're too much for him and maybe you're not. If you turn yourself off, if you never show what

you really are, how will you know? Why don't you just
be yourself and find out what happens? Take a risk."
She turned to me again. "That's it, I guess."

"Do you want to say anything about medicine?"

"Well, it was an intellectual challenge—especially, I
suppose, since I'm a woman. It was an outlet for something, I'm not sure what. But I'm not happy practicing.
But what else can I do? Become a housewife?"

"I can imagine alternatives." She remained silent. I
added, "You did very well today."

"I don't feel like getting out of this chair."

"Could you say that some other way?"

"I don't feel like going back to being me."

She stood up and returned to her own chair. She
seemed very elated; her face was flushed and her
movements were energetic. Not knowing how to express her excitement, she sought the outlet of humor.
"Why don't you just retire and I'll stay in that chair and
do your work?"

"Could you express that some other way?"

"I feel marvelous."

"Thank you."

During the next several weeks, she did not say a
great deal, but she seemed quietly happy and self-
contained. At one point she said, without elaboration,
"I'm getting along better with Stan."

On another occasion she suddenly asked, "Why are
people so frightened by strong emotion?"

"Are *you* frightened by it?" I asked.

"I . . . Oh, you mean . . . yes, sometimes I suppose
I am. Ah, I know—fear of losing control, fear of being
overwhelmed."

"When a person is frightened of strong emotions in
himself, he's often frightened by the sight of strong emotions in others—because it stirs up what he's repressed
and denied. He feels threatened from within—but he
thinks he's being threatened by the other person."

"That's why it upsets me when I see someone being
angry—even if the person is not angry at me. It triggers
off some awareness of my own repressed anger. Well,
well."

Then, one day, she said, "I'm learning to assert myself. To express what I think, or what I'm feeling, or what I want or don't want. You know, it's a big job—just to be aware of what I think or feel or want. I'm not used to it. Sometimes it's exciting. I'm not sure if Stan is liking it or not. Sometimes he seems to, sometimes not. We've given up a lot of our friends. Mother is very upset with me, and I hope she's enjoying her misery, because I couldn't care less. That's one change I *know* Stan likes. I've thrown out most of my old wardrobe because of you. Know what that's cost me? Self-awareness and self-assertiveness—that's it, correct?"

"Self-awareness—self-responsibility—self-assertiveness."

"The holy trinity."

"That's right."

"Well, I don't think I'm going to remain in medicine—which is no surprise to you, I'll bet. I need another six months to get the nerve to quit."

"You've got it all figured out—even the time schedule."

"I don't know whether I'll stay with Stan or not. It's less frightening now—I mean, if I don't."

"Uh-huh."

"I think . . . uh . . . that . . . maybe I want to write."

"Could you say that some other way, please?"

"I want to write. I want to write . . . uh . . . you know . . . stories . . . fiction." She looked around the room at the faces of the group. "Nobody is laughing."

"Is there anything else you want to say?"

"I'm scared."

"It will be interesting to see what you choose to do about it."

*

* *

Self-awareness, self-responsibility, self-assertiveness—such is the process by which one takes repossession of a disowned self.

When a person acts without knowledge of what he thinks, feels, needs or wants, he does not yet have the option of choosing to act differently. That option comes into existence with self-awareness. That is why self-awareness is the basis of change.

When a person becomes self-aware, he is in a position to acknowledge responsibility for that which he does, including that which he does to himself, to acknowledge that *he* is the cause of his actions—and thus to take ownership of his own life. Self-responsibility grows out of self-awareness.

When a person becomes aware of what he is and takes responsibility for what he does, he experiences the freedom to express his authentic thoughts and feelings, to express his authentic self. Self-assertiveness becomes possible with the achievement of self-awareness and the acknowledgement of self-responsibility.

The extent to which a person commits himself to self-awareness, self-responsibility and self-assertiveness is the extent to which he attains self-esteem. It is also the measure of his mental health.

I do not wish to conclude this book without acknowledging explicitly certain of the moral premises that underly my approach to therapy.

There are, for example, psychotherapists who subtly or not so subtly would pressure Cora to remain in her marriage, regardless of whether or not that marriage was personally fulfilling to her. They would do so on the assumption that there are higher values, such as "the sanctity of the family relationship," that properly must be placed ahead of an individual's self-interest or personal happiness. I regard this view as criminally wrong.

The approach to psychotherapy presented in this book rests on the premise that a human being—every human being—is an end in himself, not a means to the ends of others; that he has a right to exist for his own sake; that honest self-interest is the moral purpose of his life. It rests on the premise that every person is responsible for the attainment of his own happiness; that just as he does not exist to serve others, so others do not exist to serve him; that he cannot live anyone else's life and no one else can lead his life; and that it is equally wrong to sacrifice himself to others or to demand that others sacrifice themselves to him. These principles are discussed in detail in *The Psychology of Self-Esteem*. Here, I wish merely to name them, so they are not left only to implication.

Nothing is easier than for men to practice self-renunciation; they do so every day; it is not a difficult feat or a moral achievement; it is a disease. Not selfishness but the absence of self, not self-esteem but self-alienation, makes possible the barbaric cruelty that men practice against one another. A concentration camp guard is the ultimate example of alienated man.

In the practice of therapy I have observed with unfailing consistency that when a client learns to take responsibility for his own life, when he achieves autonomy and authenic self-esteem, when he ceases to practice self-denial and self-sacrifice, he experiences a degree of benevolence toward other human beings that was unknown to him in his alienated state.

In proportion as a person is in touch with his actual self, with his real needs, with his authentic feelings—and in proportion as he acknowledges ownership of his own person—he experiences a sense of inner strength, a sense of personal efficacy, a sense of being alive physically, emotionally and mentally, that frees him of that fear of others which underlies all hostility and destructiveness. To achieve that state is the highest form of *selfishness*. It is man's greatest challenge. It is his greatest reward.

Epilogue

INTERVIEW* WITH

NATHANIEL BRANDEN
Appearing in Reason Magazine, May, 1973.

REASON: In reading *The Psychology of Self-Esteem,
Breaking Free* and *The Disowned Self,* one is struck
by how different each of these books is, in abstract
level, in approach, and so forth. How do you see their
relationship to one another?
BRANDEN: *The Psychology of Self-Esteem* is, of
course, the most theoretical and the most comprehensive
in the subjects it treats. In it, I attempted to lay the
foundation of my way of thinking about psychology.

Today, my understanding has gone considerably beyond what I said in that book, but it still functions as
my basic frame of reference. I tend to define my more
recent identifications in relation to the views expressed
there, as extensions of those views, or new applications,
or modifications, or corrections.

*Copyright © 1973 by Reason Magazine. The interviewer is George H. Smith author of Atheism: The Case Against God-Nash Publishing, 1973.

Breaking Free is a different kind of book entirely. I think of it as an exercise, an experiment. As you know, it consists almost entirely of edited transcripts of therapy sessions. So much has been written about child-parent relations, but I wanted in that book to capture the child's perspective and experience in the words of the clients themselves—in effect, to let them tell their own stories—to tell how it was for them—and also to show how this information was elicited—and thereby to disclose how parents contribute to neurosis, to the formation of negative self-concepts, to the undermining of a child's self-esteem. My purpose was not to blame parents, or to deny the individual's responsibility for his own life, but to illuminate what happens in early child-parent transactions. The book is thus intended to be a help to self-understanding, as well as a warning to parents.

R: You don't deal with childhood very much in *The Psychology of Self-Esteem*.

B: That's right. At the time of writing the book, I recognized that childhood is where almost all neurotic problems begin, but that's not what I focused on. My focus was more on the present, just as it used to be, in earlier years, when doing psychotherapy.

But more recently, several years ago, I found myself compelled to plunge deeper into childhood experiences, in the course of working with clients, and then to work to integrate those experiences with the present. I found I achieved better results that way. And that shift of focus is expressed in *Breaking Free*. During the past several years, I have become far more interested in childhood.

As to *The Disowned Self*, I really regard it as a sequel to *The Psychology of Self-Esteem*. The important breakthrough for me in that book was the treatment of the relationship of reason and emotion. I see this as a significant advance over my earlier approach.

Psychologists who emphasize the intellect, cognition, reason, tend to take a disparaging attitude toward emotions, though few of them will admit it. Often their attitude is implicit rather than explicit. Psychologists who emphasize emotions, and specialize in emotional-release types of therapy, tend to be hostile to reason and the intellect—though, again, few of them will admit it. I reached a point where I saw that a new integration was necessary. I wanted, in *The Disowned Self,* to provide that integration—to show a better way of thinking about the relationship of reason and emotion.

Now, the desirability of achieving such an integration is not arguable. The question is: How is it to be done? How does one implement it? That is what I wanted to answer in *The Disowned Self.*

Explicitly, of course, the theme of the book is the problem of self-alienation—the state that results when an individual represses and disowns certain of his needs, feelings, desires, hurts, frustrations, fears, longings, and so forth. That problem is the vehicle though which the issue of reason and emotion is explored.

R: Is there any connecting link that unites the three books?

B: The three books are united by their concern with self-esteem. They may all be viewed as variations on the theme of self-esteem. They deal, in different ways and from different perspectives, with the conditions necessary for the attainment of self-esteem, the factors that result in the undermining of self-esteem, and the ways in which the presence or absence of self-esteem affects an individual's personality and life.

R: You characterize your approach to psychology as "biocentric." Can you elaborate on the meaning of this?

B: "Biocentric" means: life-centered. So a biocentric psychology is one that approaches the study of human beings from a biological or a life-centered perspective.

Man is a living organism. Like all other organisms, his primary task is to exercise his capacities in dealing with his environment so as effectively to satisfy his needs, to preserve and enhance his well-being. The way in which an individual deals with this task is, I believe, the key to his psychology.

An understanding of the nature of man must begin with the study of the nature of life. Man's psychological nature can only be grasped in the context of his nature as a living organism. Man's nature, needs and capacities as a specific kind of organism are the source both of his unique achievements and of his potential problems. This is the view that dictated the general approach in *The Psychology of Self-Esteem*.

On a more concrete level, here are examples that might help to illuminate what I mean:

When I began my studies of self-esteem, it seemed clear that self-esteem was an inherent need of human beings. What is a need, in the basic biological sense? It is a condition of an organism's survival and well-being, a condition of its continued efficacious functioning. So in order to establish that self-esteem was a need, I asked myself: In what way is self-esteem vital to a human being's survival and well-being? What does it have to do with the effectiveness of his functioning? That's the biocentric approach.

Or take my treatment of the question of mental health. By what standard is mental health or illness to be gauged? I answer that question by working from the premise that the mind has a clear survival-function: to keep the human organism in good cognitive contact with internal and external reality, with the self and with the world, and thereby to guide and regulate behavior. This led to the conclusion that a person is mentally healthy to the extent that the functioning of his consciousness is unimpeded by blocks, and that he is mentally unhealthy to the extent that blocks obstruct the functioning of his consciousness. That, again, is the biocentric approach.

To carry this last point a bit further: On a very general level, we can say that a person is neurotic to the extent that his perception of reality is distorted by wishes and fears. On a deeper level, neurosis can be understood as representing an interference with, an obstruction of, the normal integrative and self-regulating functions of mind. "Integration" is the key concept here. It's a key concept both in biology and psychology. Integration is central and basic to all living processes and to all cognitive processes. Neurosis is interference with cognitive integration—and thus interference with the life process.

Another illustration of the biocentric approach may

be found in my treatment of the issue of volition or "free will" versus determinism. I attempted there to step outside the traditional philosophical context in which that problem is debated, and to approach volition biologically and to place man's power of choice in a biological context.

But beyond such examples—and I could give you many more—I am enormously interested in studying the parallels that I believe to exist between biological processes and psychological processes.

R: Do you plan to write about this?

B: Eventually.

R: Can you relate this approach to your views concerning the development of psychological problems?

B: Well, let's consider how psychological problems begin. I am convinced that the root of neurosis—always or almost always—is the process of disowning, of repressing important aspects of one's own experience, repressing needs, emotions and perceptions.

The disowning process begins in childhood. A child may find himself in an environment that is frightening or even terrifying, frustrating, bewildering, perhaps excruciatingly painful. In effect, he feels himself trapped in a nightmare. Intolerable emotions threaten to overwhelm him and to render him incapable of functioning. How is he to protect himself? To preserve his sanity? To preserve his ability to function? That is the problem he confronts. He generates a solution, and within the limits of his knowledge it may be the only solution he can conceive: he learns to disconnect from his own emotions, to block his feelings, to become alienated from his own body.

Naturally, this process does not happen on a fully conscious or verbal level, and it does not happen to the same extent in everyone. Some degree of repression, however, seems to be a universal of childhood.

Later in life, the child's repression may give him no end of trouble; it may be reinforced again and again and may lay the foundation of future neurosis. If he does not learn to reconnect with his feelings, to discover his needs, his functioning will certainly be impaired.

But here is the point: as a child, *his repression had survival-value*. In a special sense, one can say it was adaptive. Or the child *felt* it was.

Whether I am dealing with a child or an adult, my first question about a symptom is: What purpose does it serve? What is its *felt* or *experienced* survival-value? *Objectively*, neurotic symptoms reflect self-destructive processes; but *subjectively*, in the context of the individual's own experience and development, they represent an attempt at self-preservation, the protection of sanity or self-esteem, or protection of the person against pain. Symptoms are always goal-directed. They represent attempted solutions to problems.

So, when attempting to understand a symptom, I invite the client to consider: What is or was the problem to which your symptom represents an attempted solution? Is the solution a satisfactory one? Is it constructive? Does it enhance and contribute to your life? If it harms and diminishes your life, are alternative solutions possible?

The characteristic of a neurotic is that he clings to solutions that don't work; he is caught in a rut; he is rigid and inflexible. The essence of the creative approach to life, in contrast to the neurotic approach, lies precisely in the freedom to change, to leap beyond an outmoded context, or rut, to experiment, to improvise, to grasp new connections, to try something one has not done before.

A neurotic, if he doesn't correct his problems, is something like the dinosaur. Early in life, the neurotic develops certain mechanisms that may have been adaptive at the time, given his particular environment. But now he has grown up, his environment has changed, and those old mechanisms are clearly maladaptive: they do not fit his new environment; he is no longer a helpless child dependent on his parents. But he clings to the old mechanisms, and sometimes goes down with them to destruction, like the dinosaur who perished when he found himself in an environment for which his adaptive mechanisms were inadequate.

The dinosaur was incapable of generating new solutions, new adaptive mechanisms. But a human being, by virtue of his intelligence and his conceptual faculty, has an option: he can question the adaptiveness of his responses to life and, in the case of maladaptive responses, can develop better alternatives.

R: You speak of symptoms as being "goal directed." Could you give illustrations?

B: Let me tell you about two cases that exemplify what I mean—and, at the same time, will show you something of the way I work.

Once, when I was giving an all-day workshop in New York City, a young man presented the following problem. In his attempts to establish relationships with girls, he said, he invariably was unsuccessful; he went to parties, he went to bars, he approached women and tried to talk to them, but nothing ever went right. The women turned away, or else they gave him phone numbers where they did not live. He was twenty-five years old, he did not consider himself bad looking—and he wasn't—but he had never slept with a girl and, he claimed, this was making him desperately unhappy as well as absolutely bewildered as to why he always failed. He wanted to give me more of his life history but I stopped him at that point and said that I thought we had enough to begin.

The workshop group consisted of twenty-three participants, sitting in a circle. I suggested that we try an exercise that might prove productive. I would give him the first part of a sentence; he would go around to each person in the room in turn, look directly at the person, and repeat the first part of my sentence plus any ending he cared to give it; he was not to worry whether or not his endings were true or false, reasonable or ridiculous. When he positioned himself before the first person, I gave him the phrase I wanted him to work with: "I willfully and deliberately turn girls off by—" He turned to me indignantly. How could I give him such a phrase? Didn't I understand his problem? Hadn't I been listening?

I told him this was only an experiment; an experiment means doing something for the purpose of discovering what will happen when you do it. He turned back to the first person, but instead of looking at that person as I had requested, he looked two feet above at the wall, and his first sentence was: "I willfully and deliberately turn girls off by—never looking at them when I speak to them!" He moved to the next person: "I willfully and deliberately turn girls off by—always acting like a clown and a jerk in their presence." He moved to the next person: "I willfully and deliberately turn girls off by—talking and talking and talking and never listening to a word they say and making it perfectly clear I couldn't care less about what they have to say." While the rest of the room looked on with astonishment, this young man went around to each person and announced twenty-two ways in which he willfully and deliberately turned girls off.

When he had finished, he appeared a bit dazed, almost punchy, and I asked him, "By the way, are any of these statements true?" Incredulously he muttered, "They're all true."

"Fine," I said to him. "Now I want you to try something else. I'm going to give you a number of different phrases now and I want you to come right back with the very first completion of the sentence that occurs to you. Never mind whether or not it makes sense." He indicated that he understood and we proceeded as follows.

I said to him, "I willfully and deliberately turn girls off so that—" He replied, "—so that I won't have to sleep with them." I said, "The prospect of sleeping with a girl is frightening, perhaps, because—" He replied, "I'll be overwhelmed, I'll be annihilated, I'll be wiped out, I'll be pulverized."

Hearing that, the next line of inquiry was obvious. I said, "Mother was always—" He replied, "—domineering, trying to control me in everything I did." I said, "Mother never—" He replied, "—would let me do anything my way; everything had to be her way." I said, "Mother always seemed to expect—" He replied, "—that I be subordinate to her in everything." I said, "That made me feel—" He replied, "—weak, helpless, inadequate, annihilated, pulverized." I said, "Women are to me—" He turned to me in astonishment as he completed the sentence: "—all just like Mother!"

I might mention, in passing, that this full exercise took about nine minutes. When I told this story to one physician he commented, "There goes a year of psycho-analytic therapy."

Anyway, the point is that at the same time the young man was complaining about his failure with women, he was in fact engineering his own defeat—to protect himself in a situation in which he felt weak, helpless and inadequate. Within the context of his neurotic perspective, his bungling with women had survival-value—even though, objectively speaking, it stood in the way of his happiness and fulfillment as a man.

Now, of course, we could go deeper into the roots of his problems and discuss their origin; but that's not really essential in this context. If we did, however, we would find that his dependence on his mother was also goal-directed; it served to keep him a child—and thus to avoid the responsibilities of adulthood.

But let me tell you about another case that's far more dramatic.

R: Go ahead.

B: This was also a man in his middle twenties—highly intelligent, sensitive, but very passive, very timid, very soft-spoken, very withdrawn and very self-pitying. He was holding down a fairly meaningless job—meaningless, that is, relative to his intellectual potential. He couldn't seem to get his life started. He complained of not knowing how to focus his energies. He complained of not having any friends and of not knowing how to relate to other people. He projected a quality of forlorn helplessness and hopelessness.

One day, in group, he said that he wanted to work on the problem of why he wasn't getting anywhere with his life.

I asked him to begin with what I call "the death-bed exercise"—as described in *The Disowned Self*—which meant that I asked him to lie on the floor, to close his eyes, and to imagine that he was in a hospital room

bed and that he was dying. His life was over; he had
only a few more hours to live; all of his chances had
been used up. Then I asked him to look up, in imagination, and see his father—who was a Lutheran minister
—standing by the side of his bed. "There is so much
that you have never said to him," I suggested, "so much
that you've kept locked up inside of you. If ever your
father would want to hear you, it would be now. If ever
it would be possible to reach him, it would be now.
Talk to him. Tell him what it was like to be his son."

Slowly and reluctantly he began to talk to his father
and to describe various childhood incidents that had
been very painful or frightening. He spoke about ways
in which he felt his father had been cruel to him—
neglecting him in order to be free to do "good works"
in the community, and so forth. But his manner was
very cerebral, he was obviously disconnected, cut off
from his emotions; his words were without feeling. One
could see, from looking at him, that he was tensing his
body and making himself numb to hold back an immense amount of rage that he felt he dared not express.
So I knew we couldn't get anywhere until he could
release, express and confront that rage.

I asked him to stop, and shifted into a different
exercise. I asked him to remain lying on the floor, to
begin shaking his head from side to side, and to say
"No!" as he did so. When a person is angry and is
holding that anger back, he tenses up the muscles in his
back and shoulders—the very muscles that would be
mobilized should the anger be released. By having him
move his head from side to side, I was making it impossible for his neck muscles to lock completely, and
thereby I was hoping to facilitate the release of feeling.
Gradually his "Nos" became stronger and angrier—
until he was stamping his feet, pounding his fists, and
shouting "No!" at the top of his lungs.

Then I asked him to re-enter the hospital fantasy and
to talk to his father again. He was emotionally con-
nected now and he began to scream and to cry and to
rage and to tell his father about the many hurts and
frustrations that he had endured at his father's hands.

When I began the first exercise, I did so on the hypothesis that his relationship with his father was relevant to his problem; but I did not have a firm conviction as to the direction in which the work was going to take us. Now, suddenly, I had a hunch—an idea struck me—and I asked him to stay in contact with his father in fantasy and simply to say to his father, over and over again, "But I'm getting back at you!"

He began shouting this sentence and as he did so his rage kept climbing to higher and higher peaks of intensity. Then I switched to another exercise; I asked him to do sentence-completions beginning with the phrase: "I'm getting back at you by—"

He screamed, "I'm getting back at you by—being unhappy! I'm getting back at you by—sitting in my room all day alone! I'm getting back at you by—crying all the time! I'm getting back at you by—making a mess of my life! I'm getting back at you by—holding stupid, senseless jobs that don't lead anywhere! I'm getting back at you by—not having any friends! I'm getting back at you by—never letting myself be happy! I'm getting back at you by—never for a minute forgetting how much you hurt me! I'm getting back at you by—keeping my anger for you alive! I'm getting back at you by—never giving you anything to be proud of!"

So here you can see that the very symptoms of which he was complaining were serving a specific purpose; they were goal-directed.

R: Prior to the exercise, was he conscious of what he was doing?

B: Not in the ordinary sense of the word "conscious." Obviously the knowledge was in his brain in some form, or the exercise wouldn't have worked as it did, but the information was blocked from conscious awareness.

Once I walked into the waiting room of my office and there was a very pretty girl of seven or eight years old, whose father was being seen by another therapist in my office. She said to me, "Mr.—what do you do in there?" I really felt puzzled for a moment: how was I going to explain to a child the nature of my work? Then I said to her, "Well . . . what I do is . . . I teach people that they know all kinds of things they think they don't know." She smiled and thought for a moment and said, "Gee, that's pretty good." "I think so too," I told her.

These two case histories demonstrate what I mean.

R: Is it characteristic of your way of working to move very rapidly from one exercise or technique to another, as you did with the second case?

B: I call that method "compounding"—riding on a kind of momentum that crashes through walls and defenses. Sometimes I work that way; sometimes not; it's not standard operating policy—it depends upon the particular problem.

R: Let's go a little bit deeper into this second case. What was the man really after by acting as he did?

B: I would say that his self-defeating behavior had two immediate goals: it was an act of revenge, a way of inflicting pain on his father—and, at the same time, a scream for help, a way of signaling to his father: "See what you've done to me? See how unhappy I am? *Now* will you be a father to me and satisfy my needs?"

Now why was he unwilling to accept the past and put it behind him? Why was he unwilling to say, in effect, "Okay, I had a rotten, miserable, frustrating childhood. But I'm not a child any longer. So what am I going to make of my life?"

R: We were wondering about that.

B: Part of the reason is that he had never adequately dealt with his childhood pain, never got it out of his system; he had frozen himself emotionally in order to avoid feeling it—and had paralyzed himself intellectually in the process.

But deeper than that was the longing to remain a child—in the hope that somehow those frustrated childhood needs would be fulfilled by someone. To put the past behind him would mean to accept the fact that those needs were never going to be fulfilled, that it was too late, that there is nothing more to be done, except to get on with his life. He couldn't or wouldn't tolerate that.

In the end, we are dealing here—as always—with the issue of a person's willingness or unwillingness to assume full responsibility for his own existence. This is the real meaning of adulthood and of maturity. It is a state that few people reach—or reach completely.

R: Probably many people who are familiar with your earlier work, with its heavy philosophical emphasis, would be surprised at the kind of therapy you are practicing.

B: I suppose so. Occasionally a person comes to therapy imagining that our work is going to consist of philosophical discussions. I don't say that philosophical analysis has no place in therapy—sometimes it can be very valuable—but only after a person has begun to confront and re-own the repressed split-off aspects of his own personality.

Clients have to learn to challenge and attack false ideas, true enough. But so long as a person is self-alienated, so long as he is cut-off from his own feelings, intellectual analysis or discussion tends to be rather unproductive. Sometimes, it only serves to strengthen his defenses, to take him farther and farther away from himself.

R: What's striking about the cases you cite is that the clients made the discoveries themselves. You didn't act as the interpreter of their reports.

B: Precisely. That's essential to the way I work. Interpretation on the part of the therapist must be kept to an absolute minimum, and avoided whenever possible. It's too easy to suggest mistaken interpretations to a vulnerable and susceptible client. But what the client discovers and confronts for himself has the marvelously satisfying stamp of authenticity. And the therapist doesn't fall into the trap of playing the omniscience game.

R: What you do is rather different from what one usually thinks of as group therapy.

B: Most group therapy consists of the various participants psychologizing on one another. They tell one another what's wrong with them and what to do. I don't believe in that. I have never been convinced of its effectiveness. And sometimes it can be harmful. What I do is really a kind of individual therapy in a group context; however, the presence of the group is necessary and helpful for many of my exercises. And when an individual has finished working, I invite the group to give him feedback in terms of each member's own feelings and experiences while watching the person who is working. The various group members might discuss what they heard in the person's work that is relevant to themselves.

R: Does a client ever refuse to try one of your exercises?
B: Occasionally. Not often. But everything is voluntary. If he doesn't want to try something, no one is going to insist.

No one even asks the client to work. The initiative for working on a problem is left entirely to the individual. When he feels ready to work, he asks to work. Nobody plays Big Daddy and leads him by the hand. If a client wants to sit in group for two months and never open his mouth, that's his privilege. But when he does open his mouth, it's a big step—and he did it himself.

R: Your therapy doesn't consist entirely of exercises?
B: No. But I use them a great deal. I try to devise exercises that will allow an individual to discover truths he needs to know, with a minimum of comment or interpretation from me. But when a comment or explanation is necessary, of course I give it.

Also, I like to propose exercises or experiments for a person to do outside of therapy, in normal life situations, that hopefully will contribute to his growth. When a client has been behaving in a self-destructive manner, I encourage him to experiment with alternative ways of acting—and to discover what happens when he abandons his self-defeating maneuvers.

Sometimes in therapy—not too often—I will talk, just talk, about the wider meanings and principles to be found in the work we are doing or in the work of a particular client. Or I will talk about philosophical or religious ideas prevalent in our culture that encourage the development of neurotic symptoms. Or I will talk about principles of clear and effective thinking. But such discussions are generally kept to a minimum. It's too easy to waste time with verbal exchanges that have no therapeutic value. On some days I will simply move from one exercise to another, with virtually no discussion or conversation at all.

R: In *The Disowned Self,* you speak of three concepts that are central to your work: self-awareness, self-responsibility, self-assertiveness. Could you amplify the meaning of these terms?

B: Let me insert a fourth concept: self-acceptance. The pillar of self-esteem and mental health is these four ideas: self-awareness, self-acceptance, self-responsibility, self-assertiveness. Now what do they mean?

Self-awareness. Awareness of what? I would answer: awareness of feelings, needs, desires, emotions, ideas, evaluations and behavior. So therapy begins with teaching clients how to be self-aware, how to know what they are feeling and what they are doing.

Self-acceptance. Acceptance of what? Acceptance of all the items I have just named. Acceptance of the fact that all of these feelings, ideas, behavior and so forth are expressions of the self *at the time they occur*. Self-acceptance entails the refusal to disown any of these aspects of the self, any of these instances of self-expression. Not necessarily to approve of all of them, but to accept them as real and as one's own. Acceptance of the reality of one's own being, of one's own inner experience and one's own behavior. So, self-acceptance literally means: full realism applied to the realm of inner experience as well as to behavior. You know, people can verbally or intellectually acknowledge their feelings or reactions while denying them emotionally and psychologically, refusing to accept and integrate them. So self-acceptance means more than merely verbal acknowledgement; it means integration.

Self-responsibility. Responsibility for what? Responsibility for being the cause of one's own choices and one's own acts. Not responsibility in the sense of moral blame, but responsibility in the sense of recognizing one's self as the chief causal agent in one's life and behavior. Further, self-responsibility means: acceptance of responsibility for one's own existence. Acceptance of one's basic—metaphysical—aloneness. Acceptance of responsibility for the attainment of one's own goals. This last is extremely important. This is a theme I hit again and again in therapy. No one plays the "helplessness game" on a desert island; we can tell ourselves and others that we are helpless only if we expect someone to pick up the responsibility we have dropped.

Self-assertiveness. Assertiveness of what? Of one's desires and judgments. Of one's needs. Of one's right to exist and to be happy. Sometimes, as an exercise, I will ask a client to face the group and simply say, again and again, "I have a right to exist." For some clients, this is very difficult. It's interesting to observe what happens. First, the statement may be made hesitantly and tearfully; later, it may be made angrily; then, eventually, it is made firmly and with conviction. One can see the whole posture and demeanor of the person has changed: he has released his own power; he experiences his own strength; he asserts his own existence.

On the psychological level, these four concepts are the foundation of morality. A person can lead a moral life only to the extent that he practices self-awareness, self-acceptance, self-responsibility and self-assertiveness. Virtues such as honesty or productiveness or integrity are consequences of these principles and follow naturally from them.

These are principles children should be taught from the start of their life. These are attitudes parents must learn to cultivate, encourage and develop in their children.

The consequence of these principles is self-esteem.

R: Coming back to your opposition to what might be described as "didactic therapy," do you never directly argue with a client's ideas if you think those ideas are mistaken and are harming him?

B: I never argue. If a client expresses a moral or philosophical notion I think is wrong, I may express my own view, but then I will invite him to explore the roots of his. If he really is mistaken, my job is to devise a means to help him to discover that fact by himself—not because I have talked him into it.

I think that, a great deal of the time, psychotherapists who argue with their client's mistaken ideas are naive. Let me give an example that may help to explain why.

Suppose a married couple comes to therapy for counseling. Their relationship is in trouble because the woman is very inhibited sexually. She claims to believe that there is something bad or sinful about sex.

Now many therapists at this point will decide that the first step of treatment is to get her to revise her thinking about sex, to persuade her that her ideas about sex are wrong. So they begin to work at educating her or propagandizing her about how good and wonderful sex is. That would not be my approach—at least, not generally.

R: What would you be likely to do?

B: Well, since she is a human being who presumably has normal human needs and feelings and capacities, I assume that the ability and the desire to respond to sex positively already exists in her, only something is blocking it. Sex can be such a profound source of joy to human beings that I find it difficult to believe that a person authentically and all the way down regards sex as evil. Often, a person *knows,* intellectually, that sex is not evil, but claims for some reason to *feel* it's evil. So that's what has to be explored.

I might have the woman do a sentence completion exercise, beginning with the phrase, "The bad thing about sex is—" Or I might use the phrase, "Bad to me means—" And do you know what kind of completion I'm very likely to get? "The bad thing about sex is—Mother says it's dirty and rotten and sinful." "Bad to me means—disobeying Mother's wishes."

If this is the way the woman's responses developed—and this is not the only possibility, of course—she is led to reformulate her problem. She no longer says that she is sexually inhibited because she thinks or feels that sex is evil. She says that she inhibits herself sexually because she is frightened to do anything that might invoke her mother's disapproval. That is an altogether different proposition.

Now she is ready to explore the problem of her

dependence on her mother. And we have saved ourselves hours and hours of discussions about the merits of sex. And when she is free of dependence on her mother, free to acknowledge and act on her own honest feelings, she is unlikely to need lectures from me on sex.

I want to make one qualification concerning what I have just said. In matters of sex, it is true that people are often dreadfully ignorant and misinformed and that therapists and marriage counselors often do have to educate their clients concerning "the facts of life." But that is a somewhat different matter from arguing philosophically about the meaning of sex. I hope this distinction is clear.

R: It is. But are you saying that all philosophically mistaken ideas are psychologically or neurotically motivated?

B: Certainly not. That would be an absurd position to maintain. No. I am thinking of certain basic highly irrational and highly self-destructive notions, such as the notion that pleasure is evil, that have no conceivable basis in reality, no even superficial plausibility. In such cases, what has to be explored is why the person feels compelled to cling to such ideas, what purpose such ideas serve for him.

R: In working with clients, you are known to sometimes use techniques of Gestalt therapy. How prominently do they figure in your work?

B: I do use Gestalt techniques, sometimes, when they seem appropriate to the situation. Or my own modifications of Gestalt techniques. But I am not a Gestalt therapist. Far from it. I have many disagreements with the Gestalt orientation, although some of the individual techniques are very effective.

I lean toward what Arnold Lazarus calls in his book, *Behavior Therapy and Beyond,* "technical eclecticism." Not *theoretical* eclecticism, but *technical* eclecticism. Ultimately, there can be only one theoretically correct way of understanding human psychology, motivation, neurosis and so forth. But many different techniques, originating in many different schools, may prove useful in attacking particular problems.

A therapist should have as wide a repertoire of techniques at his command as possible, so that he can fit what he does to the specific client and the specific problem, rather than cling rigidly to one particular method whether or not it is the most suitable method in a particular case. So, aside from the techniques I have developed myself, I employ techniques developed by other schools when and as they seem suitable.

I think what probably distinguishes my way of working is my integration of the cognitive and the emotional, my method of constantly moving back and forth between the conceptual and the experiential, which is not a matter of a single technique but rather reflects a basic attitude, a philosophy, that is expressed through a multiplicity of techniques and the way in which they are interrelated practically, when I am working on specific problems.

Coming back to Gestalt therapy for a moment, I think that by itself it is very limited. It is not enough. One of my main objections is that it is so very anti-intellectual. "Thinking" is a bad word in Gestalt therapy. No distinction is made between authentic, rational thinking and phony, defensive intellectualizing. I once attempted to discuss the anti-intellectualism of Gestalt therapy with a prominent leader in the Gestalt movement, and do you know what he said to me? He earnestly assured me that Gestalt therapy couldn't possibly be anti-intellectual since its founder, Fritz Perls, was a high educated and cultured man.

R: Do you see any value in Behavior therapy?

B: We have to distinguish between Behaviorism as a psychological theory, to which I am profoundly opposed, and Behavior therapy as a set of techniques, some of which are very useful. "Behavior therapy" is not a unified school, and means different things to different practitioners. But some of the techniques associated with this orientation have demonstrated their effectiveness and have a valid place in a therapist's repertoire. One can agree that a particular technique is effective without necessarily agreeing with someone's theoretical interpretation of *why* it is effective. So at times I cer-

tainly do what can be described as "Behavior therapy."
I would venture to guess that in some sense most therapists do.

R: Is it correct that you now exclusively do group
therapy?

B: Yes. For a number of years I did only individual
therapy and was enormously skeptical about the value
of group therapy. I couldn't imagine how working in a
group setting could produce profound results. But a
friend of mine, Dr. Roger Callahan, was doing group
therapy as well as individual therapy and he invited me
to sit in and watch him work. I was very impressed; I
saw possibilities that simply hadn't occurred to me. That
was in the mid-1960's.

Subsequently, in New York City, I did some experi-
mental work with a few groups and became enormously
excited by that way of working. It took me some time
after that to develop my own distinctive method of
group therapy which, as we mentioned earlier, is rather
different than what most people think of as group
therapy. In my experience, group therapy is for the
majority of clients *more* effective, not *less* effective, than
individual therapy. Now obviously this depends on the
specific kind of therapy practiced and the particular
skills of the therapist. There are many different kinds of
group therapy, just as there are many different kinds of
individual therapy. There are very competent psychotherapists who work only on an individual basis. There
is no reason why everyone has to work the same way.
The way a therapist chooses to work is in part, of
course, an expression of his own personality. The only
point is to get results. For myself, I enjoy group therapy
enormously and am convinced that I do my best work
in that setting.

The range of experience offered to clients in groups
is much wider and richer than that offered in individual
therapy, and can be used to facilitate growth.

I think of my groups in effect as personal growth
seminars. *Experiential* seminars, as contrasted with
didactic seminars. I don't even think so much in terms
of therapy, but rather in terms of growth, of helping the

individual to discover and release his potential, intellectually, creatively, emotionally, sexually.

Sometimes a person comes to see me who I feel is not right for group therapy or not right for the specific kind of work I do, in which case I refer him to a colleague for individual work.

I have two special groups of clients, who, instead of meeting once a week for two hours, as in my regular groups, meet once a month for two days, on a week-end, for concentrated work. I started this more or less at the request of a number of clients who felt that their growth and development was better facilitated in the context of two-day workshops than in once-a-week regular groups. So I started one week-end group as a trial project, and the results were so satisfying that I began a second week-end group. It's very demanding, but very, very rewarding.

R: In addition to which, you give two-day workshops in various cities around the country?

B: Yes.

R: Are clients ever turned off by your approach to therapy?

B: Of course. If they don't mean business, if they don't really want to get into their problems, if they just want to play at therapy, I'm the wrong man to come to. Once, after doing an exercise that was very self-revealing, a client said to me, "You don't leave a person any place to hide." The next day he quit therapy. It's too bad. He was an intelligent person. But he had great resistance to knowing what he was feeling and what purposes were motivating his actions. When the exercise revealed some of this information to him, he had a choice: to deal with it—or to run. In therapy, courage is the name of the game. Courage to feel and confront and know and accept, and to take responsibility.

R: I'd like to return to an earlier point in our discussion. When you were talking about self-responsibility, you said that no one plays the "helplessness game" on a desert island. What do you mean by that? Don't you believe that people can genuinely feel and be helpless?

B: If an avalanche is falling on you and there is no

place to run, you are absolutely helpless; there is nothing to do but die. But that is not the condition of most people most of the time.

Of course we can sometimes feel helpless, in a specific situation, when we don't immediately know what to do or how to cope; but if we struggle to preserve the clarity of our mind, if we take the responsibility of looking for a solution, we are not surrendering to helplessness in a deeper, metaphysical sense, and we are not abandoning our will to efficacy.

The "helplessness game" consists of parading one's feelings of helplessness as a means of manipulating others into taking responsibility for the solution of one's problems or the burden of one's existence.

Sometimes when a client complains of feelings of helplessness, I will have him do a sentence completion exercise, "The good thing about feeling helpless is—" And then we hear such sentences as, "The good thing about feeling helpless is—people will feel sorry for me." "The good thing about feeling helpless is—I won't have to do anything." "The good thing about feeling helpless is—I don't have to get angry." "The good thing about feeling helpless is—someone will do something." "The good thing about feeling helpless is—I won't have to act and risk making a mistake." And so on.

In a similar way, people often produce confusion in themselves. I remember a young woman who complained that, at parties, when people began to discuss politics, she found herself becoming very confused and unable to follow or understand what they were saying. I gave her an exercise and she came out with such sentences as, "The good thing about being confused is— nobody will get mad at me for my political opinions." "The good thing about being confused is—I don't have to take a stand." "The good thing about being confused is—I won't be able to understand what people are saying and so I won't have to challenge them."

R: So we're back to the goal-directedness of symptoms again.

B: That's right.

R: You seem very partial to the sentence completion technique.

B: If I could use only one technique, that is the one I would choose. I have many different versions of it. One version is explained at length in *The Disowned Self*. But there are many other ways of working with sentence completion that I have developed. This technique is very complex and sophisticated; it may look easy, but it isn't; to use it well, to use it imaginatively and effectively, takes considerable practice and experience.

One of the things I like about the technique, in any of its variations, is that, when a client is properly into the exercise and working well, it becomes simultaneously a cognitive and emotional experience for him—sometimes a very explosive one. In some circumstances this exercise is sufficient, by itself, to produce dramatic changes in a person, to eliminate neurotic symptoms and inspire radical improvements in behavior.

R: When people are led to realize the goal-directedness of their symptoms, does that produce feelings of guilt?

B: No. Emphatically not. Nor should it. For many clients, the reaction is one of relief and a sense of freedom—as though the client feels that his life's been given back into his own hands or, more precisely, he comes to realize that it always was in his own hands.

The client is encouraged to be, in effect, a good friend to himself and try to understand why he felt that his particular symptoms or neurotic method of behaving was *necessary*—in other words, why he felt his survival and self-esteem required it. Then he is ready to question the assumption of such necessity and is open to consider alternatives.

Speaking of guilt, you know, that's an emotion I tend to be suspicious of. I'm suspicious of self-condemnation in general. It, too, can be goal directed.

R: What possible purpose can it serve?

B: "I'm no good—so expect nothing of me." "I'm no good—I said it first, so I don't have to wait in terror for you to say it." "I'm no good—so I don't have to try, I don't have to struggle, there's no point in struggling, since I'm worthless anyway."

R: Is all guilt motivated by such considerations?

B: No. But it's a possibility one has to be aware of.

Sometimes, a person wants to believe he's worthless in order to justify his parents' cruel treatment. By taking the blame on himself, he absolves his parents.

R: Why does he do that?

B: Because, as a child, it feels too terrifying to regard himself as innocent, in view of how his parents treat him. That would mean, from his point of view, that they must be monsters. And he can't live with that idea—it's too frightening. So, paradoxically, out of self-protection, he takes the blame on himself—and may go on doing so for the rest of his life.

R: Can you relate your theory of self-esteem to the goal-directedness of symptoms?

B: On the biological level, the ultimate goal and standard of the organism's activity—metabolic activity, self-repairing activity, and so forth—is the life of the organism itself, the preservation of its ability to function.

On the psychological level, the ultimate goal and standard is preservation of self-esteem, by which I mean: of a person's confidence in the efficacy of his mind, in his sense of control, and in his worth as a person.

If, for instance, a person disowns and represses various feelings, emotions, desires, he does so because he experiences them as threatening, threatening to his mental equilibrium, to his sense of control, to his effective functioning, or to his sense of personal worth. If a person retreats into fantasy rather than deal with the challenges of life, if he avoids testing his capabilities in action, he does so to preserve the illusion of a self-esteem he does not in fact possess.

The fear of aloneness, of self-responsibility, of loss of love, of rejection, are all related to fear of a basic feeling of powerlessness, ineffectiveness, helplessness in the face of reality. As I said in *The Psychology of Self-Esteem,* man's deepest fear is not in dying but of feeling unfit to live, inadequate to the challenges of life, unworthy of existence.

R: In all three of your books you stress the fact that the teachings of religion are inimical to self-esteem and mental health. Do you plan to write on this subject at greater length in the future?

B: I don't plan a specific book on the subject, but I do have more I would like to say and I rather think I will create some opportunity, at some point, to say it.

Many people are readily able to recognize the psychologically harmful effects of religion's antagonism to sex. That *has* been written about. But that is far from the whole story. Religion is much more than anti-sex. It is anti-mind, anti-self-esteem, anti-intellectual self-confidence, anti-self-assertiveness, anti-pleasure, anti-self-interest. Which means, basically, that religion is anti-life.

Philosophers have expressed themselves on the destructiveness of religion. Disgracefully, psychologists and psychiatrists have not, with very rare exceptions. Almost invariably they have chosen to remain silent on a subject of life-and-death importance to their profession.

Imagine a noxious agent in the environment that is infecting and killing millions of people, and the medical profession knows about it, but remains silent. What would you think? That is the state of psychology and psychiatry today—with religion, of course, being the noxious agent.

R: Is it possible that psychologists and psychiatrists are unaware of the harmful effects of religion?

B: No, it is not possible. Anyone who engages in the practice of psychotherapy confronts every day the devastation wrought by the teachings of religion.

R: Then how do you explain the fact that you are one of the very few writers, in your field, who has chosen to deal with this issue in print?

B: I can suggest two reasons. The first is that most psychologists and psychiatrists are—at least, such is my impression—very unphilosophical, very unaccustomed to thinking philosophically or dealing with philosophical issues. So I suspect that many therapists feel "over their heads" in this territory.

But I don't think that is the major reason. I believe the chief reason is moral cowardice. I remember my astonishment, many years ago, when I heard the head of a department of psychology say, "Imagine having the courage to announce over television that you are an atheist!" On another occasion, trying to discuss the subject with a prominent psychiatrist, I was told, "If you try to challenge people on religion, they'll kill you."

Most of the time, what I have encountered when I try to discuss this subject is some of the most incredible rationalizing and double-talk I have ever heard.

In my view, psychologists and psychiatrists who know the truth on this subject and who have access to public communication, but remain silent, are traitors to their profession. If preventive therapy is every psychologist's and psychiatrist's professed dream, then an exposé of the harmful consequences of childhood exposure to the teachings of religion is a pretty good place to begin.

R: One final question. Are there any political implications to the work you do as a psychotherapist? Or to express the question differently, is there any connection between your psychological theories and your political convictions?

B: All political theories rest, explicitly or implicitly, on a view of human nature, a concept of what man is, as well as a view of the values and code of conduct appropriate to him. My political convictions are a consequence and expression of my psychological and ethical convictions.

If, as a psychotherapist and as a human being, I value autonomy, individuality, self-responsibility, then it is not surprising that, in the sphere of politics, I am an advocate of political freedom—of libertarianism—of a social system based on the invioliability of individual rights.

Since you ask about the relationship between psychology and politics, I would like to make this observation. There is an interesting situation in psychology and psychiatry today. On the one hand, there is a growing endorsement of the ideals of autonomy and self-responsibility, which, naturally, I think is a very healthy and desirable trend. But, on the other hand, most psychologists and psychiatrists are, according to available studies, predominantly inclined to collectivism and statism. Here, then, is a very radical contradiction.

In their offices, these psychotherapists maintain that the individual must learn to be responsible for his own existence. But in political discussions they support the notion that no one should have to bear the burden of his own existence and that it is the task of "society" or "the state" to assume that responsibility. In their capacity as psychotherapists, they recognize the phoniness and warn of the destructiveness of self-sacrifice. But in their capacity as social commentators, they do not hesitate to advocate the sacrifice of the individual for "the good of society."

It is therapists of the so-called "third force" or "humanistic" orientation that talk most about autonomy and self-responsibility, and it is among this group that the contradiction is most apparent.

It is remarkable how they manage to avoid confronting it. But sooner or later they will have to confront it; the contradiction will explode in their faces. Then it will be interesting to see which half of their contradiction they retain and which half they discard.

Appendix A
Emotions

[The psychology of emotions is so basic to the theme of this work that I have chosen to reprint, from *The Psychology of Self-Esteem,* the chapter that deals with this issue. I have added a number of annotations which are in brackets and italics directly following the sentences to which they pertain.]

I

Emotions and Values

Throughout the preceding discussion, I have stressed that his ability to reason is man's essential attribute—the attribute which explains the greatest number of his other characteristics.

This fact is often obscured by the widespread confusion about the nature and role of *emotions* in man's life. One frequently hears the statement, "Man is not merely a rational being, he is also an emotional being" —which implies some sort of dichotomy, as if, in effect, man possessed a *dual* nature, with one part in opposition to the other. In fact, however, the content of man's emotions is the product of his rational faculty; his emotions are a derivative and a consequence, which, like all of man's other psychological characteristics, cannot be understood without reference to the conceptual power of his consciousness. [*The characterization of "the content of man's emotions" as "the product of his rational faculty" is possibly misleading; I do not wish to imply that emotions are the product of rational deliberation; later in the chapter I specifically state the opposite.*]

As man's tool of survival, reason has two basic functions: cognition and evaluation. The process of cognition consists of discovering what things *are,* of identifying their nature, their attributes and properties. The process of evaluation consists of man discovering the relationship of things to himself, of identifying what is beneficial to him and what is harmful, what should be sought and what should be avoided.

"A 'value' is that which one acts to gain and/or keep."[1] It is that which one regards as conducive to one's welfare. A value is the object of an action. Since man must act in order to live, and since reality confronts him with many possible goals, many alternative courses of action, he cannot escape the necessity of selecting values and making value-judgments.

"Value" is a concept pertaining to a relation—the relation of some aspect of reality to man (or to some other living entity). If a man regards a thing (a person, an object, an event, a mental state, etc.) as good for him, as beneficial in some way, he *values* it—and, when possible and appropriate, seeks to acquire, retain and use or enjoy it. If a man regards a thing as bad for him, as inimical or harmful in some way, he *dis*values it— and seeks to avoid or destroy it. If he regards a thing as of no significance to him, as neither beneficial nor harmful, he is *indifferent* to it—and takes no action in regard to it.

Although his life and well-being depend on man selecting values that are *in fact* good for him, i.e., con-

[1] Ayn Rand, *The Virtue of Selfishness* (New York: New American Library, 1964), p.5.

sonant with his nature and needs, conducive to his continued efficacious functioning, there are no internal or external forces compelling him to do so. Nature leaves him free in this matter. As a being of volitional consciousness, he is not biologically "programmed" to make the right value-choices automatically. He may select values that are incompatible with his needs and inimical to his well-being, values that lead him to suffering and destruction. But whether his values are life-serving or life-negating, it is a man's values that direct his actions. Values constitute man's basic motivational tie to reality.

In existential terms, man's basic alternative of "for me" or "against me," which gives rise to the issue of values, is the alternative of life or death. [*This issue is discussed in Chapter XII of* The Psychology of Self-Esteem.] But this is an adult, conceptual identification. As a child, a human being first encounters the issue of values through the experience of physical sensations of *pleasure* and *pain.*

To a conscious organism, pleasure is experienced, axiomatically, as a value—pain, as a disvalue. The biological reason for this is the fact that pleasure is a life-enhancing state and that pain is a signal of danger, of some disruption of the normal life process.

There is another basic alternative, in the realm of consciousness, through which a child encounters the issue of values, of the desirable and the undesirable. It pertains to his cognitive relationship to reality. There are times when a child experiences a sense of cognitive *efficacy* in grasping reality, a sense of cognitive *control,* of mental *clarity* (within the range of awareness possible to his stage of development). There are times when he suffers from a sense of cognitive *inefficacy,* of cognitive *helplessness,* of mental *chaos,* the sense of being out of control and unable to assimilate the data entering his consciousness. To experience a state of efficacy is to experience it as a value; to experience a state of inefficacy is to experience it as a disvalue. The biological basis of this fact is the relationship of efficacy to survival.

The value of a sense of efficacy *as such,* like the value

of pleasure *as such,* is introspectively experienced by man as a primary. One does not ask a man: "Why do you prefer pleasure to pain?" Nor does one ask him: "Why do you prefer a state of control to a state of helplessness?" It is through these two sets of experiences that man first *acquires* preferences, i.e., values.

A man may choose, as a consequence of his errors and/or evasions, to pursue pleasure by means of values that *in fact* can result only in pain; and he can pursue a sense of efficacy by means of values that can only render him impotent. But the value of pleasure and the disvalue of pain, as well as the value of efficacy and the disvalue of helplessness, remain the psychological base of the phenomenon of valuation.

A man's values are the product of the thinking he has done or has failed to do [*within the context of his particular life experiences and his basic nature and needs*]. Values can be a manifestation of rationality and mental health or of irrationality and neurosis. They can be an expression of psychological maturity or of arrested development. They can grow out of self-confidence and benevolence or out of self-doubt and fear. They can be motivated by the desire to achieve happiness or by the desire to minimize pain. They can be born out of the desire to use one's mind or the desire to escape it. They can be acquired independently and by deliberation or they can be uncritically absorbed from other men by, in effect, a process of osmosis. They can be held consciously and explicitly or subconsciously and implicitly. They can be consistent or they can be contradictory. They can further a man's life or they can endanger it. These are the alternatives prossible to a being of volitional consciousness.

There is no way for man to regress to the state of an animal, no stereotyped, biologically prescribed pattern of behavior he can follow blindly, no "instincts" to whose control he can surrender his existence. If he defaults on the responsibility of reason, if he rebels against the necessity of thought—the distortions, the perversions, the corruption that become his values are still a twisted expression of the fact that his is a conceptual form of consciousness. [*It must be understood, in this context, that the revolt against the responsibility of reason and thought includes a revolt against the responsibility of self-awareness.*] His values are still the product of his mind, but of a mind set in reverse, set against its own proper function, intent on self-destruction. Like rationality, *ir*rationality is a concept that is not applicable to animals; it is applicable only to man.

An animal's basic values and goals are biologically "programmed" by nature. An animal does not face such questions as: What kind of entity should I seek to become? For what purpose should I live? What should I make of my life? Man does—and men answer these questions in vastly different ways, depending on the quantity and quality of their thinking.

Differences in men's basic values reflect differences in their basic premises, in their fundamental views of themselves, of other men, of existence—their views of what is possible to them and what they can expect of life.

Since values involve the relation of some aspect of reality to the valuer, to the acting entity, a man's view of himself plays a crucial role in his value-choices. To illustrate this by means of a simple example: a man regards a falling bomb as bad for him because he is aware of his own mortality; if he were physically indestructible, he would appraise the bomb's significance differently. One's (conscious or subconscious) view of one's own person, one's nature and powers—whether one appraises oneself correctly or not—is implicit in one's value-judgments.

The degree of a man's self-confidence or lack of it, and the extent to which he regards the universe as open or closed to his understanding and action—will necessarily affect the goals he will set for himself, the range of his ambition, his choice of friends, the kind of art he will enjoy, etc. [*This theme is elaborated in Chapter VII of* The Psychology of Self-Esteem.]

For the most part, the process by which a man's view of himself affects his value-choices, does not take place on a conscious level; it is *implicit* in his evaluations, reflecting earlier conclusions which, in effect, are "filed" in his subconscious.

The subconscious is the sum of mental contents and processes that are outside of or below awareness. Man's subconscious performs two basic tasks which are crucial to his intellectual development and efficient functioning. The subconscious operates as a storehouse of past knowledge, observations and conclusions (it is obviously impossible for man to keep all of his knowledge in focal awareness); and it operates, *in effect,* as an electronic computer, performing super-rapid integrations of sensory and ideational material. Thus, his past knowledge (provided it has been properly assimilated) can be instantly available to man, while his conscious mind is left free to deal with the *new*.

This is the pattern of all human learning. Once, a man needed his full mental attention to learn to walk; then the knowledge became automatized—and he was free to pursue new skills. Once, a man needed his full mental attention to learn to speak; then the knowledge became automatized—and he was enabled to go forward to higher levels of accomplishment. Man moves from knowledge to more advanced knowledge, automatizing his identifications and discoveries as he proceeds—turning his brain into an ever more efficacious instrument, *if* and to the extent that he continues the growth process.

Man is a *self-programmer*. Just as this principle operates in regard to his cognitive development, so it operates in regard to his value development. As he acquires values and disvalues, these, too, become automatized; he is not obliged, in every situation he encounters, to recall all of his values to his conscious mind in order to form an estimate. In response to his perception of some aspect of reality, his subconscious is triggered into a lightning-like process of integration and appraisal. For example, if an experienced motorist perceives an oncoming truck veering toward a collision, he does not need a new act of conscious reasoning in order to grasp the fact of danger; faster than any thought could take shape in words, he registers the significance of what he perceives, his foot flies to the brake or his hands swiftly turn the wheel.

One of the forms in which these lightning-like appraisals present themselves to man's conscious mind is his *emotions.*

His emotional capacity is man's automatic barometer of what is *for* him or *against* him (within the context of his knowledge and values). The relationship of value-judgments to emotions is that of *cause* to *effect.* An emotion is a value-response. It is the automatic psychological result (involving both mental and somatic features) of a super-rapid, subconscious appraisal.

An emotion is the psychosomatic form in which man experiences his estimate of the beneficial or harmful relationship of some aspect of reality to himself.

The sequence of psychological events is: from perception to evaluation to emotional response. On the level of immediate awareness, however, the sequence is: from perception to emotion. A person may or may not be consciously aware of the intervening value-judgment. A separate act of focused awareness may be required to grasp it, because of the extreme rapidity of the sequence. That a person may fail to identify either the judgment or the factors involved in it, that he may be conscious only of the perception and of his emotional response, is the fact which makes possible men's confusion about the nature and source of emotions.

There are many reasons why a person may remain unaware of the evaluative processes underlying his emotions. Among the most important of these reasons are the following:

1. Competence at introspecting and identifying one's own mental processes has to be *acquired;* it has to be *learned.* Most people have not formed the habit of seeking to account to themselves for the reasons of their beliefs, emotions and desires; consequently, when they do attempt it, they frequently fail—and do not persevere.

2. Most people do not hold their values and convictions in clearly defined form. Vagueness and obscurity characterize a good deal of their mental contents. Their

beliefs and values have never been formulated in precise,
objective language, and are stored in the subconscious
only as *approximations,* by means of pre-verbal symbols,
such as images, which their owners cannot easily trans-
late into objective, articulate speech.

3. Sometimes, an emotion and the value-considera-
tions underlying it are extremely complex. For example,
suppose a wife is emotionally upset; she knows that the
feeling involves her husband. Perhaps he has been in-
considerate of her in some way; but he is working very
hard and is under a strain; but she, too, is under a strain
and is tired of bearing the emotional burden of his work
pressures; still, she knows she is inclined to be oversensi-
tive; on the other hand, she wants to be honest with him
about her feelings; but she does not want to upset
him and, perhaps, make the situation worse. All of
these considerations may be clashing in her subconscious. On the conscious level, she feels an emotion of
diffuse irritation at the universe in general and at her
husband in particular, plus some amount of guilt—and
she cannot untangle the reasons.

4. Sometimes, one responds emotionally to things of
which one is not aware. For example, one may meet a
person for whom one feels an almost instant dislike;
yet if one searches one's mind, one can think of nothing
objectionable that he has said or done. It may be the
case that one was *peripherally* aware of affectations in
his posture and way of moving; or of some subtle in-
sincerity in his voice; or of some negative implications
in his remarks that one did not pause to identify fully—
and one's subconscious reacted accordingly.

5. The single most formidable obstacle to identifying
the roots of one's emotions is *repression.* Since the
values that underlie some people's emotional reactions
are offensive to their self-respect and conscious convictions, the causes of such reactions may be barred from
awareness. An artist who has a block against admitting
the envy he feels toward a more talented rival, may be
quite unaware—and ferociously resistant to recognizing
—that the elation he feels was caused by news of the
failure of his rival's art show.

It is interesting to observe that those who are most prone to rhapsodize about their emotions and to speak disparagingly of reason, are those who are most incompetent at introspection and most ignorant of the *source* of their emotions. They regard their emotions as the given, as mystical revelations, as the voice of their "blood" or of their "instincts," to be followed blindly.

For example, consider the following statement by D. H. Lawrence: "My great religion is a belief in the blood, the flesh, as being wiser than the intellect. We can go wrong in our minds. But what our blood feels and believes and says, is always true. The intellect is only a bit and a bridle. What do I care about knowledge? All I want is to answer to my blood, direct, without fribbling intervention of mind or moral, or what not."[1]

Lawrence expresses the position in an extreme form. But, in a milder, less flamboyant manner, many people live by—more precisely, die by—this doctrine every day.

Man is an integrated organism, his nature (*qua* living entity) does not contain contradictory elements; reason and emotion—thinking and feeling—are not mutually inimical faculties. But they perform radically different functions, and their functions are not interchangeable. *Emotions are not tools of cognition.* To treat them as such is to put one's life and well-being in the gravest danger. What one *feels* in regard to any fact or issue is irrelevant to the question of whether one's judgment is true or false. It is not by means of one's emotions that one apprehends reality. [*However, emotions in effect contain information that one's conscious mind may need to consider in arriving at a valid judgment; but reason remains the final arbiter.*]

One of the chief characteristics of mental illness is the policy of letting one's feelings—one's wishes and fears—determine one's thinking, guide one's actions and serve as one's standard of judgment. This is more than a *symptom* of neurosis, it is a *prescription* for neurosis. It is a policy that involves the wrecking of one's rational

[1] Quoted by Brand Blanshard, in *Reason and Analysis* (La Salle, Ill.: Open Court, 1962), p. 47.

faculty. [*It must be stressed that the neurotic is not
in fact in good contact with his feelings in any but the
most superficial sense; he is characteristically alienated
from his emotional life. I do not wish to leave any implication, however slight, of a reason/emotion dichotomy; either they function in harmony—or both
faculties are sabotaged.*]

It is not accidental, but logical and inevitable, that
the predominant emotions an irrationalist is left with—
after he has put this policy into practice—are depression,
guilt, anguish and fear. The notion of the happy irrationalist, like that of the happy psychotic, is a myth—as
any psychotherapist is in a position to testify.

Whether or not they regard their emotions as reliable
guides to action, the majority of people tend to regard
them, in effect, as primaries, as "just there." Yet the
evidence to refute such an error is overwhelming and
readily available.

The mere perception of an object has no power to
create an emotion in man—let alone to determine the
content of the emotion. The emotional response to an
object is inexplicable, except in terms of the *value-
significance* of the object to the perceiver. And this
necessarily implies a process of appraisal. For example,
three men look at a scoundrel: the first man recognizes
to what extent this person, in his craven irrationality, has
betrayed his status as a human being—and feels contempt; the second man wonders how he can be safe in
a world where such persons can prosper—and feels fear;
the third man secretly envies the scoundrel's "success"
—and feels a sneaking admiration. All three men *perceive* the same object. The differences in their emotional
reactions proceed from differences in their evaluation of
the *significance* of what they perceive.

Just as emotions are not created by objects of perception as such, so they are not the product of any sort
of innate ideas. Having no innate knowledge of what is
true or false, man can have no innate knowledge of
what is good for him or evil. A man's values—to repeat
—are a product of the quantity and quality of his thinking.

An emotional response is always the reflection and product of an estimate—and an estimate is the product of a person's values, *as the person understands them to apply to a given situation.*

This last must be stressed. Quite aside from the question of the objective validity of his values, a man may misapply them in a given case, so that his appraisal is incorrect even by his own terms. For example, a man may misapprehend the nature of the facts to be judged. Or he may focus on one aspect of a situation, failing to grasp the full context, so that his involuntary evaluation is grossly inappropriate. Or his evaluative process may be distorted by internal pressures and conflicts that are irrelevant to the issue confronting him. Or he may not recognize that his past thinking and conclusions are inadequate to a judgment of the present situation, which contains new and unfamiliar elements.

In making value-judgments, man does not hold in mind automatically the full, appropriate context. Brief, out-of-context reactions are not uncommon. One of the penalties of an improper reliance on one's emotions, is a tendency to attach undue importance to such responses. People sometimes reproach themselves for momentary emotions, felt out of context, that have no significance whatever. Suppose, for example, a happily married man, deeply in love with his wife, meets another woman for whom he experiences a sexual desire; he is tempted, for the space of a few moments, by the thought of an affair with her; then, the full context of his life comes back to him and he loses his desire; the abstract sexual appreciation remains, but that is all; there is no temptation to take action. Such an experience can be entirely normal and innocent. But many men would mistakenly reproach themselves and wonder about possible defects in their character revealed by their sexual response. Enduring and persistent emotions that clash with one's conscious convictions *are* a sign of unresolved conflicts. Occasional, *momentary* feelings need not be. [*Referring back to the example above, should such a man reproach himself for his momentary feeling of sexual attraction, should he, in effect, forbid himself to ex-*

*perience it, the attraction is very likely to persist—if
only subconsciously—regardless of any intellectual
analysis he may perform.*]

As to enduring and persistent emotions that clash
with one's convictions and/or one's other values, these
can be made the means of increased self-understanding
and self-improvement—*if* one recognizes the nature
and source of emotions. By analyzing the roots of his
feelings and desires, a man can discover ideas he has
held without conscious awareness, he can be led to a
knowledge of values he has formed without verbal identification, to concepts he has accepted without thought,
to beliefs that represent the opposite of his stated conclusions. [*The "analysis" of feelings and desires can
be effective only after one permits oneself freely and
openly to experience them; should this process of self-
accepting self-awareness be aborted or blocked, any
subsequent "analysis" is unlikely to be of significant
practical value.*]

Reason and emotion are not antagonists; what may
seem like a struggle between them is only a struggle
between two opposing ideas, one of which is not conscious and manifests itself only in the form of a feeling.
The resolution of such conflicts is not always simple;
it depends on the complexity of the issues involved. But
resolutions are achievable—and the necessary first step
is to recognize the actual nature of that which needs to
be resolved.

The guiltless emotional spontaneity that men long for
—the freedom from torturing self-doubt, enervating depression and paralyzing fears—is a proper and achievable goal. But it is possible only on the basis of a rational view of emotions and of their relation to thought.
It is possible only if one's emotions are not a mystery,
only if one does not have to fear that they may lead one
to destruction. It is the prerogative and reward of a person who has assumed the responsibility of identifying
and validating the values that underlie his emotions—
the person for whom emotional freedom and openness
do *not* mean the suspension of awareness. [*Awareness,
and specifically self-awareness, is the precondition of*

emotional freedom and openness—for all the reasons discussed earlier in this book.]

II

Emotions and Actions

The pleasure-pain mechanism of man's consciousness —the capacity to experience joy and suffering—performs a crucial function in regard to man's survival. This function involves the *motivational* aspect of man's psychology.

Imagine a living entity so constituted that every time it took an action beneficial to its life, it experienced pain —and every time it took an action inimical to its life, it experienced pleasure. Clearly, such an entity could not exist; it would be a biological impossibility. But if, impossibly and miraculously, it were to come into existence, it would quickly perish. With its pleasure-pain mechanism set in reverse, against its own life, it could not survive. Nothing could prompt or motivate it to perform the actions its survival required.

Pleasure (in the widest meaning of the term, as both a physical and an emotional experience) is a concomitant of life—a concomitant of efficacious action. Pain is a signal of danger—a concomitant of *in*efficacious action.

Such is the basic biological function of pleasure and pain. Pleasure is the reward of successful (life-serving) action and is an incentive to act further. Pain is the penalty of unsuccessful (life-negating) action and is an incentive to act differently.

On the physical level, i.e., on the level of sensations, it is a man's physiology that determines what he experiences as pleasurable or painful (although psychological factors are often involved). On the level of emotions, it is a man's values that determine what gives him joy or suffering. His physiology is not open to his choice. His values are.

As I discussed above, it is through his values that man programs his emotional mechanism. Short-term, man can pervert this mechanism by programming irrational values. Long-term, he cannot escape the logic implicit in its biological function. The protector of the biological function of man's emotional mechanism is the law of contradiction. A man whose values were *consistently* irrational (i.e., incompatible with his nature and needs) could not continue to exist. Most men's values are a mixture of the rational and the irrational—which, necessarily, creates an inner conflict. Such a conflict means that the satisfaction of one value entails the frustration of another.

The simplest example of the foregoing is the "pleasure" of getting drunk—followed by the misery of a hangover. One of the cardinal characteristics of irrational values is that they *always* entail *some* form of "hangover"—whether the loss of one's health, one's job, one's wife, one's intellectual competence, one's sexual capacity or one's self-esteem. According to the values he selects, his emotions are a man's reward—or his nemesis. Nature and reality always have the last word.

Happiness or joy is the emotional state that proceeds from the achievement of one's values. Suffering is the emotional state that proceeds from a negation or destruction of one's values. Since the activity of pursuing and achieving values is the essence of the life-process—happiness or suffering may be regarded as an *incentive system* built into man by nature, a system of reward and punishment, designed to further and protect man's life.

The biological utility, i.e., the survival value, of *physical* pain is generally recognized. Physical pain warns man of danger to his body and thus enables him to take appropriate corrective action. It is not sufficiently recognized that *psychological* pain—anxiety, guilt, depression—performs the same biological function in regard to man's consciousness. It warns him that his mind is in an improper state and that he must act to correct it. He may, of course, choose to ignore the warning—but not with impunity.

There is another aspect involved in the biological utility of emotions. Man can draw conclusions, can acquire many values and premises, *implicitly,* without conscious awareness of doing so. He would be in danger if he had no means of being aware of their existence, if they affected his actions with no warning signs available to his conscious mind. But it is via his emotions that man is given the evidence of such subconscious premises —so that he can revise or correct them if necessary.

The motivational power and function of emotions is evident in the fact that every emotion contains an inherent action tendency, i.e., an impetus to perform some action related to the particular emotion. Love, for example, is a man's emotional response to that which he values highly; it entails the action tendency to achieve some form of contact with the loved person, to seek the loved person's presence, to interact intellectually, emotionally, physically, etc. The emotion of fear is a man's response to that which threatens his values; it entails the action tendency to avoid or flee from the feared object. Values by their very nature entail action. So do value-responses, i.e., emotions.

The action involved is not always physical. For example, there are feelings of quiet happiness that invoke in a man the desire only to remain still and contemplate the source of his happiness—or the beauty of the world around him; his sought-for values have been achieved and all he wants is to dwell on and experience the reality of their existence. But every emotion carries *some* implication for action. (This does not mean, of course, that the action should necessarily be taken; it may not be possible or appropriate in a given context.)

The action implication of some emotions is *negative,* i.e., they tend specifically to retard or inhibit action. This is evident in the case of acute depression. The person feels that nothing is worth doing, that action is futile, that he is helpless to achieve happiness. The impulse is toward stillness, passivity, withdrawal.

Implicit in every emotional response is a *dual* value judgment, both parts of which have action implications. Every emotion reflects the judgment "for me" or "against me"—and also "to what extent." Thus, emotions differ according to their *content* and according to their *intensity*. Strictly speaking, these are not two *separate* value-judgments, they are integral aspects of the same value-judgment; they may be separated only by a process of abstraction. They are experienced as one response. But the intensity aspect obviously influences the strength of the impulse to action as well as, sometimes, the nature of the action taken.

An action tendency, as an emotional experience, can be distinguished from the wider emotional field in which it occurs. Considered as a separate experience, it is the emotion of *desire* or of *aversion*.

Every emotion proceeds from a value-judgment, but not every value-judgment leads to an emotion. An emotion is experienced only when the value-judgment is considered, by the person involved, to have significance for his own life, to have *relevance to his actions*.

Suppose, for example, that a research scientist reads about some new discovery in a field remote from his own, unconnected to his professional or personal interests and having no implications for his own actions or goals. He may appraise the discovery as "good," but the appraisal would not invoke any significant or discernible emotion in him.

Now suppose that he sees in the discovery a possible lead to the solution of a research problem of his own— then his appraisal of "good" is accompanied by an emotion, a sense of excitement and an eagerness to pursue the lead.

If he sees in the discovery an *unmistakable* and *major* key to the solution of his own problem—then the emotion of elation is more intense and so is the urgency of his desire to rush to his laboratory.

Now consider a different kind of example. A man is in love with a woman and feels sexual desire for her. Then some physical accident renders him impotent. He does not lose the capacity to experience sexual desire, but that desire now has a significantly different emotional quality—because the alteration in his own physical state has affected the action implications of his evaluation of the woman. The estimate of her value as such has not changed; what has changed is its relevance to himself, to his own actions.

In order to feel love for some object, be it a human being, a pet or a new house, a man must see some possibility of action he can take in regard to it; otherwise, his appraisal of "good" is merely an abstract judgment, without *personal* significance.

The same principle is clearly evident in the case of the emotion of fear. When, in response to the perception of some danger to his values, a person feels fear—he feels it on the premise that there is some counteraction he could or should or might be able to take. If he were firmly, fully convinced that no action was possible, he might feel sadness or regret, but not fear. (Observe that fear always involves uncertainty: if a person knows clearly what action to take and is able to take it, he does not feel fear.)

Sometimes, the emotions a person feels, and the action implications they entail, are very abstract; the value-response is, in effect, metaphysical in character. A person may respond to some great achievement or to a great work of art, and draw emotional inspiration from it: he sees in it an expression of man's creative power, he sees the triumph of man's efficacy, he sees the heroic, the noble, the admirable—and this sight provides emotional fuel for the pursuit of his own values.

It is interesting to observe that both profound happiness and profound suffering are experienced as "metaphysical." Implicit in a feeling of profound happiness is the sense of living in a "benevolent" universe, i.e., a universe in which one's values are attainable, a universe open to the efficacy of one's effort. Implicit in profound suffering is the opposite feeling: the sense of living in a universe in which one's values are unreachable, a universe in which one is helpless, where no action is worth taking because nothing can succeed.

Unresolved contradictions in a man's values lead to psychologically destructive consequences. The action tendency inherent in emotional responses is pertinent to an understanding of this issue.

Contradictions cannot exist in reality. But a man can hold ideas, beliefs, values which, with or without his knowledge, are contradictory. Contradictory ideas cannot be integrated; they sabotage the integrative function of man's mind and undercut the certainty of his knowledge in general.

The disastrous consequence of holding contradictory values is the short-circuiting of the value-emotion-action mechanism. *A man is hit by two contradictory and conflicting impulses to action.* He knows or senses, in effect, that the impossible is being demanded of him. The more profound the values involved, the worse the psychological disaster—if the conflict is evaded and repressed rather than identified and resolved.

Consider, as a classic illustration of this problem, a case such as the following. A priest has taken vows of celibacy and feels deeply committed to his vows. But a woman in his congregation begins to attract him sexually. Walking up to his pulpit one Sunday, he sees her—and suddenly feels violent sexual desire. For a brief moment, he feels himself driven to a course of action that conflicts intolerably with the course of action to which he has committed his life. In the next instant, he faints. When he regains consciousness, he has no memory of his desire for the woman (he has repressed it); but he feels acute, seemingly causeless anxiety.

In cases of value-conflict, the short-circuit occurs in the transition from consciousness to reality, i.e., via the emotional mechanism that translates evaluations (events of consciousness) into actions (events of reality).

Whether a man's emotional mechanism brings him happiness or suffering depends on its programming. It depends on the validity and consistency of his values. His emotional apparatus is a machine. Man is its driver. According to the values he selects, he makes the motivational power of his emotions work in the service of his life—or against it.

III

Emotions and Repressions:
The Repression of Negatives

Repression is a subconscious mental process that forbids certain ideas, memories, identifications and evaluations to enter conscious awareness.

Repression is an *automatized avoidance reaction*, whereby a man's focal awareness is involuntarily pulled away from any "forbidden" material emerging from less conscious levels of his mind or from his subconscious.

Among the various factors that may cause a man to feel alienated from his own emotions, repression is the most formidable and devastating.

But it is not emotions as such that are repressed. An emotion as such cannot be repressed; if it is not *felt*, it is not an emotion. Repression is always directed at thoughts. What is blocked or repressed, in the case of emotions, is either evaluations that would lead to emotions or identifications of the nature of one's emotions. [*It would be more precise to say: what is blocked is one's awareness of one's emotions.*]

A man can repress the knowledge of what emotion he is experiencing. Or he can repress the knowledge of its extent and intensity. Or he can repress the knowledge of its object, i.e., of who or what aroused it. Or he can repress the reasons of his emotional response. Or he can repress conceptual awareness that he is experiencing any particular emotion at all; he can tell himself that he feels nothing.

For example, hearing of the success of a friend who is also a business rival, a man may repress the awareness that the emotion he feels is envious resentment, and assure himself that what he feels is pleasure. Or, failing to be admitted to the college of his choice, a student may tell himself that he feels "a little disappointed," and repress the fact that he feels devastatingly crushed. Or, feeling sexually rebuffed by his sweetheart and repressing his pain out of a sense of humiliation, a youth may account to himself for his depression by the thought that no one understands him. Or, repressing her guilt over an infidelity, a wife can explain her tension and irritability by the thought that her husband takes no interest in her or their home. Or, burning with unadmitted frustration and hostility because he was not invited to join a certain club, a man may tell himself that the subject leaves him completely indifferent. [*In all these cases, the person involved is blocking or repressing awareness of his feelings; often, what the person characterizes as a "feeling" is not a feeling at all, but a thought, an idea, a notion of what he would like to feel or is "supposed" to feel.*]

Repression differs from evasion in that evasion is instigated consciously and volitionally; repression is subconscious and involuntary. In repression, certain thoughts are blocked and inhibited from reaching conscious awareness; they are not *ejected* from focal awareness, they are prevented from *entering* it. [*They may have been ejected from focal awareness at an earlier point in time; but that process as such is not repression.*]

In order to understand the mechanism of repression, there are three facts pertaining to man's mind that one must consider.

1. All awareness is necessarily selective. In any particular moment, there is far more in the world around him than a man could possibly focus on—and he must choose to aim his attention in a given direction to the exclusion of others. This applies to introspection no less than to extrospection.

Focal awareness entails a process of *discriminating* certain facts or elements from the wider field in which they appear, and considering them *separately*. This is equally true of the perceptual and the conceptual levels of consciousness.

2. There are degrees of awareness. There is a gradient of diminishing mental clarity along the continuum from

focal awareness to peripheral awareness to total un-awareness or unconsciousness. To use a visual meta-phor, the continuum involved is like that between two adjoining colors on the spectrum, say, blue and violet; the area of pure blue (focal awareness) shades off by almost imperceptible degress of blue-violet (peripheral awareness), which shades into pure violet (unconscious-ness).

The phenomenon of degrees of awareness makes it possible for a man not to let his left hand know what his right hand is doing. A man can be aware of some-thing very dimly—but aware enough to know that he does not want to be aware more clearly.

The mind can contain material which, at a given moment, is neither subconscious nor a focal aware-ness, but is in that wider field of consciousness whose elements must be distinguished and identified by a directed effort which will *bring* them into focal aware-ness—an act that a man may or may not choose to per-form.

3. Man is a self-programmer. To an extent immeasur-ably greater than any other living species, he has the ability to retain, integrate and *automatize* knowledge.

As a man develops, as he learns to form concepts and then still wider concepts, the quantity of pro-grammed data in his brain grows immeasurably, ex-panding the range and efficacy of his mind. Cognitions, evaluations, physical skills—all are programmed and automatized in the course of normal human develop-ment. It is this programming, retained on a subcon-scious level, that makes possible not only man's con-tinued intellectual growth, but also the instantaneous cognitive, emotional and physical reactions without which he could not survive.

When a man's mind is in active focus, the goal or purpose he has set determines what material, out of the total content of his knowledge, will be fed to him from the subconscious. If, for instance, a man is think-ing about a problem in physics, then it is the material relevant to that particular problem which will normally flow into his conscious mind. Focal awareness controls the subconscious process by setting the appropriate goal(s)—by grasping the requirements of the situation and, in effect, issuing the appropriate orders to the subconscious.

The subconscious is regulated, not only by the orders it receives in any immediate moment, but by the "standing orders" it has received—i.e., by a man's long-term interests, values and concerns. These affect how material is retained and classified, under what conditions it is reactivated and what kind of subconscious connections— in response to new stimuli or data—are formed.

This is very evident in the case of creative thinking. Creative thinking rests on the establishment of a standing order to perceive and integrate everything possible relevant to a given subject of interest. The problem with which he is concerned may not occupy a thinker's mind day and night; at times he will focus on other issues; but his subconscious holds the standing order to maintain a state of constant readiness, and to signal for the attention of the conscious mind should any significant data appear. The phenomenon of the sudden "inspiration" or "flash of insight" is made possible by a final, split-second integration which rests on innumerable earlier observations and connections retained in the subconscious and held in waiting for the final connection that will sum them up and give them meaning.

Now let us turn to the psychology of repression.

Repression, mechanically, is simply one of the many instances of the principle of automatization. Repression entails an automatized standing order exactly opposite to the one involved in creative thinking: it entails an order *forbidding* integration. [*Such repression is often implemented and reinforced by means of chronic muscular tension which serves to block the free flow of inner experience.*]

The simplest type of repression is the blocking from conscious awareness of painful or frightening memories. In this case, some event that was painful or frightening when it occurred *and would be painful or frightening if recalled,* is inhibited from entering conscious awareness.

The phenomenon of forgetting as such, is not, of course, pathological; memory, like awareness, is necessarily selective; one normally remembers that to which one attaches importance. But in cases of repression, memories do not simply "fade away"; they are actively blocked.

Consider the following example. A twelve-year-old boy succumbs to the temptation to steal money from a friend's locker in school. Afterward, the boy is tremblingly fearful that he will be found out; he feels humiliated and guilty. Time passes and his act is not discovered. But whenever the memory of his theft comes back to him, he re-experiences the painful humiliation and guilt; he strives to banish the memory, he hastily turns his attention elsewhere, telling himself, in effect, "I don't want to remember. I wish it would go away and leave me alone!" After a while, *it does.*

He no longer has to eject the memory from conscious awareness; it is inhibited from entering. It is repressed. The act of banishing the memory has become automatized.

Should the memory ever begin to float toward the surface of awareness, it is blocked before it can reach him. A kind of psychological alarm-signal is set off and the memory is again submerged.

Twenty years later, he may encounter the friend from whom he stole the money and greet him cheerfully; he remembers nothing of his crime. Or he may feel vaguely uncomfortable in his friend's presence and disinclined to renew the acquaintance—but with no idea of the reason.

Repressed memories are not always as localized and specific as in this example. Repression has a tendency to "spread out," to include other events associated with the disturbing one—so that memories of entire areas or periods of a man's life can be affected by the repressive mechanism.

People with traumatically painful childhoods sometimes exhibit something close to amnesia concerning their early years. They do not simply repress individual incidents; they feel that they want to forget the events of an entire decade, and they often succeed to a remarkable extent. If any questions about their childhood are raised, they may feel a heavy wave of pain or depression, with very meager, if any, ideational content to account for it.

Thoughts and evaluations, like memories, may be barred from awareness because of the pain they would invoke.

A religious person, for example, might be appalled to find himself entertaining doubts about his professed beliefs; he condemns himself as sinful and, in effect, tells these doubts, "Get thee behind me, Satan"—and the doubts retreat from his field of awareness. At first, he evades these doubts; later, it is not necessary: he has repressed them. He may then proceed to reinforce the repression by intensified expressions of religious fervor, which will help to divert his attention from any lingering uneasiness he cannot fully dispel.

Or consider the case of a neurotically dependent woman who is married to a cruel, tyrannical man. She dares not let any criticism of him enter her awareness —because she has surrendered her life to him, and the thought that her owner and master is irrational and malevolent would be terrifying to her. She observes his behavior, her mind carefully kept empty, her judgment suspended. She has automatized a standing order forbidding evaluation. Somewhere within her is the knowledge of how she would judge her husband's behavior if it were exhibited by any other man—but this knowledge is not allowed to be integrated with the behavior she is observing in her husband. Her repression is reinforced and maintained by considerable evasion; but her blindness is not caused *only* by evasion; to an important extent, she has *programmed* herself to be blind.

Not uncommonly, one can see a similar pattern of repression among children whose parents are frighteningly irrational. Children often repress negative evaluations of their parents, finding it more bearable to reproach themselves in the case of a clash, than to consider the possibility that their parents are monsters. One can observe this same phenomenon among the citizens of a dictatorship, in their attitude toward the rulers. [*A child, given his vulnerability, is not necessarily reproachable; the citizens of a dictatorship who refuse to judge the actions of their rulers, are.*]

Perhaps the most complex instances of repression are those involving the attempt to negate emotions and desires.

An emotion can be attacked through the repressive mechanism in two ways: The repression can occur *before* the emotion is experienced, by inhibiting the evaluation that would produce it—or it can occur *during* and/or *after* the emotional experience, in which case the repression is directed at a man's knowledge of his own emotional state.

(As we noted earlier, emotions as such cannot be repressed; whenever I refer to "emotional repression," I mean it in the sense of the above paragraph.)

A man seeks to repress an emotion because in some form he regards it as threatening. The threat involved may be simply pain, or a sense of loss of control, or a blow to his self-esteem.

Consider the case of a mild, amiable woman, who tends to be imposed upon and exploited by her friends. One day, she experiences a violent fit of rage against them—and she is shocked and made anxious by her own feeling. She is frightened for three reasons: she believes that only a very immoral person could experience such rage; she is afraid of what the rage might drive her to do; and she is apprehensive lest her friends learn of her feeling and abandon her. She tells herself fiercely, in effect, "Do not judge their actions—above all, do not judge their behavior toward you—be agreeable to everything." When this order is automatized on the subconscious level, it acts to paralyze her evaluative mechanism; she no longer feels rage—at the price of no longer feeling much of anything. She does not know what any events really mean to her. She then proceeds to compound her repression by instigating an additional block to prevent her from recognizing her own emotional emptiness; she assures herself that she feels all the emotions she believes it appropriate to feel.

Or: A man finds himself spending more and more
time with a married couple who are friends. He does
not note the fact that he is far more cheerful when the
wife is present than when he and the husband are alone.
He does not know that he is in love with her. If he knew
it, it would be a blow to his sense of personal worth
—first, because he would see it as disloyalty to the
husband; second, because he would see it as a reflection
on his realism and "hard-headedness," since the love
is hopeless. If brief flashes of love or desire enter his
awareness, he does not pause on them or appraise
their meaning; their significance does not register; the
normal process of integration has been sabotaged. He
no longer remembers when the first dim thoughts of love
rose to disturb him, and his mind slammed tightly closed
before they reached full awareness, and a violent "No!"
without object or explanation took their place in his
consciousness. Nor does he know why, when he leaves
his friends' home, his life suddenly seems unaccount-
ably, desolately arid.

Or: A man who has never made much of himself is
resentful and envious of his talented, ambitious younger
brother. But the man has always professed affection for
him. When his brother is drafted into the army, there
is one brief moment when the man feels triumphant
pleasure. Then, in the next moment, the knowledge of
the nature of his emotion is evaded—and then repressed
—and he jokes with his brother about the army "making a man of him." Later, when he receives the news
that his brother has been killed in action, he does not
know why all he can feel is a heavy numbness and a
diffuse, objectless guilt; he tells himself that his grief
is too profound for tears; and he drags himself around,
strangely exhausted, not knowing that all of his energy
is engaged in never letting himself identify the repressed
wish which some enemy bullet has fulfilled.

Or: A woman sacrifices her desire for a career to her
husband's desire for children and a wife who has
no interests apart from the family. Then, after a while,
she feels an occasional spurt of hatred for her children,
which horrifies her. She represses such feelings and is

not aware of them again—except that sometimes she is inexplicably and uncharacteristically careless of her children's physical safety. Then she is horrified to discover feelings of contempt for her husband. She represses them, she throws herself with renewed fervor into the role of devoted wife—except that sexual relations with her husband become empty and boring. She takes great pains to present to their friends the picture of a cheerful, "well-adjusted" wife and mother—except that she begins to drink when she is alone.

Or: Since childhood, a man has regarded the emotion of fear as a reflection on his strength, and has struggled never to let himself know when he is afraid. He has instituted a block against recognizing the emotion when it appears. His manner is superficially calm, but he tends to be somewhat stiff and monosyllabic; he backs away from any sort of personal involvement. No values seem to arouse any response in him. An enormous amount of his energy goes into simply maintaining the illusion of inner equilibrium—into keeping his face pleasantly inscrutable and his mind cautiously empty. He feels safest when social conversation involves "small talk"—or some neutral subject where no moral judgments are expected of him or are expressed by anyone else. At home, he practices body-building stolidly and earnestly, and admires the emptiness of his face in the mirror, and feels manly—except that he tends to avoid women because he is close to being impotent.

There are two particularly disastrous errors that can drive a person to repression. [*The discussion that follows is far from exhaustive; it needs to be supplemented by the material presented earlier in this book.*]

1. Many people believe that the fact of experiencing certain emotions is a moral reflection on them.

But a man's moral worth is not to be judged by the content of his emotions; it is to be judged by the degree of his rationality: only the latter is directly in his volitional control. [*This subject is discussed at length in Chapters VII and XII of* The Psychology of Self-Esteem.]

A man may make errors, honestly or otherwise, that

result in emotions he recognizes as wrong and undesirable; it may be the case that some of these inappropriate emotions are the result of *past* errors or irrationality. But what determines his moral stature in the *present* is the policy he adopts toward such emotions.

If he proceeds to defy his reason and his conscious judgment and to follow his emotions blindly, acting on them while knowing they are wrong, he will have good grounds to condemn himself. If, on the other hand, he refuses to act on them and sincerely strives to understand and correct his underlying errors, then, in the present, he is following the policy of a man of integrity, whatever his past mistakes.

If a man takes the content of his emotions as the criterion of his moral worth, repression is virtually inevitable. For example, the Bible declares that a man's sexual desire for his neighbor's wife is the moral equivalent of his committing adultery with her; if a man accepts such a doctrine, he would feel compelled to repress his desire, even if he never intended to act on it.

All of the foregoing applies equally to the repression of "immoral" thoughts.

Freudian psychoanalysts teach that irrational and immoral desires are inherent in man's nature (i.e., contained in man's alleged "id"), and that man cannot escape them; he can only repress them and sublimate them into "socially acceptable" forms. The Freudians teach that repression is a necessity of life. Their secularized version of the doctrine of Original Sin compels them to do so. Since they do not recognize that a man's emotions and desires are the product of acquired (not innate) value-premises which, when necessary, can be altered and corrected—since they regard certain immoral and destructive desires as inherent in human nature at birth—they can have no solution to offer man except repression.

To quote from psychoanalyst A. A. Brill's *Lectures on Psychoanalytic Psychiatry:*

Please note that it is not repression, but the *failure* of it, which produces the (neurotic) symptom. People constantly misinterpret Freud as having said that one gets sick because of repression, and, *ergo,* they deduce that the best way to remain healthy is never to repress. Now only a complete fool could believe or say such a thing. No one—not even an animal—can do just what he pleases; and certainly Freud and his school never advocated such nonsense.[1]

This leads us to the second major error that prompts man to repress:

2. Many people believe that if one feels an emotion or desire, one will and must act on it.

This premise is implicit in the above quotation from Brill. Note the alternative he sets up: either a man represses certain desires, i.e., makes himself unconscious of them—or else he does "just what he pleases," i.e., surrenders to any impulse he happens to experience. This is absurd.

A rational man neither represses his feelings nor acts on them blindly. One of the strongest protections *against* repression is a man's conviction that he will not act on an emotion merely because he feels it; this allows him to identify his emotions calmly and to determine their justifiability without fear or guilt. [*"Justifiability" in this context refers, strictly speaking, not to emotions as such but rather to the evaluations they reflect.*]

It is an interesting paradox that repression and emotional self-indulgence are often merely two sides of the same coin. The man who is afraid of his emotions and represses them, sentences himself to be pushed by subconscious motivation—which means, to be ruled by feelings whose existence he dares not identify. And the man who indulges his emotions blindly, has the best reason to be afraid of them—and, at least to some extent, is driven to repress out of self-preservation.

If, then, a man is to avoid repression, he must be prepared to face any thought and any emotion, and to consider them rationally, secure in the conviction that

[1] A.A. Brill *Lectures on Psychoanalytic Psychiatry* (New York: Vintage Books, 1955), pp. 42-43.

he will not act without knowing what he is doing and why. [*Sometimes, under certain circumstances, in the absence of full understanding and faced with the necessity to act, a man may choose to take a calculated risk and proceed to act on the basis of an emotion; but that choice should be made consciously, with willingness to accept the consequences.*]

Ignorance is not bliss, not in any area of man's life, and certainly not with regard to the contents of his own mind. Repressed material does not cease to exist; it is merely driven underground, to affect a man in ways he does not know, causing reactions he is helpless to account for, and, sometimes, exploding into neurotic symptoms.

There are occasions in a man's life when it is necessary for him to *suppress* thoughts and feelings. But suppression and repression are different processes. Suppression is a conscious, deliberate, nonevasive expelling of certain thoughts or feelings from focal awareness, in order to turn one's attention elsewhere. Suppression does not involve a denial of any facts, or a pretense that they do not exist; it involves the implicit premise that one will focus on the suppressed material later, when appropriate.

For example, if a student is studying for an examination, he may have to suppress his thoughts and feelings about an eagerly awaited vacation; he is not evading or repressing; but he recognizes that at present his attention is required elsewhere, and he acts accordingly. Or: a man finds himself becoming angry in the midst of a discussion; he suppresses the anger, he does not deny its existence—in order to think more clearly and to address his mind exclusively to the issues that need to be resolved. [*It could happen, of course, that the underlying causes of his anger are so relevant to the dispute that it would be advisable for him not to suppress his anger but to pay very close attention to it, to experience it fully; in effect, his emotions may be trying to tell him something he needs to know, something his conscious mind has overlooked.*]

Sometimes, however, there is a certain danger in

suppression: a man may suppress thoughts or feelings when there are still unresolved conflicts involved that require further attention and analysis. He may do so with no intent of dishonesty. But a suppression that is repeated consistently can turn into a repression; in effect, the suppression becomes automatized.

Although repression is often preceded and reinforced by evasion, evasion is not a necessary and instrinsic part of the repressive process. A person may mistakenly (but not necessarily dishonestly) believe that he can (and should) *order* undesirable or painful emotions out of existence; such orders, repeated often enough, can result in an automatized block.

However, the more a man practices evasion i.e., the more firmly he establishes in his mind the principle that the unpleasant or disturbing need not be looked at—the more susceptible he becomes to the instantaneous repression of negatively charged material. In such a case, the policy of repression becomes generalized— it becomes a characteristic, automatic response.

IV

Emotions and Repressions:
The Repression of Positives

The Freudian view of human nature has caused the concept of repression to be associated primarily with negatives, i.e., with the repression of the irrational and immoral. But there are many tragic instances of men who repress thoughts and feelings which are rational and desirable. [*Strictly speaking, feelings should not be characterized as "rational" or "irrational," as these designations are inapplicable.*]

When a person represses certain of his thoughts, feelings or memories, he does so because he regards them as threatening to him in some way. When, specifically, a person represses certain of his emotions or desires, he does so because he regards them as *wrong,* as unworthy of him, or inappropriate, or immoral, or unrealistic, or indicative of some irrationality on his part—and as *dangerous,* because of the actions to which they might impel him. [*Even more important is that a person represses certain of his emotions because he experiences them as intolerably painful.*]

Repression, as we have discussed, is not a rational solution to the problem of disturbing or undesirable mental contents. But it is particularly unfortunate when the repressed ideas or feelings are, in fact, *good,* right, normal and healthy.

A person may judge himself by a mistaken standard, he may condemn emotions and desires which are entirely valid—and if he does so, it is not vices he will attempt to drive underground, but virtues and legitimate needs.

As an example of this error, consider the psychology of a man who represses his desire to find rationality and consistency in people, and who represses his pain and frustration at their absence—under the influence of the fallacious belief that a placid, uncondemning expectation and acceptance of irrationality in people is a requirement of maturity and "realism."

The encounter with human irrationality, in childhood, is one of the earliest psychological traumas in the lives of many people, and one of the earliest occasions of repression. At a time when a young mind is struggling to acquire a firm grasp of reality, it is often confronted —through the actions of parents and other adults—with what appears to be an incomprehensible universe. It is not inanimate objects that appear incomprehensible, but people. It is not nature that appears threatening, but human beings. And, more often than not, the problem is submerged by him, repressed, ignored, never dealt with, never understood, never conquered.

In the case of the man we are considering, the irrationality to which he was exposed as a child was not the expression of intentional cruelty or ill-will. It was simply the "normal" manner of functioning, on the part of his parents, which most adults take for granted.

It consisted of such things as: making promises capri-

ciously, and breaking them capriciously—oversolici-
tude when the parent was in one mood, and callous
remoteness when the parent was in another—answering
questions pleasantly one day, and irritably dismissing
them the next—sudden expressions of love followed by
sudden explosions of resentment—arbitrary unexplained
rules and arbitrary, unexplained exceptions—unexpected rewards and unprovoked punishments—subtle
pressures, gentle sarcasms, smiling lies, masquerading as
affection and parental devotion—switching, irreconcil-
able commandments—vagueness and ambiguity and
impatience and coldness and hysteria and indulgence
and reproaches and anxious tenderness.

It was not the trauma of a single moment or episode,
but a long accumulation of blows delivered to a victim
who was not yet able to know he was a victim, or of
what. He could not understand his elders' behavior; he
knew only that he felt trapped in a world that was
unintelligible and menacing.

As he grew older, this impression was confirmed and
reinforced by many other people he encountered, by
the irrational behavior of playmates, teachers, etc.

The process of repressing his feelings began early.
His bewilderment and dread were painful and he did
not like to experience them. He could not understand his
feelings; he could not yet conceptualize the factors
involved. He could not yet be fully confident of his
ability to judge his parents and other people correctly;
his judgments lacked the conviction of certainty. At
times, he experienced his feeling of horror as overwhelming and paralyzing. And so, to reduce his anguish
and to maintain a sense of control, he strove to deny
the reality of the problem. This meant: when faced
with dishonesty, hypocrisy, inconsistency, evasiveness,
to feel nothing—to be an emotional blank. *This* meant:
to inactivate his capacity to pass moral judgments.

Now, as an adult, he has learned to "accept" human
irrationality. "Acceptance," in this context, does not
mean the knowledge that a great many men behave
irrationally and that he must be prepared to meet
this problem; it means he accepts irrationality as the

normal and *natural,* he ceases to regard it as an aberration, he does not condemn it.

If a friend whom he had every reason to trust commits some act of betrayal, and he cannot escape feeling hurt and shocked, he *reproaches himself* for this reaction: he feels that he is naive and out of touch with reality.

To the extent that he cannot fully extinguish his frustrated, anguished desire for rationality, he feels guilty. Such is the corruption that repression has worked on his thinking.

Now consider another case: a man who represses his *idealism,* i.e., his aspiration to any values above the level of the commonplace.

When he was a boy, no one understood or shared his feelings about the books he read or the things he liked; no one shared or understood his feeling that a man's life should be important, that he should achieve something difficult and great. What he heard from people was: "Oh, don't take yourself so seriously. You're impractical." He did not strive to conceptualize his own desires and values, to weigh the issue consciously and rationally; he was hurt by people's attitudes; he felt like an outcast; he did not want to feel that way; so he gave up. If he saw a romantic movie about some man's heroic achievement, he would remark to his friends, indifferently: "Not bad. But pretty corny, wasn't it?"—and repress the memory of what he had felt in the theatre for two hours, protected by darkness. Now, as a middle-aged Babbitt, he listens with empty eyes and an emptier soul while his son speaks of the great things he wants to do when he grows up, and he tells his son to go mow the lawn, and then, sitting alone, why, he wonders, why should I be crying?

Or: The man who, in adolescence, has been desperately lonely. He had found no one whom he could like or admire, no one to whom he could talk. The one girl he cared for had deserted him for another boy. He came to believe that his loneliness was a weakness; that the pain of his frustrated longing for a person he could value was a flaw which he must conquer in himself;

that a truly strong, independent man could have no such longing. He became progressively more repressed emotionally. His public manner became more remote and more cheerful. Now, at the age of thirty, he meets a woman with whom he falls desperately in love. But a subconscious block forbids him to know how much he loves her: to know it would unlock the pain of his past and expose him to new pain, should his love not be reciprocated. Since his repression seals off the knowledge of her meaning to him, he cannot communicate it to her. He sees her frequently, but assumes a manner of detached, amused affection: he feels that this manner expresses strength. At first, she responds to him. But eventually she withdraws, alienated by a passionless remoteness which she perceives as weak and unmasculine.

Or: The man who represses his desire for an appreciation and admiration he has earned, because, mistakenly, he views his desire as a failure of independence—and does not understand the feelings of loneliness and a strange, unwanted bitterness that hit him at times.

Or: The woman who represses her femininity, because she is afraid of shocking her timid, conventional husband—and does not understand the apathy that invades more and more areas of her life.

Or: The woman who represses her femininity, because she has accepted the popular notion that femininity and intellectuality are incompatible—and who does not understand her subsequent tension and hostility in the realm of sex. (Or: The woman who represses her intellectuality, because she has accepted the same dichotomy, and is left with the same bitterness.)

Or: The man of authentic self-esteem who represses the strength of his impulse to self-assertiveness, out of consideration for the neurotic sensibilities of people who are less secure psychologically—and does not understand his periodic explosions of rebellious, seemingly unprovoked anger.

When a person represses, his intention is to gain an increased sense of control over his life; invariably and inevitably, he achieves the opposite. Observe that in every one of the above cases, repression leads to increased frustration and suffering, not to their amelioration. Whether a person's motive is noble or ignoble, facts cannot be wiped out by self-made blindness; the person who attempts it merely succeeds in sabotaging his own consciousness.

Repression devastates more than a man's emotions; it has disastrous effects on the clarity and efficiency of his thinking. When a man tries to consider any problem in an area touched by his repression, he finds that his mind tends to be unwieldy and his thinking distorted. His mind is straight-jacketed; it is not free to consider all possibly relevant facts; it is denied access to crucial information. As a consequence, he feels helpless to arrive at conclusions, or the conclusions he reaches are unreliable.

This does not mean that, once a man has repressed certain thoughts or feelings, he is permanently incapacitated: with sustained effort, it is possible for him to *de*-repress. Since the represser's mind is only *partially* disabled by blocks, the unobstructed area of his mind retains the capacity to work at removing them.

Repressed material does not vanish completely; it reveals itself in countless indirect ways. The two broadest categories of clues by which repressed material can be traced are: (1) the presence of emotions and desires that appear causeless and incomprehensible in terms of one's conscious convictions; (2) the presence of contradictions in one's responses—contradictions between one's desires, or between one's emotions and one's actions. A concern with detecting such contradictions is the necessary precondition of successful de-repression; it is the starting point of one's introspective efforts to remove mental blocks. [*Another category is contradictions between one's words and one's feelings.*]

The details of the process of de-repression are outside the scope of this discussion. It must be noted, however, that the process can be extremely difficult. Sometimes, such complexities are involved that a man may require the aid of a competent psychotherapist.

In order to avoid repression—or in order to *de*-repress—it is imperative that a man adopt the policy of *being aware* of his emotions: that he take note of and *conceptualize* his emotional reactions and that he identify their reasons. This policy, practiced consistently, makes repression almost impossible; the chief reason why it is often so easy for men to repress is their policy of unconcern with, and obliviousness to, their own mental states and processes. [*One must be aware, however, of the error of premature conceptualization, that is, the attempt to conceptualize emotions ahead of fully experiencing them.*]

If his emotions are to be a source of pleasure to man, not a source of pain, he must learn to *think* about them. Rational awareness is not the "cold hand" that kills; it is the power that liberates.

Appendix B

Alienation

[There is a growing tendency among psychologists and psychiatrists to treat the problem of man's self-alienation as a social or political issue. I wrote on this subject some years ago, in the July-August-September 1965 issues of *The Objectivist Newsletter*. My article is reprinted here in slightly abridged form. I have added a number of annotations that appear in brackets and italics directly following the sentences to which they pertain.]

> And how am I to face the odds
> of man's bedevilment and God's?
> I, a stranger and afraid
> in a world I never made.

In the writings of contemporary psychologists and sociologists, one encounters these lines from A. E. Housman's poem more and more today—quoted as an eloquent summation of the sense of life and psychological plight of twentieth-century man.

In book after book of social commentary, one finds the same message: modern man is overwhelmed by anxiety, modern man suffers from an "identity crisis," modern man is *alienated*. " 'Who am I?' 'Where am I going?' 'Do I belong?': these are the crucial questions man asks himself in modern mass society," declares the sociologist and psychoanalyst Hendrik M. Ruitenbeek, in *The Individual and the Crowd—A Study of Identity in America*.[1]

The concept of *alienation*, in its original psychiatric usage, denoted the mentally ill, the severely mentally ill—often, particularly in legal contexts, the insane. It conveyed the notion of the breakdown of rationality and self-determination, the notion of a person driven by forces which he cannot grasp or control, which are experienced by him as compelling and alien, so that he feels estranged from himself.

Centuries earlier, medieval theologians had spoken with distress of man's alienation from God—of an over-concern with the world of the senses that caused man to become lost to himself, estranged from his proper spiritual estate.

It was the philosopher Hegel who introduced the concept of alienation (outside of its psychiatric context) to the modern world. The history of man, maintained Hegel, is the history of man's self-alienation: man is blind to his true essence, he is lost in the "dead world" of social institutions and of property, which he himself has created, he is estranged from the Universal Being of which he is a part—and human progress consists of man's motion toward that Whole, as he transcends the limitations of his individual perceptions.

"Alienation" was taken over by Karl Marx and given a narrower, less cosmic meaning. He applied the concept primarily to the worker. The worker's alienation was inevitable, he asserted, with the development of the division of labor, specialization, exchange, and private property. The worker must sell his services; thus he comes to view himself as a "commodity," he becomes alienated from the product of his own labor, and his work is no longer the expression of his powers, of his inner self. The worker, who is alive, is ruled by that which is "dead" (i.e., capital, machinery). The consequence, says Marx, is spiritual impoverishment and mutilation: the worker is alienated from himself, from nature and from his fellow-men; he exists only as an animated *object,* not as a human being.

Since the time of Marx, the idea of alienation has been used more and more extensively by psychologists, sociologists, and philosophers—gathering to itself a wide variety of usages and meanings. But from Hegel and Marx onward, there appears to be an almost universal reluctance, on the part of those who employ the term, to define it precisely; it is as if one were expected to *feel* its meaning, rather than to grasp it conceptually. In a two-volume collection of essays entitled *Alienation,* the editor, Gerald Sykes, specifically scorns those who are too eager for a definition of the term; haste for definition, he declares, reveals that one suffers from "an advanced case of—alienation."[1]

Certain writers—notably those of a Freudian or Jungian orientation—declare that the complexity of modern industrial society has caused man to become "over-civilized," to have lost touch with the deeper roots of his being, to have become alienated from his "instinctual nature." Others—notably those of an existentialist or Zen Buddhist orientation—complain that our advanced technological society compels man to live too intellectually, to be ruled by abstractions, thus alienating him from the real world which can be experienced in its "wholeness" only via his emotions. Others—notably those of a petulant mediocrity orientation—decry specifically the alienation of the artist; they assert that, with the vanishing of the age of patrons, with the artist thrown on his own resources to struggle in the marketplace—which is ruled by "philistines"—the artist is condemned to fight a losing battle for the preservation of his spiritual integrity: he is too besieged by material temptations.

[1] New York: George Braziller, 1964, Vol. 1, p. xiii.

Most of these writers declare that the problem of alienation—and of man's search for identity—is not new, but has been a source of anguish to man in every age and culture. But they insist that today, in Western civilization—above all, in America—the problem has reached an unprecedented severity. It has become a crisis.

What is responsible for this crisis? What has alienated man and deprived him of identity? The answer given by most writers on alienation is not always stated explicitly, but—in their countless disparaging references to "the dehumanizing effects of industrialism," "soul-destroying commercialism," "the arid rationalism of a technological culture," "the vulgar materialism of the West," etc.—the villain in their view of things, the destroyer whom they hold chiefly responsible is not hard to identify. It is *capitalism.*

This should not be startling. Since its birth, capitalism has been made the scapegoat responsible for almost every real or imagined evil denounced by anyone. As the distinguished economist Ludwig von Mises observes:

Nothing is more unpopular today than the free market economy, i.e., capitalism. Everything that is considered unsatisfactory in present-day conditions is charged to capitalism. The atheists make capitalism responsible for the survival of Christianity. But the papal encyclicals blame capitalism for the spread of irreligion and the sins of our contemporaries, and the Protestant churches and sects are no less vigorous in their indictment of capitalist greed. Friends of peace consider our wars as an off-shot of capitalist imperialism. But the adamant nationalist warmongers of Germany and Italy indicted capitalism for its "bourgeois" pacifism, contrary to human nature and to the inescapable laws of history. Sermonizers accuse capitalism of disrupting the family and fostering licentiousness. But the "progressives" blame capitalism for the preservation of allegedly out-dated rules of sexual restraint. Almost all men agree that poverty is an outcome of capitalism. On the other hand many deplore the fact that capitalism, in catering lavishly to the wishes of people intent upon getting more amenities and a better living, promotes a crass materialism. These contradictory accusations of capitalism cancel one another. But the fact remains that there are few people left who would not condemn capitalism altogether.[1]

It is true that a great many men suffer from a chronic feeling of inner emptiness, of spiritual impoverishment, the sense of lacking personal identity. It is true that a great many men feel alienated—*from something*—even if they cannot say from what—from themselves or other men or the universe. And it is profoundly significant that capitalism should be blamed for this. Not because there is any justification for the charge, but because, by analyzing the reasons given for the accusation, one can learn a good deal about the nature and meaning of men's sense of alienation and non-identity—and, simultaneously, about the psychological motives that give rise to hostility toward capitalism.

The writers on alienation, as I have indicated, are not an intellectually homogeneous group. They differ in many areas: in their view of what the problem of alienation exactly consists of, in the aspects of modern industrial society and a free-market economy which they find most objectionable, in the explicitness with which they identify capitalism as the villain, and in details of their own political inclinations. Some of these writers are socialists, some are fascists, some are medievalists, some are supporters of the welfare state, some scorn politics altogether. Some believe that the problem of alienation is largely or entirely solvable by a new system of social organization; others believe that the problem, at bottom, is metaphysical and that no entirely satisfactory solution can be found.

Fortunately for the purposes of this analysis, however, there is one contemporary writer who manages to combine in his books virtually all of the major errors

[1] Ludwig von Mises, *Socialism,* New Haven, Connecticut: Yale University Press, 1951, p. 527.

perpetrated by commentators in this field: psychologist and sociologist Erich Fromm. Let us, therefore, consider Fromm's view of man and his theory of alienation in some detail.

*

*   *

Man, declares Erich Fromm, is "the freak of the universe."

This theme is crucial and central throughout his writings: man is radically different from all other living species, he is "estranged" and "alienated" from nature, he is overwhelmed by a feeling of "isolation" and "separateness"—he has lost, in the process of evolution, the undisturbed tranquillity of other organisms, he has lost the "pre-human harmony" with nature which is enjoyed by an animal, a bird, or a worm. The *source* of his curse is the fact that he possesses a mind.

"Self-awareness, reason, and imagination," Fromm writes in *Man for Himself,* "have disrupted the 'harmony' which characterizes animal existence. Their emergence has made man into an anomaly, into the freak of the universe." Man cannot live as an animal: he is not equipped to adapt himself automatically and unthinkingly to his environment. An animal blindly "repeats the pattern of the species," its behavior is biologically prescribed and stereotyped, it "either fits in or it dies out"—but it does not have to *solve* the problem of survival, *it is not conscious of life and death as an issue.* Man does and is; this is his tragedy. "Reason, man's blessing, is also his curse . . ."[1]

In *The Art of Loving,* he writes:

What is essential in the existence of man is the fact that he has emerged from the animal kingdom, from instinctive adaptation, that he has transcended nature—although he never leaves it; he is part of it—and yet once torn away from nature, he cannot return to it; once thrown out of paradise—a state of original oneness with nature—cheru-

[1] Erich Fromm, *Man for Himself,* New York: Rinehart & Co. 1947, pp. 39, 40.

bim with flaming swords block his way, if he should try to return.[1]

That man's rational faculty deprives man of "paradise," alienating and estranging him from nature, is clearly revealed, says Fromm, in the "existential dichotomies" which his mind dooms man to confront—"contradictions" inherent in life itself. What are those tragic "dichotomies?" He names three as central and basic. Man's mind permits him to "visualize his own end: death"—yet "his body makes him want to be alive."[2] Man's nature contains innumerable potentialities yet "the short span of his life does not permit their full realization under even the most favorable circumstances."[3] Man "must be alone when he has to judge or to make decisions solely by the power of his reason" —yet "he cannot bear to be alone, to be unrelated to his fellow men."[4]

These "contradictions," says Fromm, constitute the dilemma of the "human situation"—contradictions with which man is compelled to struggle, but which he can never resolve or annul, *and which alienate man from himself, from his fellow men, and from nature.*

If the logic of the foregoing is not readily perceivable, the reason does not lie in the brevity of the synopsis. It lies in the unmitigated arbitrariness of Fromm's manner of presenting his ideas; he writes, not like a scientist, but like an oracle who is not obliged to give reasons of proof.

It is true that man differs fundamentally from all other living species, by virtue of possessing a rational, conceptual faculty. It is true that, for man, survival is a problem to be solved—by the exercise of his intelligence. It is true that no man lives long enough to exhaust his every potentiality. It is true that every man is alone, separate, and unique. It is true that thinking re-

---

[1] Erich Fromm, *The Art of Loving,* New York: Harper & Brothers, 1956 p. 7.

[2] *Man for Himself,* p. 40.

[3] Ibid., p. 42.

[4] Ibid., p. 43.

quires independence. These are the facts that grant glory to man's existence. Why would one choose to regard these facts as a terrifying cosmic paradox and to see in them the evidence of monumentally tragic human problems?

Fromm does not tell us. Nowhere does he establish any logical connection between the facts he observes and the conclusions he announces.

If we are *not* to regard his conclusions as arbitrary—as mystical revelations, in effect—then we must assume that he does not bother to give reasons for his position because he regards his conclusions as virtually self-evident, as irresistibly conveyed by the facts he cites, easily available to everyone's experience and introspection. But if he feels it is readily apparent, by introspection, that the facts he cites constitute an agonizing problem for man—the most appropriate answer one can give is: "Speak for yourself, brother!"

Reason, Fromm insists, and the self-awareness which reason makes possible, turns man's "separate, disunited existence" into an "unbearable prison"—and man "would become insane could he not liberate himself from this prison and reach out, unite himself in some form or other with men, with the world outside."[1]

The following paragraph is typical of what Fromm considers an explanation:

The experience of separateness arouses anxiety; it is, indeed, the source of all anxiety. Being separate means being cut off, without any capacity to use my human powers. Hence to be separate means to be helpless, unable to grasp the world—things and people—actively; it means that the world can invade me without my ability to react. Thus, separateness is the source of intense anxiety. Beyond that, it arouses shame and the feeling of guilt. This experience of guilt and shame in separateness is expressed in the Biblical story of Adam and Eve. After Adam and Eve have eaten of the "tree of knowledge of good and evil," after they have disobeyed . . . after they have become

---

[1] *The Art of Loving*, p. 8.

human by having emancipated themselves from the original animal harmony with nature, i.e., after their birth as human beings—they saw "that they were naked—and they were ashamed." Should we assume that a myth as old and elementary as this has the prudish morals of the nineteenth-century outlook, and that the important point the story wants to convey to us is the embarrassment that their genitals were visible? This can hardly be so, and by understanding the story in a Victorian spirit, we miss the main point, which seems to be the following: after man and woman have become aware of themselves and of each other, they are aware of their separateness, and of their difference, inasmuch as they belong to different sexes. But while recognizing their separateness they remain strangers, because they have not yet learned to love each other (as is also made very clear by the fact that Adam defends himself by blaming Eve, rather than by trying to defend her). *The awareness of human separation, without reunion by love—is the source of shame. It is at the same time the source of guilt and anxiety.*[1]

All social institutions, all cultures, all religions and philosophies, all progress, asserts Fromm, are motivated by man's need to escape the terrifying sense of helplessness and aloneness to which his reason condemns him.

The necessity to find ever-new solutions for the contradictions in his existence, to find ever-higher forms of unity with nature, his fellowmen and himself, is the source of all psychic forces which motivate man . . .[2]

In *Man for Himself,* Fromm states that only through "reason, productiveness and love" can man solve the problem of his "separateness" and achieve a "new union" with the world around him. Fromm's claim to be an advocate of *reason* is disingenuous, to say the least. He speaks of reason and love as being "only two

---

[1] Ibid., pp. 8-9.
[2] Erich Fromm, *The Sane Society,* New York; Rinehart & Co. 1955, p. 25.

different forms of comprehending the world."[1] As if this were not an unequivocal proof of his mysticism, he goes on to speak, in *The Art of Loving,* of the "paradoxical logic" of Eastern religions, which, he tells us approvingly, is not encumbered by the Aristotelian law of contradiction and which teaches that "man can perceive reality only in contradictions."[2] (Hegel and Marx, he asserts—correctly—belong to this "paradoxical" epistemological line.) His discussion of what he means by "productiveness" is scarcely more gratifying.

In *The Art of Loving,* written some years after *Man for Himself,* he declares that reason and productive work, though certainly important, provide only partial and, by themselves, very unsatisfactory solutions: the "unity" they achieve is "not interpersonal," and the "desire for interpersonal fusion is the most powerful striving in man."[3] Fromm pulls an unexplained switch at this point. What began as a problem between man and nature is now to be solved (in some unspecified manner) by human "togetherness." One is not surprised; in reading Fromm, this is the sort of pronouncement for which one is waiting—there is a sense of inevitability about it. Love and love alone, he tells us with wonderful originality, can allay man's terror— "Love is the only sane and satisfactory answer to the problem of human existence."[4]

Only through "relating" oneself positively to others, only through feeling "care and responsibility" for them —while preserving one's personal integrity, he adds somewhat mysteriously—can man establish new ties, a new union, that will release him from alienated aloneness.

The cat is now ready to be let fully out of the bag. The preceding is Fromm's view of alienation as a *metaphysical* problem; its full meaning and implication become clear when one turns to his *social-political*

---

[1] *Man for Himself,* p. 97.
[2] *The Art of Loving,* p. 77.
[3] Ibid., p. 18.
[4] Ibid., p. 133.

analysis of alienation. In the context of the latter, one can see clearly what sort of "ties," what sort of "union" and what sort of "love" Fromm has in mind.

*

* *

Every society, as a system of human relationships, may be evaluated by how well it satisfies man's basic psychological needs, says Fromm—i.e., he explains, by the possibilities for love, relatedness, and the experience of personal identity which it offers man.

Capitalism, Fromm declares, has been disastrous in this regard: far from solving the problem of man's alienation, it worsens it immeasurably in many respects. In liberating man from medieval regulation and authority, in breaking the chains of ecclesiastical, economic and social tyranny, in destroying the "stability" of the feudal order, capitalism and individualism thrust upon man an unprecedented freedom that was "bound to create a deep feeling of insecurity, powerlessness, doubt, aloneness, and anxiety."[1]

Scratch a collectivist and you will usually find a medievalist. Fromm is not an exception. Like so many socialists, he is a glamorizer of the Middle Ages. He perfunctorily acknowledges the faults of the historical period—but in contrasting it with the capitalism that succeeded it, he is enchanted by what he regards as its virtues.

What characterizes medieval in contrast to modern society is its lack of individual freedom. . . . But although a person was not free in the modern sense, neither was he alone and isolated. In having a distinct, unchangeable, and unquestionable place in the social world from the moment of birth, man was rooted in a structuralized whole, and thus life had a meaning which left no place, and no need, for doubt. A person was identical with his role in society; he *was* a peasant, an artisan, a knight, and not *an individual* who *happened* to have this or that occupation. The social order was conceived as a natural order, and

[1] Erich Fromm, *Escape from Freedom,* New York: Rinehart & Co., 1941. p. 63.

being a definite part of it gave man a feeling of security
and of belonging. There was comparatively little com-
petition. One was born into a certain economic position
which guaranteed a livelihood determined by tradition,
just as it carried economic obligations to those higher in
the social hierarchy. But within the limits of his social
sphere the individual actually had much freedom to
express his self in his work and in his emotional life. Although there was no individualism in the modern sense
of the unrestricted choice between many possible ways of
life (a freedom of choice which is largely abstract), there
was a great deal of *concrete individualism in real life*.[1]

It is not uncommon to encounter this sort of perspective on the Middle Ages, among writers on alienation. But what makes the above passage especially
shocking and offensive, in the case of Fromm, is that
he repeatedly professes to be a lover of freedom and
a valuer of human life.

The complete lack of control over any aspect of one's
existence, the ruthless suppression of intellectual freedom, the paralyzing restrictions on any form of individual initiative and independence—these are cardinal
characteristics of the Middle Ages. But all of this is
swept aside by Fromm—along with the famines, the
plagues, the exhausting labor from sunrise to sunset the
suffocating routine, the superstitious terror, the attacks
of mass hysteria afflicting entire towns, the nightmare
brutality of men's dealings with one another, the use of
legalized torture as a normal way of life—all of this
is swept aside, so entranced is Fromm by the vision of
a world in which men did not have to invent and compete, they had only to submit and obey.

Nowhere does he tell us what specifically the medieval man's *"concrete individualism"* consisted of. One
is morbidly curious to know what he would say.

With the collapse of medievalism and the emergence
of a free-market society, Fromm declares, man was
compelled to assume total responsibility for his own
survival: he had to produce and to trade—he had to

[1] *Ibid.*, pp. 41-42.

think and to judge—he had no authority to guide him, and nothing but his own ability to keep him in existence. No longer could he, by virtue of the class into which he was born, *inherit* his sense of personal identity: henceforward, he had to *achieve* it. This posed a devastating psychological problem for man, intensifying his basic feeling of isolation and separateness.

"It is true," Fromm remarks, "that the capitalistic mode of production is conducive to political freedom, while any centrally planned social order is in danger of leading to political regimentation and eventually to dictatorship."[1] Capitalism, he further concedes, has proven itself superlatively capable of producing goods and of raising men's material standard of living to undreamed-of heights. But a "sane society" must have more to offer man than political freedom and material well-being. Capitalism, Fromm insists, is destructive of man's *spirit*. He offers several reasons for this charge, which are very revealing.

(1) Like Marx, Fromm decries the humiliating predicament of the worker who has to *sell* his *services*. Capitalism condemns the worker to experience himself, not as a man, but as a commodity, as a thing to be traded. Furthermore, since he is only a tiny part of a vast production process, since, for example, he does not build an entire automobile himself (and then drive home in it), but builds only a small part of it (the total being subsequently sold to some unknown, distant party), the worker feels alienated from the product of his own labor and, therefore, feels alienated from his own labor as such—unlike the artisan of the Middle Ages, whose labor could express the "full richness" of his personality.

It is an elementary fact of economics that specialization and exchange, under a division of labor, make a level of productivity possible which otherwise would not be remotely attainable. In pre-capitalist centuries, when a man's economic well-being was limited by the goods he himself could produce with his own primitive

[1] *The Sane Society*, p. 138.

tools, an unconscionable amount of labor was required to make or acquire the simplest necessities—and the general standard of living was appallingly low: human existence was a continual, exhausting struggle against imminent starvation. About half of the children born, perished before the age of ten. But with the development of the wages system under capitalism, the introduction of machinery and the opportunity for a man to sell his labor, life (to say nothing of an ever-increasing standard of material well-being) was made possible for millions who could have had no chance at survival in pre-capitalist economies. However, for Fromm and those who share his viewpoint, these considerations are, doubtless, too "materialistic." To offer men a chance to enjoy an unprecedented material well-being, is, evidently, to sentence them to alienation; whereas to hold them down to the stagnant level of a medieval serf or guildsman, is to offer them spiritual fulfillment.

(2) Fromm decries the "anonymity of the social forces . . . inherent in the structure of the capitalistic mode of production."[1] The laws of the market, of supply and demand, of economic cause and effect, are ominously impersonal: no single individual's *wishes* control them. Is it the worker who determines how much he is to be paid? No. It is not even the employer. It is that faceless monster, the market. It determines the wage level in some manner beyond the worker's power to grasp. As for the capitalist, his position is scarcely better: he, too, is helpless. "The individual capitalist expands his enterprise not primarily because he *wants* to, but because he *has* to, because . . . postponement of further expansion would mean regression."[2] If he attempts to stagnate, he will go out of business. Under such a system, asks Fromm, how can man *not* feel alienated?

Consider what Fromm is denouncing. Under capitalism, the wages paid to a man for his work are determined *objectively*—by the law of supply and de-

[1] Ibid.

[2] Ibid., p. 86.

mand. The market—reflecting the voluntary judgments of all those who participate in it, all those who buy and sell, produce and consume, offer or seek employment—establishes the general price level of goods and services. This is the context which men are obliged to consider in setting the prices they will ask for their work or offer for the work of others; if a man demands more than the market value of his work, he will remain unemployed; if a particular employer offers him less than the market value of his work, the man will seek—and find—employment elsewhere. The same principle applies to the capitalist who offers his goods for sale. If the prices and quality of his goods are comparable or preferable to those of other men in the same field of production, he will be able to compete; if others can do better than he can, if they can offer superior goods and/or lower prices, he will be obliged to improve, to grow, to equal their achievement, or else he will lose his customers. The standard determining a producer's success or failure is the *objective* value of his product—as judged, within the context of the market (and of their knowledge), by those to whom he offers his product. This is the only rational and just principle of exchange. But *this* is what Fromm considers evil.

What he rebels against is *objectivity*. How—he demands—can a man not feel alienated in a system where his wishes are not omnipotent, where the unearned is not to be had, where growth is rewarded and stagnation is penalized?

It is clear from the foregoing that Fromm's basic quarrel is with *reality*—since nature confronts man with the identical conditions, which a free economy merely reflects: nature, too, holds man to the law of cause and effect; nature, too, makes constant growth a condition of successful life.

There are writers on alienation who recognize this and do not bother to center their attacks on capitalism: they damn nature out-right. They declare that man's life is intrinsically and inescapably *tragic*—since reality is "tyrannical," since contradictory desires cannot be satisfied, since objectivity is a "prison," since time is a

"net" that no one can elude, etc. Existentialists, in
particular, specialize in this sort of pronouncement. [*In
recent years there has been a growing tendency among
certain writers on alienation to call for the abolition of
all known social systems, while evading the question of
what new system they propose to substitute; they continue, predictably, to reserve their harshest criticisms
not for totalitarian political systems but for the American system of semi-capitalism.*]

(3) As consumer in a capitalist economy, Fromm
contends, man is subject to further alienating pressures.
He is overwhelmed with innumerable products among
which he must choose. He is bewildered and brain-
washed by the blandishments of advertisers, forever
urging him to buy their wares. This staggering multiplicity of possible choices is threatening to his sanity.
Moreover, he is "conditioned" to consume for the sake
of consuming—to long for an ever-higher standard of
living—merely in order to keep the "system" going.
With automatic washing machines, automatic cameras,
and automatic can openers, modern man's relationship
to nature becomes more and more remote. He is increasingly condemned to the nightmare of an *artificial*
world.

No such problem confronted the feudal serf.

This much is true: sleeping on an earthen floor, the
medieval serf—to say nothing of the cavemen—was
much *closer* to nature, in one uncomfortable and un-
hygienic sense of the word.

The above criticism of capitalism has become very
fashionable among social commentators. What is remarkable is that almost invariably, as in the case of
Fromm, the criticism is made by the same writers who
are loudest in crying that man needs more *leisure*. Yet
the purpose of the "gadgets" they condemn is, specifically, to liberate man's time. Thus they wish to provide
man with more leisure, while damning the material
means that make leisure possible.

As for the charge—equally popular—that the multiplicity of choices offered to man in capitalistic society

is threatening to his mental equilibrium, it should be remembered that *fear* of choices and decisions is a basic symptom of mental illness. To whose mentality, then, do these critics of capitalism demand that society be adjusted?

(4) The development of a complex, highly industrialized society requires an extreme degree of quantification and abstraction in men's method of thinking, observes Fromm—and this, in still another way, estranges man from the world around him: he loses the ability to relate to things in "their concreteness and uniqueness."[1]

One can agree with Fromm in part: an industrial technological society demands the fullest development and exercise of man's *conceptual* faculty, i.e., of his distinctively *human* form of cognition. The *sensory-perceptual* level of consciousness—the level of an animal's cognition—will not do.

Those who assert that the conceptual level of consciousness alienates man from the real world, merely confess that their concepts bear no relation to reality— or that they do not understand the relation of concepts to reality. But it should be remembered that the capacity to abstract and conceptualize offers man—to the extent that he is rational—a means of "relating" to the world around him immeasurably superior to that enjoyed by any other species. It does not "alienate" man from nature, it makes him nature's master: an animal obeys nature *blindly;* man obeys her *intelligently*—and thereby acquires the power to command her. [*To prevent any possible misunderstanding, perhaps it should be stressed that the foregoing remarks are not intended to imply any hostility or antagonism between man and nature; the notion of such hostility or antagonism would be thoroughly irrational; man is part of nature, a fact that he forgets only at his peril.*]

(5) Finally, most alienating of all, perhaps, are the sort of relationships that exist among men under capitalism, says Fromm.

[1] Ibid., p. 114.

What is the modern man's *relationship to his fellow man?*
It is one between two abstractions, two living machines,
who use each other. The employer uses the ones whom
he employs; the salesman uses his customers. . . . There is
not much love or hate to be found in human relations of
our day. There is, rather, a superficial friendliness, and
a more than superficial fairness, but behind that surface
is distance and indifference. . . . The alienation between
man and man results in the loss of those general and
social bonds which characterize medieval as well as most
other precapitalist societies.[1]

Fromm is claiming that there existed, in pre-capitalist
societies, a mutual good will among men, an attitude of
respect and benevolent solidarity, a regard for the value
of the human person, that vanished with the rise of a
free-market society. This is worse than false. The claim
is absurd historically and disgraceful morally.

It is notorious that, in the Middle Ages, human relationships were characterized by mutual suspiciousness,
hostility, and cruelty: everyone regarded his neighbor
as a potential threat, and nothing was held more cheap-
ly than human life. Such invariably is the case in *any*
society where men are ruled by brute force. In putting
an end to slavery and serfdom, capitalism introduced a
social benevolence that would have been impossible under earlier systems. Capitalism valued a man's life as
it had never been valued before. Capitalism is the
politico-economic expression of the principle that a
man's life, freedom, and happiness are his by moral
right.

Under capitalism, men are free to *choose* their "social bonds"—meaning: to choose whom they will associate with. Men are not trapped within the prison
of their family, tribe, caste, class, or neighborhood.
They choose whom they will value, whom they will be-
friend, whom they will deal with, what kind of relationships they will enter. This implies and entails man's
responsibility to form independent value-judgments. It
implies and entails, also, that a man must *earn* the

[1] Ibid., p. 139.

social relationships he desires. But this, clearly, is anathema to Fromm.

"Love," he has told us, "is the only sane and satisfactory answer to the problem of human existence"—but, he asserts, love and capitalism are *inimical*. "The *principle* underlying capitalistic society and the *principle* of love are incompatible."[1] The principle of capitalism, says Fromm, is that of "fairness ethics," of *trade,* of the exchange of values, without recourse to force or fraud; individuals deal with another only on the premise of mutual self-interest; they engage only in those transactions from which they expect a profit, reward, or gain. "It may even be said that the development of fairness ethics is the particular ethical contribution of capitalist society."[2]

But to approach love with any concern for one's self-interest is—he asserts—to negate the very essence of love. To love an individual is to feel care and responsibility for him; it is not to appraise his character or personality as a "commodity" from which one expects pleasure. To love "ideally" is to love "unconditionally" —it is to love a human being, not for the fact of *what* he is, but for the fact *that* he is—it is to love without reference to values or standards or judgment. "In essence, all human beings are identical. We are all part of One; we are One. This being so, it should not make any difference whom we love."[3]

It should not, in other words, make any difference whether the person we love is a being of stature or a total nonentity, a genius or a fool, a hero or a scoundrel. "We are all part of One." Is it necessary to point out who stands to gain and who to lose by this view of love?

The desire to be loved "unconditionally," the desire to be loved with no concern for his objective personal worth, is one of man's "deepest longings," Fromm insists; whereas to be loved on the basis of *merit,* "be-

[1] *The Art of Loving,* p. 131.

[2] Ibid., p. 129.

[3] Ibid., p. 55.

cause one deserves it," invokes doubt and uncertainty, since merit has to be struggled for and since such love can be withdrawn should the merit cease to exist. "Furthermore, 'deserved' love easily leaves a bitter feeling that one is not loved for oneself, that one is loved *only because one pleases* . . ."[1]

It is typical of Fromm that he should deliver what is in fact (though not in Fromm's estimate) a deadly insult to human nature, without offering any justification for his charge. He assumes that all men, by nature, are so profoundly lacking in self-esteem that they crave a love which bears no relation to their actions, achievements, or character, a love not to be earned but to be received only as a free gift.

What does it mean to be loved "for oneself"? In reason, it can mean only: to be loved for the values one has achieved in one's character and person. The highest compliment one can be paid by another human being is to be told: "Because of what you are, you are essential to my happiness." But this is the love that, according to Fromm, leaves one with "a bitter feeling."

It is the capitalistic culture, he declares, that inculcates such concepts as the "deserved" and the "undeserved"—the earned and the unearned—and thus poisons the growth of proper love. Proper love, Fromm tells us, should be given solely out of the richness of the spirit of the giver, in demonstration of the giver's "potency." Fromm nowhere reveals the exact nature of this "potency," of course. "Love is an act of faith . . ."[2] Proper love should raise no questions about the virtue or character of its object; it should desire no joy from such virtues as the object might possess— for, if it does, it is not proper love, it is only capitalistic selfishness.

But, Fromm asks, "how can one act within the framework of existing society and at the same time practice love?"[3] He does not declare that love is *impossible*

---

[1] Ibid., p. 42.
[2] Ibid., p. 128.
[3] Ibid., pp. 130-131.

under capitalism—merely that it is exceptionally difficult.

[*To love is the value; healthy love expresses admiration. Love is not alms, but a tribute. If love did not imply admiration, if it did not imply an acknowledgement of moral qualities that the recipient of love possessed— what meaning or significance would love have, and why would Fromm or anyone consider it desirable? Only one answer is possible, and it is not an attractive one: when love is divorced from values, then "love" becomes, not a tribute, but a moral blank check: a promise that one will be forgiven anything, that one will not be abandoned, that one will be taken care of.*]

To divorce love from values (and value-judgments), is to confess one's longing for the unearned. The idealization of this longing as a proper moral goal is a constant theme running through Fromm's writing.

That the underlying motive is the desire to be taken care of, the desire to be spared the responsibility of independence, is revealed explicitly in Fromm's sociopolitical "solution" to the problem of alienation.

In order that man may be enabled to conquer his feeling of aloneness and alienation, to practice love and to achieve a full sense of personal identity, a new social system must be established, Fromm declares.

Private ownership of the means of production must be abolished. The profit motive must be forbidden. Industry must be decentralized. Society should be divided into self-governing industrial guilds; factories should be owned and run by all those who work in them.

Why—according to Fromm's social philosophy— should a janitor in an industrial plant not have the same right to determine its management as the man who happened to create the plant? Does not the janitor's personality require as much self-expression as anyone else's?

Under capitalism, says Fromm, men are overwhelmed by and are the pawns of a complex industrial machine whose omnipotent forces and laws are beyond their comprehension or control. Under the decentralized, "democratic" system he proposes—which is some sort of blend of guild socialism and syndicalism—industrial establishments will be broken down into units whose function is within everyone's easy comprehension, with no "alienating" demands made on anyone's abstract capacity.

Under this system, he explains, every person will be provided with his minimum subsistence, whether the person wishes to work or not. This is necessary if man is to develop healthily and happily. However, to discourage parasitism, Fromm suggests that this support should not extend beyond two years. Who is to provide this support, whether they will be willing to do so, and what will happen if they are not willing, are questions Fromm does not discuss.

So long as men are occupied with the problem of survival, Fromm feels, their spiritual concerns—the concerns that really *matter*—are almost inevitably neglected. How can the worker's personality not be impoverished, if he must face daily the necessity of earning a livelihood? How can the businessman develop his creative potentialities, if he is in bondage to his obsession with production? How can the artist preserve his soul's integrity, if he is plagued with temptations by Hollywood and Madison Avenue? How can the consumer cultivate individual tastes and preferences, if he is surrounded by the standardized commodities begotten by mass production?

If one wishes to understand the relevance of epistemology to politics, one should observe what is gained for Fromm by that "paradoxical logic" of which he writes so approvingly. If, as it teaches, "man can perceive reality only in contradictions," then Fromm does not have to be troubled by the conflict between his claim to be an advocate of reason and his enthusiasm for Eastern mysticism—nor does he have to be troubled by the conflict between his claim to be a defender of individualism and his advocacy of political collectivism. His disdain for the law of contradiction permits him to announce that true individualism is possible only in the collectivized community—that true freedom is possible only when production is taken out of the hands of private individuals and placed under the absolute control of the group—that men will cease to be objects of "use" by others, only when they are willing to renounce personal profit and make *social usefulness* the goal of their lives."[1]

Fromm calls his proposed system "Humanistic Communitarian Socialism." Under it, he maintains, man will achieve "a new harmony with nature" to replace the one he has lost—man will enjoy the tranquillity and self-fulfillment of the animals whose state Fromm finds so enviable.

If, often, Fromm is more than a little disingenuous in the presentation of his views, he is, nonetheless, extremely *explicit*. This is what is unusual about him. Most writers of his persuasion twist themselves for pages and pages in order to obscure their advocacy of the ideas—and contradictions—which he announces openly. With rare exceptions, one will find comparable candor only among the existentialists and Zen Buddhists, many of whose premises Fromm shares.

His explicitness notwithstanding, he is very representative culturally and should be recognized as such. The recurrent themes running through the literature on alienation—and through today's social commentary generally—are the themes which Fromm brings into naked focus: that reason is "unnatural," that a noncontradictory, objective reality "restricts" one's individuality, that the necessity of *choice* is an awesome burden, that it is "tragic" not to be able to eat one's cake and have it, too, that self-responsibility is frightening, that the achievement of personal identity is a *social* problem—that "love" is the omnipotent solution —and that the political implementation of this solution is socialism.

*

*   *

The problem of alienation and the problem of personal identity are inseparable. The man who lacks a

[1] For the most detailed presentation of these doctrines, see Fromm's *The Sane Society*.

firm sense of personal identity feels alienated; the man who feels alienated lacks a firm sense of personal identity.

Pain is an organism's alarm-signal, warning of danger; the particular species of pain which is the feeling of alienation announces to a man that he is existing in a psychological state improper to him—*that his relationship to reality is wrong*.

No animal faces such questions as: What should I make of myself? What manner of life is proper to my nature? Such questions are possible only to a rational being, i.e., a being whose characteristic method of cognitive functioning (of apprehending reality) is conceptual, who is not only conscious but also self-conscious, and whose power of abstraction enables him to project many alternative courses of action. Further, such questions are possible only to a being whose cognitive faculty is exercised *volitionally* (thinking is not automatic)—a being who is self-directing and self-regulating in thought and in action, and whose existence, therefore, entails a constant process of *choice*.

As a living entity, man is born with specific needs and capacities; these constitute his *species* identity, so to speak—i.e., they constitute his human nature. How he exercises his capacities to satisfy his needs—i.e., how he deals with the facts of reality, how he chooses to function, in thought and in action—constitutes his *personal* or *individual* identity. His sense of himself— his implicit concept or image of the kind of person he is (including his self-esteem or lack of it)—is the cumulative product of the choices he makes.

A man's "I," his ego, his deepest self, is his faculty of awareness, his capacity to think. To choose to think, to identify the facts of reality—to assume the responsibility of judging what is true or false, right or wrong—is man's basic form of *self-assertiveness*. It is his acceptance of the responsibility of intellectual independence, his commitment to the efficacy of his own mind.

The essence of *selflessness* is the suspension of one's consciousness. When and to the extent that a man chooses to evade the effort and responsibility of thinking, of seeking knowledge, of passing judgment, his action is one of *self-abdication*. To relinquish thought, is to relinquish one's ego—and to pronounce oneself unfit for existence, incompetent to deal with the facts of reality.

To the extent that a man chooses to think, his premises and values are acquired first-hand and they are not a mystery to him; he experiences himself as the *active cause* of his character, behavior, and goals. To the extent that a man attempts to live without thinking, [*to the extent that he attempts to live without awareness of relevant aspects of external reality as well as of internal reality*], he experiences himself as *passive,* his person and actions are the accidental products of forces he does not understand, of his range-of-the-moment feelings and random environmental influences. When a man defaults on the responsibility of thought, he is left at the mercy of his involuntary, subconscious reactions—and *these* will be at the mercy of the outside forces impinging upon him, at the mercy of whoever and whatever is around him. By his default, such a person turns himself into the social determinists' view of man: into an empty mold waiting to be filled, into a will-less robot waiting to be taken over by any environment and any conditioners.

A strong sense of personal identity is the product of two things: a policy of independent thinking [*including the self-awareness described earlier in this book*]—and, as a consequence, the possession of an integrated set of values. Since it is his values that determine a man's emotions and goals, and give direction and meaning to his life, a man experiences his values as an extension of himself, as an integral part of his identity, as crucial to that which makes him himself.

"Values," in this context, refers to fundamental and abstract values, not to concrete value-judgments. For example, a man holding rationality as his abstract value may choose a friend who appears to embody this value; if, subsequently, he decides that he was mistaken in his judgment, that his friend is not rational and that their relationship should be ended, this does not alter his personal identity; but if, instead, he decides that he no longer values rationality, his personal identity *is* altered.

If a man holds contradictory values, these necessarily do violence to his sense of personal identity. They result in a splintered sense of self, a self broken into unintegratable fragments. To avoid this painful experience of a splintered identity, a man whose values are contradictory will commonly seek to escape knowledge of his contradictions by means of evasion, repression, rationalization, etc. Thus, to escape a problem created by a failure of thought, he suspends thinking. To escape a threat to his sense of personal identity, *he suspends his ego*—he suspends his self *qua* thinking, judging entity.

Moved by feelings whose source he does not understand, and by contradictions whose existence he does not acknowledge, he suffers a progressive sense of self-estrangement, of self-alienation. A man's emotions are the product of his premises and values. But the man who is run by his emotions, attempting to make them a substitute for rational judgment, experiences them as alien forces. The paradox of his position is this: his emotions become his only source of personal identity, but his experience of identity becomes: *a being ruled by demons.* [*Such a man does not, in any but a superficial sense, experience his emotions; what he is aware of are seemingly inexplicable impulses—which is not the same thing.*]

It is important to observe that the experience of self-alienation and the feeling of being alienated from reality, from the world around one, proceed from the same cause: one's default on the responsibility of thinking. The suspension of proper cognitive contact with reality and the suspension of one's ego, are a single act. A flight from reality is a flight from self. [*Chronologically, a flight from reality follows rather than precedes a flight from self; thereafter, the process becomes reciprocal.*]

One of the consequences is a feeling of alienation from other men, the sense that one is not part of the human race—that one is, in effect, a freak. In betraying one's status as a human being, one makes oneself a metaphysical outcast. This is not altered by the knowledge that many other human beings have committed the same betrayal. One feels alone and cut off—cut off by the unreality of one's own existence, by one's desolate inner sense of spiritual impoverishment.

The same failure of rationality and independence by which men rob themselves of personal identity leads them, most commonly, to the self-destructive policy of seeking a *substitute* for identity—or, more precisely, seeking a second-hand identity—through mindless conformity to the values of others. This is the psychological phenomenon which I have designated as social metaphysics. [*In the chapter on "Social Metaphysics," in* The Psychology of Self-Esteem, *discussing the phenomenon of the second-hand identity*], I commented on the type most relevant to the present context, the "Conventional" social metaphysician:

This is the person who accepts the world and its prevailing values ready-made; his is not to reason why. What is true? What others say is true. What is right? What others believe is right. How should one live? As others live. . . . (This is) the person whose sense of identity and personal worth is *explicitly* a function of his ability to satisfy the values, terms and expectations of those omniscient and omnipresent "others." . . . In a culture such as the present one, with its disintegrating values, its intellectual chaos, its moral bankruptcy—where the familiar guideposts and rules are vanishing, where the authoritative mirrors reflecting "reality" are splintering into a thousand unintelligible subcults, where "adjustment" is becoming harder and harder—the Conventional social metaphysician is the first to run to a psychiatrist, crying that he has lost his identity, because he no longer knows unequivocally what he is supposed to do and be.

It would never occur to a person of self-esteem and independent judgment that one's "identity" is a thing to be gained from or determined by others. To a person untouched by self-doubt, the wails heard today about the anguish of modern man as he confronts the question "Who am I?" are incomprehensible. But in the light of the above, the wailing becomes more intelligible. It is the cry of social metaphysicians who no longer know which authorities to obey—and who are moaning that it is *someone's* duty to herd them to a sense of self, that "The System" must provide them with self-esteem. [*When a person defaults on the responsibility of independent thought, and when he cuts himself off from awareness of his own needs, desires, frustrations and longings, then inevitably he experiences himself as dependent on external forces for any sense of personal identity; identity becomes "recognition," "status," a rank or award to be conferred by the omnipotent Others.*]

This is the psychological root of the modern intellectuals' mystique of the Middle Ages, of the dazed longing for that style of life—and of the massive evasion concerning the actual conditions of existence during that period. The Middle Ages represents the social metaphysician's unconfessed dream; a system in which his dread of independence and self-responsibility is proclaimed to be a virtue and is made a social imperative.

When—in any age—a man attempts to evade the responsibility of intellectual independence, and to derive his sense of identity from "belonging," he pays a deadly price in terms of the sabotaging of his mental processes thereafter. The degree to which a man substitutes the judgment of others for his own, failing to look at reality directly, is the degree to which his mental processes are alienated from reality. He functions, not by means of concepts, but by means of memorized cue-words, i.e., learned *sounds* associated with certain contexts and situations, but lacking authentic cognitive content for their user. This is the unidentified, unrecognized phenomenon that prompts unthinking people today to grant validity to the charge that modern man lives "too abstractly," "to intellectually," and that he needs to "get back to nature." They sense dimly that they are out of contact with reality, that something is wrong with their grasp of the world around them. But they accept an entirely fallacious interpretation of their problem. The truth is not that they are lost among "abstractions," but that they have failed to discover the nature and proper use of abstractions; they are not lost among concepts, they are lost among *cue-words.* They are cut off from reality not because they attempt to grasp it too intellectually, but because they attempt to grasp it *only as seen by others;* they attempt to grasp it *second-hand.* And they move through an unreal world of verbal rituals, mouthing the slogans and phrases they hear repeated by others, falsely imagining that those empty words are concepts, and never apprehending the proper use of their conceptual faculty, never learning what first-hand, conceptual knowledge consists of. Then they are ready for the Zen Buddhist who tells them that the solution to their alienation from reality is to empty their mind of all thought and sit for an hour, crosslegged, contemplating the pattern of veins on a leaf. [*It might be argued that this aspect of Zen Buddhism represents a misguided attempt to help men become reconnected with the ignored reality of inner experience and that certain Zen Buddhist exercises do result in enhanced self-awareness; but what is so disastrous about the Zen Buddhist approach is its hostility to reason and conceptual thought. Whoever sets himself against reason, sets himself against reality and against nature and, consequently, against man's survival. I refer the reader to my discussion of man's conceptual function in* The Psychology of Self-Esteem.]

It is a well-known psychological fact that when men are neurotically anxious, when they suffer from feelings of dread for which they cannot account, they often attempt to make their plight more tolerable by directing their fear at some external object: they seek to persuade themselves that their fear is a rational response to the threat of germs, or the possible appearance of burglars, or the danger of lightning, or the brain-controlling radiations of Martians. The process by which men decide that the cause of their alienation is capitalism, is not dissimilar.

There are reasons, however, why capitalism is the target for their projection and rationalization.

The alienated man is fleeing from the responsibility of a volitional (i.e., self-directing) consciousness: the freedom to think or not to think, to initiate a process of reason or to evade it, is a burden he longs to escape. But since this freedom is inherent in his nature as man, there is no escape from it; hence his guilt and anxiety when he abandons reason and sight in favor of feelings and blindness. But there is another level on which man confronts the issue of freedom: the existential or social level—and here escape *is* possible. *Political freedom is not a metaphysical given: it has to be achieved*— hence it can be rejected. The psychological root of the revolt against freedom in one's existence, is the revolt against freedom in one's consciousness. *The root of the revolt against self-responsibility in action is the revolt against self-direction in thought.* The man who does not want to think, does not want to bear responsibility for the consequences of his actions nor for his own life.

Today, of course, capitalism has largely been abandoned in favor of a mixed economy, i.e., a mixture of freedom and statism—moving steadily in the direction of increasing statism. Today, we are far closer to the "ideal society" of the socialists than when Marx first wrote of the worker's "alienation." Yet with every advance of collectivism, the cries concerning man's alienation grow louder. The problem, we are told, is getting worse. In communist countries, when such criticisms are allowed to be voiced, some commentators are beginning to complain that the Marxist solution to the worker's alienation has failed, that man under communism is still alienated, that the "new harmony" with nature and one's fellow men has not come.

It didn't come to the medieval serf or guildsman, either—the propaganda of commentators such as Erich Fromm notwithstanding.

Man cannot escape from his nature, and if he establishes a social system which is inimical to the requirements of his nature—a system which forbids him to function as a rational, independent being—psychological and physical disaster is the result.

A free society, of course, cannot automatically guarantee the mental well-being of all its members. Freedom is not a *sufficient* condition to assure man's proper fulfillment, but it is a *necessary* condition. And capitalism—laissez-faire capitalism—is the only system which provides that condition.

The problem of alienation is not metaphysical; it is not man's natural fate, never to be escaped, like some sort of Original Sin; it is a *disease*. It is not the consequence of capitalism or industrialism or "bigness"—and it cannot be legislated out of existence by the abolition of property rights. The problem of alienation is *psycho-epistemological:* it pertains to how man chooses to use his own consciousness. It is the product of man's revolt against thinking—which means: against reality.

If a man defaults on the responsibility of seeking knowledge, choosing values and setting goals—if this is the sphere he surrenders to the authority of others—*how is he to escape the feeling that the universe is closed to him?* It is. By his own choice.

[*As to any sense of alienation forced on man by the social system in which he lives, it is not freedom but the lack of freedom—brought about by the rising tide of statism, by the expanding powers of the government and the increasing infringement of individual rights—that produces in man a sense of powerlessness and helplessness, the terrifying sense of being at the mercy of malevolent forces.*]

A NOTE TO MY READERS

For more than twenty years the central theme of my work has been the importance of self-esteem and the process of its attainment. Now, in an increasing number of cities throughout the United States, I am offering a 40-hour Intensive on SELF-ESTEEM AND THE ART OF BEING. The purpose of this Intensive is to raise—radically—the level of the participant's self-esteem.

Since first announcing this Intensive, I have received many requests for further details about the nature of the program. The problem in responding is that the Intensive is a unique learning experience and there is nothing to compare it to. It is not a lecture course, although it does contain elements of teaching. It is not psychotherapy, not a form of clinical treatment, although it does include a number of psychological exercises and processes that facilitate personal growth. And it is not like other "personal development" programs currently being offered—either in approach, methods, philosophy, or goals.

It is a special kind of adventure, like no other I have ever offered—a voyage into inner space, produced by the complex orchestration of a wide variety of personal growth processes. The goal is a profoundly enhanced experience of self-acceptance, self-trust, self-assertion and self-esteem—and an increased capacity for honesty and authenticity in human relationships. The corollary of increased, self-understanding is increased understanding of others—and the consequence of both is an increased capacity for intimacy and effectiveness in love relationships.

Readers are invited to write to: The Biocentric Institute, P.O. Box 4009, Beverly Hills, CA. 90213 (213) 274-6361.

Nathaniel Branden

ABOUT THE AUTHOR

Also author of *"If You Could Hear What I Cannot Say": Learning to Communicate with the Ones You Love, The Psychology of Self-esteem, Breaking Free, The Disowned Self, The Psychology of Romantic Love,* and *The Romantic Love Question & Answer Book,* Nathaniel Branden is a pioneer in his studies of self-esteem, personal transformation, and man/woman relationships. Dr. Branden is in private practice in Los Angeles and lives in Lake Arrowhead, California.

As director of the Biocentric Institute in Los Angeles, he offers Intensive Workshops throughout the United States in self-esteem and man/woman relationships. He also conducts professional training workshops for mental health professionals in his approach to personal growth and development.

Communications to Dr. Branden or requests for information about his various lectures, seminars, and Intensive Workshops should be addressed to The Biocentric Institute, P.O. Box 4009, Beverly Hills, CA 90213.

Bantam
On Psychology

☐	23874	**HOW TO BREAK YOUR ADDICTION TO A PERSON** Howard M. Halpern, Ph.D.	$3.95
☐	01419	**IF YOU COULD HEAR WHAT I CANNOT SAY . . .** Nathaniel Branden (A Large Format Book)	$8.95
☐	23043	**ACTIVE LOVING** Ari Kiev, M.D.	$2.95
☐	22576	**PATHFINDERS** Gail Sheehy	$4.50
☐	23234	**PASSAGES: PREDICTABLE CRISES OF ADULT LIFE** Gail Sheehy	$4.50
☐	23006	**THE FAMILY CRUCIBLE** Dr. Napier	$4.50
☐	23399	**THE POWER OF YOUR SUBCONSCIOUS MIND** Dr. J. Murphy	$3.95
☐	23125	**FOCUSING** E. Grendlin	$3.95
☐	23079	**LOVE IS LETTING GO OF FEAR** Gerald Jampolsky	$2.95
☐	23818	**PEACE FROM NERVOUS SUFFERING** Claire Weekes	$3.95
☐	20540	**THE GESTALT APPROACH & EYE WITNESS TO THERAPY** Fritz Perls	$3.50
☐	24064	**THE BOOK OF HOPE** DeRosis & Pellegrino	$4.50
☐	23449	**THE PSYCHOLOGY OF SELF-ESTEEM: A New Concept of Man's Psychological Nature** Nathaniel Branden	$3.95
☐	23267	**WHAT DO YOU SAY AFTER YOU SAY HELLO?** Eric Berne, M.D.	$3.95
☐	20774	**GESTALT THERAPY VERBATIM** Fritz Perls	$3.50
☐	24038	**PSYCHO-CYBERNETICS AND SELF-FULFILLMENT** Maxwell Maltz, M.D.	$3.95
☐	24557	**THE DISOWNED SELF** Nathaniel Branden	$3.95
☐	24411	**CUTTING LOOSE: An Adult Guide for Coming To Terms With Your Parents** Howard Halpern	$3.95
☐	20977	**WHEN I SAY NO, I FEEL GUILTY** Manuel Smith	$3.95